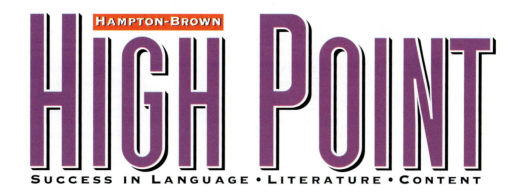

# HIGH POINT

**HAMPTON-BROWN**

## SUCCESS IN LANGUAGE • LITERATURE • CONTENT

ALFREDO SCHIFINI
DEBORAH SHORT
JOSEFINA VILLAMIL TINAJERO

HAMPTON-BROWN

800-333-3510

# Curriculum Reviewers

**Tedi Armet**
*ESL Coordinator*
Fort Bend Independent School District
Sugar Land, Texas

**Suzanne Barton**
*Teacher Director*
International Newcomer Academy
Fort Worth Independent School District
Fort Worth, Texas

**Maggie Brookshire**
*ELD Teacher, Grade 6*
Emerald Middle School
Cajon Valley Unified School District
El Cajon, California

**Raina Cannard**
*ESL Coordinator*
Elk Grove Unified School District
Sacramento, California

**Lily Dam**
*Administrator*
Dallas Independent School District
Dallas, Texas

**Judy Doss**
*ELD Teacher and Coordinator*
Burbank High School
Burbank Unified School District
Burbank, California

**Rossana Font-Carrasco**
*ESOL Teacher*
Paul W. Bell Middle School
Miami-Dade County School District 5
Miami, Florida

**Jillian Friedman**
*ESOL Teacher*
Howard Middle School
Orange County Public Schools
Orlando, Florida

**Vivian Kahn**
*ESL Teacher/Site Coordinator*
Halsey Intermediate School 296
Community School District 32
New York, New York

**Suzanne Lee**
*Principal*
Josiah Quincy School
Boston, Massachusetts

**Mary McBride**
*ELL Teacher*
Monroe Middle School
Inglewood Unified School District
Los Angeles, California

**Carolyn McGavock**
*ESL Teacher*
Rafael Cordero Bilingual Academy
Junior High School 45
Community School District 4
New York, New York

**Juan Carlos Méndez**
*ESL/Bilingual Staff Developer*
Community School District 9
Bronx, New York

**Cynthia Nelson-Mosca**
*Language Minority Services Director*
Cicero School District 99
Cicero, Illinois

**Kim-Anh Nguyen**
*Title 7 Coordinator*
Franklin McKinley School District
San Jose, California

**Ellie Paiewonsky**
*Director of Bilingual/ESL*
Technical Assistance Center of Nassau
Board of Cooperative Educational Services
Massapequa Park, New York

**Jeanne Perrin**
*ESL Specialist*
Boston Public Schools
Boston, Massachusetts

**Rebecca Peurifoy**
*Instructional Specialist*
Rockwall Independent School District
Rockwall, Texas

**Marjorie Rosenberg**
*ESOL/Bilingual Instructional Specialist*
Montgomery County Public Schools
Rockville, Maryland

**Harriet Rudnit**
*Language Arts Reading Teacher*
*Grades 6–8*
Lincoln Hall Middle School
Lincolnwood, Illinois

**Olga Ryzhikov**
*ESOL Teacher*
Forest Oak Middle School
Montgomery County, Maryland

**Dr. Wageh Saad, Ed.D.**
*Coordinator of Bilingual and*
*Compensatory Education*
Dearborn Public Schools
Dearborn, Michigan

**Gilbert Socas**
*ESL Teacher*
West Miami Middle School
Miami-Dade County Public Schools
Miami, Florida

Hampton-Brown
P.O. Box 223220
Carmel, California 93922
1-800-333-3510

Printed in the United States of America
ISBN 0-7362-1223-X

05 06 07 08 09 10

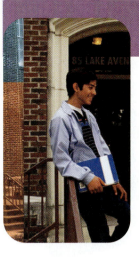

# Carlos Comes to Lakeside School

Basic Vocabulary
Language Functions
Patterns and Structures
High Frequency Words
Sounds and Letters

**THEME BOOK** 📼

**THEME BOOK** 📼

**THEME BOOK** 📼

**THEME BOOK** 📼

**THEME BOOK** 📼

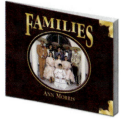

**THEME BOOK** 📼

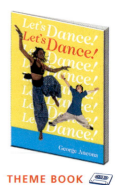

**THEME BOOK** 📼

**THEME BOOK** 📼

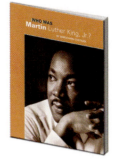

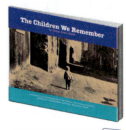

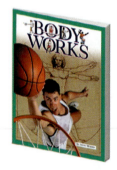

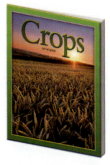

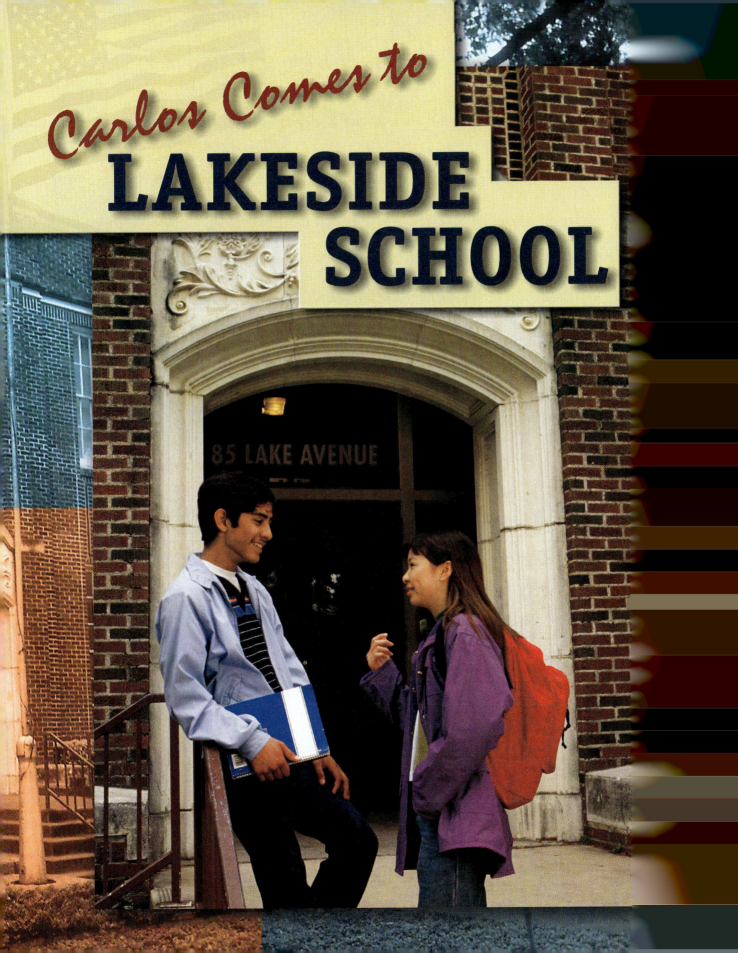

# Carlos Comes to
# LAKESIDE SCHOOL

85 LAKE AVENUE

# This is Lakeside School.

This is the main building.

- window
- flag
- front door
- steps

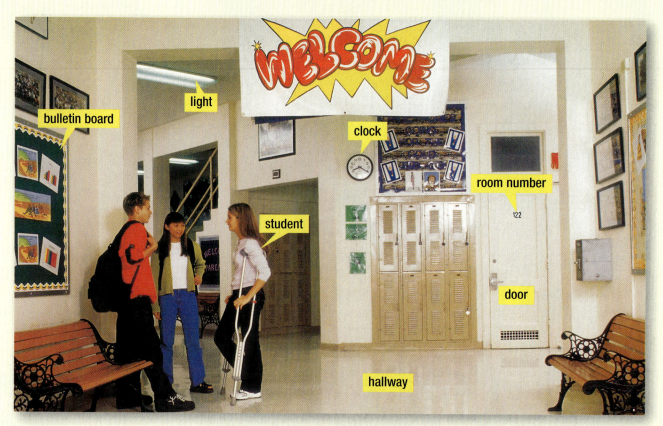

- light
- clock
- bulletin board
- room number
- student
- door
- hallway

This is the entrance hall.

12

van

truck

sidewalk

school bus

crosswalk

street

This is the parking lot.

 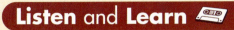

**Maylin**:  Hi, I'm Maylin.

**Carlos**:  Hello. I am Carlos.
Nice to meet you.

gym

fence

garbage can

bench

field

This is the field.

Time: 8:30 a.m.

# Here is a classroom.

a wall

a bookcase

a bookshelf

a window

a pencil sharpener

a book

paper

a notebook

a desk

**SCHOOL SUPPLIES**

a stapler

an eraser

a pencil

a pen

a highlighter

scissors

a ruler

14

a board

Mrs. Terry

a teacher

a workbook

a textbook

WELCOME!

**Maylin:** Here is Room 113.

**Carlos:** Is this my room?

**Maylin:** Yes.

**Carlos:** Is Mr. Rosario my teacher?

**Maylin:** No, Mrs. Terry is.

**Mrs. Terry:** Hi, Maylin.

**Maylin:** Hello, Mrs. Terry. This is Carlos. Carlos, this is Mrs. Terry.

**Carlos:** Hi.

**Mrs. Terry:** Welcome, Carlos. Nice to meet you.

Time:
8:40 a.m.

# This is a map of the school.

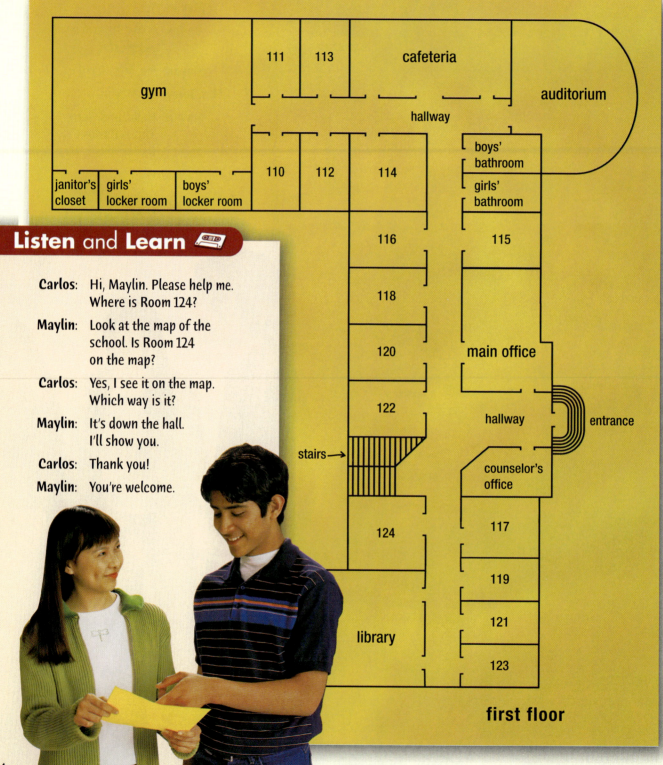

gym

111    113    cafeteria

auditorium

hallway

janitor's closet | girls' locker room | boys' locker room

110    112    114

boys' bathroom

girls' bathroom

116    115

118

120    main office

122

hallway    entrance

stairs →

counselor's office

124    117

library

119

121

123

**first floor**

## Listen and Learn

**Carlos:** Hi, Maylin. Please help me. Where is Room 124?

**Maylin:** Look at the map of the school. Is Room 124 on the map?

**Carlos:** Yes, I see it on the map. Which way is it?

**Maylin:** It's down the hall. I'll show you.

**Carlos:** Thank you!

**Maylin:** You're welcome.

16

# WHERE IS IT ON THE MAP?

THE MAIN OFFICE

THE COUNSELOR'S OFFICE

THE LIBRARY

THE GIRLS' BATHROOM

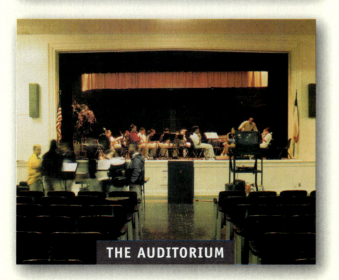

THE AUDITORIUM

THE CAFETERIA

# Here are some teachers.

light switch

transparency

overhead projector

dictionary

Numbers All Around

Clocks have them.
Stamps have them.
Buses, ships, and stores have them.
Money have them.
Balls have them.
Highways, trucks, and doors have them.
Two plus two. Ten plus four!
Do the math. Keep the score!

2+2

**MS. CHANDANI, ESL TEACHER**

uniform

mat

**MR. DUNCAN, P.E. TEACHER**

scale

**MRS. SATO, SCIENCE TEACHER**

homework assignment

**MR. ROSARIO, MATH TEACHER**

### Class Schedule

| Class | Time | Room | Teacher |
|---|---|---|---|
| Homeroom | 8:30 a.m. | 113 | Mrs. Terry |
| Math | 8:45 a.m. | 124 | Mr. Rosario |
| ESL, Lang. Arts | 9:45 a.m. | 118 | Ms. Chandani |
| ESL, Reading | 10:45 a.m. | 121 | Mr. Motts |
| P.E. | 11:45 a.m. | Gym | Mr. Duncan |
| Lunch | 12:40 p.m. | | |
| Science | 1:10 p.m. | 116 | Mrs. Sato |
| Social Studies | 2:10 p.m. | 233 | Mrs. Varela |
| Band practice | 3:10 p.m. | Auditorium | Mrs. Cally |

map

globe

**MRS. VARELA, SOCIAL STUDIES TEACHER**

## Listen and Learn

**Maylin:** It is time for math class. Who is your math teacher?

**Carlos:** Mr. Rosario.

**Maylin:** He is a good teacher.

**Carlos:** Where is your ESL class?

**Maylin:** It's in Room 118.

**Carlos:** Who is your teacher?

**Maylin:** Ms. Chandani. She is really nice!

# Here is a math class.

I work at my desk.

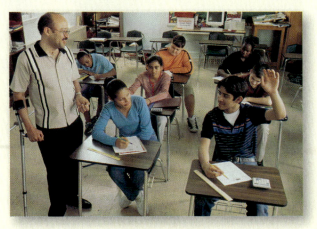

I raise my hand.

I write a problem on the board.

problem

solution

I write the answer to the problem.
I show my work.

I work with a group.

I read my textbook.

I write my name on my worksheet.

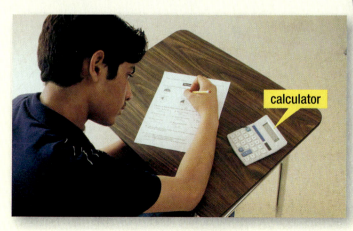

I read my worksheet.
I write the answers.

**Mr. Rosario:** Which circle shows 25% of 4? Show me.

**Carlos:** Here is the circle. It is Circle C.

**Mr. Rosario:** Good. Point to the circle that shows 50% of 4.

**Carlos:** Here is the circle. It is Circle A.

**Mr. Rosario:** Good. Now show me the circle that shows 75% of 4.

**Carlos:** Here is the circle. It is Circle D.

**Mr. Rosario:** Good job, Carlos!

# Here is the main office.

mailbox

principal

assistant principal

computer

copy machine

floor

PRINCIPAL

ceiling

bulletin board

calendar

secretary

telephone

## Listen and Learn

**Carlos:** Hi, Mrs. Cruz, my name is Carlos Parra. Where is the telephone? I need to call my mom.

**Mrs. Cruz:** What is her phone number?

**Carlos:** 555-3298.

**Mrs. Cruz:** Is this a work number?

**Carlos:** Yes. My mom is at work. She is a secretary, like you.

# What is in the library?

bookcase

700

500

00

300

800

BIOGRAPHY

top shelf

globe

middle shelves

magazine

bottom shelf

table

book return box

chair

newspaper

Book
Return

## COMPUTER STATION

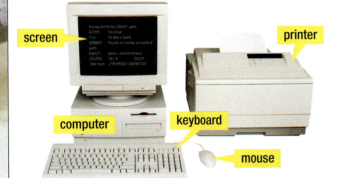

screen

printer

cart

book title

computer

keyboard

mouse

book cover

lamp

librarian

check-out desk

encyclopedias

WORLD BOOK

CIVIL WAR

Carlos: Will you help me find a book, Mrs. Jones?

Mrs. Jones: Sure. Do you like sports?

Carlos: Yes. I like sports a lot!

Mrs. Jones: Here is a good book for you. The title is *The Best in Sports*.

Carlos: Does the book show a picture of soccer?

Mrs. Jones: Yes, it does. You will like the book!

**Time:**
**12:00 p.m.**

# What do you do in P.E.?

basket

basketball

court

**A GYM LOCKER**

lock

sneakers

You can play basketball.

helmet

bat

mask

softball

umpire

glove

You can play softball.

26

You can run around the track.

You can play volleyball.

**Dan:** What sports do you like?

**Carlos:** I like soccer.

**Dan:** My friend Ron likes soccer, too. We also play basketball. Can you play basketball?

**Carlos:** Yes, I can play basketball. I like lots of sports.

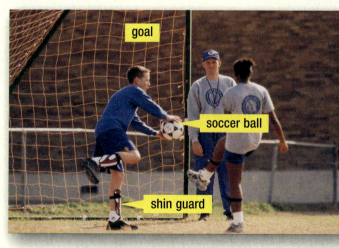

You can play soccer.

# The nurse's office is busy.

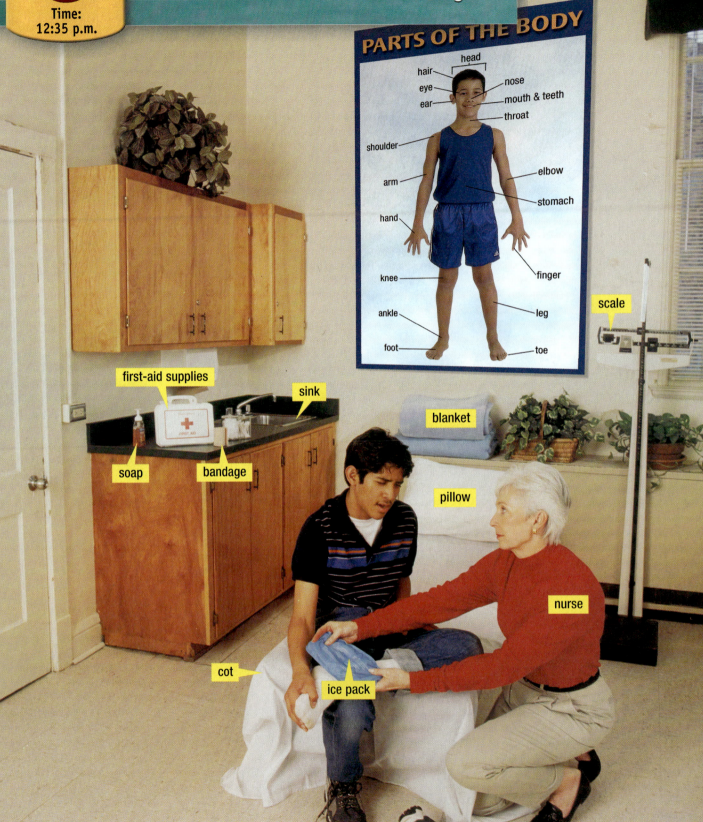

PARTS OF THE BODY

- head
- hair
- eye
- ear
- shoulder
- arm
- hand
- knee
- ankle
- foot
- nose
- mouth & teeth
- throat
- elbow
- stomach
- finger
- leg
- toe

scale

first-aid supplies

sink

soap

bandage

blanket

pillow

nurse

cot

ice pack

# HOW DO THEY FEEL?

I feel sick.

He has
a toothache.

She has
a headache.

He has an earache.

She has a
stomachache.

thermometer

They have colds.
They have fevers, too.

## Listen and Learn

**Mrs. Kent:** How do you feel?

**Carlos:** My foot hurts. I hurt it in P.E. class.

**Mrs. Kent:** I'll put ice on it. You'll feel better tomorrow.

**Carlos:** Thank you, Mrs. Kent.

# What's in the cafeteria?

## Listen and Learn

**Carlos:** How's the food?

**Maylin:** So-so.

**Carlos:** What is that on your plate?

**Maylin:** This is salad. It's not bad.

**Carlos:** I like pizza and hamburgers.

**Maylin:** Me, too.

**Carlos:** I do not like hot dogs.

**Maylin:** I don't like macaroni and cheese.

**Carlos:** What's macaroni and cheese?

**Maylin:** It's sticky and thick. Yuck.

cashier

table

cup

bowl

**MONEY**

| quarter | dime | one-dollar bill |
|---------|------|-----------------|
| 25¢ | 10¢ | $1 |

| nickel | penny | five-dollar bill |
|--------|-------|------------------|
| 5¢ | 1¢ | $5 |

# A CAFETERIA TRAY

straw

tray

milk carton

napkin

chips

paper plate

knife

fork

spoon

# HOT FOOD

| taco and beans | hot dog | soup | hamburger | macaroni and cheese | pizza |

# COLD FOOD

| cake | apple sauce | bagel | egg | cottage cheese | ice cream |

## Salad

dressing

tomato

carrot

lettuce

## Fruit

orange

banana

grapes

apple

## Sandwich

bread

meat

cheese

pickle

31

# Science class is fun!

model

cabinet

poster

**LAB SAFETY**

**Think safety first!**

Wear goggles.

Wear gloves.

Wash hands well.

This is a science lab.

I listen to the teacher.

report

I do an experiment.

I measure.

microscope

I observe.

notes

I take notes.

**Carlos:** Mrs. Sato, I need a tray for my plants. Can you give me one?

**Mrs. Sato:** I think you need more than one tray!

**Carlos:** Yes, I do.

**Mrs. Sato:** Then get two trays from the cabinet. Take them to the table.

**Carlos:** Thanks.

# The school store has good things!

# WHICH CLOTHES DO YOU LIKE?

gray sweatshirt

white cap

red jacket

tan T-shirt

blue shorts

green sweatpants

black sneakers

purple socks

## Listen and Learn

**Maylin:** You can get good things at this store! Look at this little Lakeside lion.

**Carlos:** I like its T-shirt! I need a new T-shirt, too. Do you like this one?

**Maylin:** No, I don't like that color. I do like those blue shorts.

**Carlos:** I like them too. My gym shorts are very old. I will get both the T-shirt and the shorts!

**Maylin:** I will just get my lion.

Time:
3:30 p.m.

# Lakeside School is great!

Bye!
See you soon!

See you later!

## LAKESIDE SCHOOL

LAKESIDE LIONS

THE FIRST WEEK AT LAKESIDE:

MONDAY: WELCOME BACK!

TUESDAY: TEACHER MEETING

WEDNESDAY: BACK-TO-SCHOOL NIGHT

THURSDAY: SCIENCE CLUB

FRIDAY: WELCOME BACK DANCE

SATURDAY: FOOTBALL GAME

SUNDAY: SOCCER TEAM CAR WASH

Good-bye!

See you Tuesday!

So long!

## Listen and Learn 🎙️

**Maylin**: How do you like Lakeside School?

**Carlos**: I like it a lot! There is a lot to do.

**Maylin**: Yes, there is! On Friday there is a big dance. Do you want to go?

**Carlos**: Yes!

**Maylin**: Great! I'll see you tomorrow.

**Carlos**: Okay. Good-bye!

37

# Carlos has a great year!

## September

Carlos meets lots of new friends.

## October

Carlos sees a football game at night.

## January

Carlos takes a picture of the snow.

## February

Carlos gets a valentine from a girl in his class!

## May

Carlos dances with a group at the school dance.

## June

Carlos takes final exams.

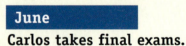

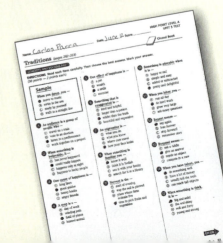

## November
**Carlos writes letters to his family.**

November 13
Dear Grandma and Grandpa,
   I really like it here at
Lakeside School. I have met lots
of new friends. I have great
teachers, too. My favorite subject
is math. I miss you.

                    Love,
                    Carlos

## December
**Carlos sings songs from a book.**

## March
**Carlos works in the school garden one day a week.**

## April
**Carlos plays softball.**

## July
**Carlos visits St. Louis.**

## August
**Carlos swims at the city pool with a boy from his class.**

I am Imran Khan.

I am from Pakistan.

I am 13 years old.

I go to Lakeside School.

I like dogs.

I also like music.

I am Lupe Valle.

I am from Nicaragua.

I am 14 years old.

I go to Lakeside School.

I like the band Loud Mouth.

I also like art.

# Glad to Meet You!

Make a card about yourself.
Put your photo on one side.
Write about yourself on the other side.
Trade cards with a classmate.
Tell your class about the card.

## In This Unit

### Vocabulary
- Personal Information
- Communication
- Numbers and Basic Operations

### Language Functions
- Exchange Greetings and Good-byes
- Give Information
- Use the Telephone

### Patterns and Structures
- Pronouns
- Present Tense Verbs
- Statements and Exclamations

### Reading
- Phonics: Short a, Short o
- Comprehension:
  Identify Sequence (sequence chain)

### Writing
- Sentences
- Postcard

### Content Area Connection
- Mathematics (basic operations)

# Nice to Meet You

**Listen and chant.** 🎞

**Hello,**
**Good-bye**

Hello.
　Hi.
How are you?
　I am fine.
　And how are you?
I am fine.
　Are you fine, too?
　Then we are fine.
　Isn't that true?
Hey, okay!
Whatever you say!
　Good-bye.
So long.
　Have a nice day!

> **Pronouns**
> Use **I** to talk about yourself.
> 　**I** am fine.
> Use **you** when you talk to someone else.
> 　Are **you** fine?
> Use **we** to talk about yourself and someone else.
> 　**We** are fine.

**EXPRESS YOURSELF** ▸ EXCHANGE GREETINGS AND GOOD-BYES

<u>1.</u> **Work with a partner. Say the chant and act it out. Add your names to the first 2 lines.**

**Example: 1.** Hello, Juan.
　　　　　　 Hi, Nikolai.

**WRITE CARDS** ✏

<u>2.–4.</u> **Work with a partner. Write each sentence below on a card. Mix your cards. Then choose a card. Finish the sentence.**

**Example: 2.** I am Nikolai.

| I am ___ . | You are ___ . | We are ___ . |

# They Are Friends

When you talk about other people or things, use the correct **pronoun**.

For a girl or a woman, use *she*. For a boy or man, use *he*.

Today **she** is 14 years old.
**He** is a great friend.

For a thing, use *it*.

**It** is a birthday cake.

Use *they* to talk about more than one person or thing.

**They** are ready to eat!

## BUILD SENTENCES

Say each sentence. Add the correct pronoun.　　　Example: **1.** He is 12 years old.

1.

_____ is 12 years old.

2.

_____ is from Nicaragua.

3.

_____ are friends.

4.

They eat soup.
_____ is hot.

5.

They share a sandwich.
_____ is big.

6.

Here are 2 bottles of milk.
_____ are for the friends.

## WRITE SENTENCES

7.–10. Write 4 sentences to tell about this picture.
Use *He is*, *She is*, *It is*, and *They are*.

Example: **7.** He is Imran.

In the Cafeteria
Lupe
tray
Imran

# We Are Friends

Use the **verbs** *am* and *are* correctly.

| Pronoun | Verb | Example |
|---------|------|---------|
| I | am | I **am** Ron. |
| you | are | You **are** Juan. |
| we | are | We **are** friends. |

## BUILD SENTENCES

Look at each picture below. Add the correct verb.
Say the new sentence.

Example: **1.** You are Anna.

1.
You _____ Anna.

2.
I _____ glad
to meet you.

3.
We _____ new
to this school.

## WRITE SENTENCES

**4.–9.** Work with a partner. Write 6 sentences.
Tell about yourself, your partner, and both
of you. Use *I am*, *You are*, and *We are*.

Example: **4.** I am 13 years old.

# They Are Ready for Class

| Use the verbs *is* and *are* correctly.

| Pronoun | Verb | Example |
|---------|------|---------|
| he<br>she<br>it | is | He **is** on the steps.<br>She **is** in front of the door.<br>It **is** closed. |
| they | are | They **are** ready for class. |

## BUILD SENTENCES

Look at each sentence below. Add the correct verb.
Say the new sentence.

Example: **1.** Lupe is in P.E. class.

Lupe

sweatshirt

sneakers

Lupe

Juan

**1.** Lupe _____ in P.E. class.

**2.** She wears sneakers. They _____ white.

**3.** She wears a sweatshirt. It _____ gray.

**4.** Now Lupe _____ in the cafeteria.

**5.** Juan _____ at the table.

**6.** They _____ ready for lunch.

## WRITE SENTENCES ✏️

**7.–9.** Where are your friends now? Write 3
sentences about them. Use *is* and *are*.

Example: **7.** Huan is in the gym.

# Fill In an Order Form

Two people want to buy some things. Read each order form.

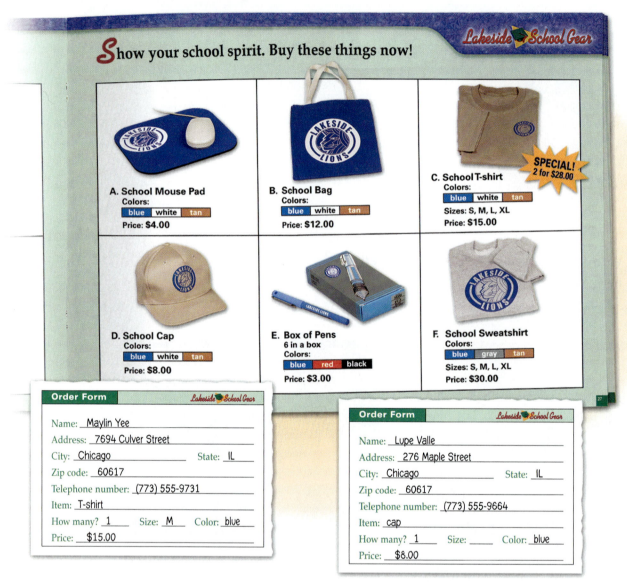

Show your school spirit. Buy these things now!

Lakeside School Gear

**A. School Mouse Pad**
Colors: blue white tan
Price: $4.00

**B. School Bag**
Colors: blue white tan
Price: $12.00

**C. School T-shirt**
SPECIAL! 2 for $28.00
Colors: blue white tan
Sizes: S, M, L, XL
Price: $15.00

**D. School Cap**
Colors: blue white tan
Price: $8.00

**E. Box of Pens**
6 in a box
Colors: blue red black
Price: $3.00

**F. School Sweatshirt**
Colors: blue gray tan
Sizes: S, M, L, XL
Price: $30.00

**Order Form** — Lakeside School Gear
Name: Maylin Yee
Address: 7694 Culver Street
City: Chicago          State: IL
Zip code: 60617
Telephone number: (773) 555-9731
Item: T-shirt
How many? 1     Size: M     Color: blue
Price: $15.00

**Order Form** — Lakeside School Gear
Name: Lupe Valle
Address: 276 Maple Street
City: Chicago          State: IL
Zip code: 60617
Telephone number: (773) 555-9664
Item: cap
How many? 1     Size: ____     Color: blue
Price: $8.00

## WHO'S TALKING? ▶ GIVE INFORMATION

1.–2. **Listen.**
Point to the correct order form. Tell the name of the person.

## WRITE PERSONAL INFORMATION

3. Choose an item from the catalog. Copy an order form and complete it for yourself. Tell a partner about the item you want.

# How Can You Communicate?

EXPRESS YOURSELF ▶ USE THE TELEPHONE

<u>1.</u> **You want to order a school T-shirt. How can you do it?**
**Act out a phone call with a partner.**

**Example: 1. Euching:** Hello, Mariana. This is Euching.

**Mariana:** Hello, Euching.

**Euching:** How can I get a school T-shirt?

**Mariana:** Send a fax to the school.

**Euching:** I don't have a fax machine.

**Mariana:** Then just call on the phone.

**Euching:** How much is a school T-shirt?

**Mariana:** It is $15.00.

**Euching:** Thanks.

**Mariana:** You're welcome. Bye!

**Euching:** See you tomorrow.

# Read and Think Together

**Make a sequence chain for *Good News*.**
**Follow these steps.**

**1** Think about the story. Who got the good news first?
Draw a box and write the name.

| Ali |
| --- |

**2** How did he get the news? Write your answer in the box.

| Ali – letter |
| --- |

**3** Draw boxes to show who got the news next. Tell how
the news came: by e-mail, fax, or phone.

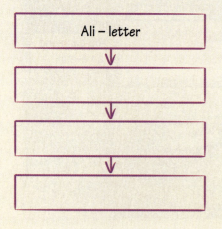

**4** Use your sequence chain to tell the
story to a friend.

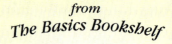

*from*
## The Basics Bookshelf

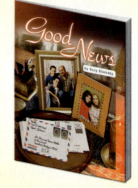

### THEME BOOK

Learn how a family
uses different forms
of communication to
share good news with
each other.

# Words to Know

## REVIEW WORDS YOU KNOW

**Read the words aloud. Which word goes in the sentence?**

| soon | school |
|------|--------|
| The  | They   |
| has  | help   |

1. The girls are at _____.
2. _____ eat lunch.
3. She _____ a lot of food.

## LEARN TO READ

**Learn new words.**

| from | I am **from** Russia. |
|------|------------------------|
| home | My **home** is now in Detroit. |
| new | I have a **new** school, too. |
| go | I will **go** to school with my friend Rob. |
| there | My school schedule is **there** on the table. |
| many | I have **many** different classes! |
| first | **First** I have English class. |
| next | **Next** I have science class. |
| then | **Then** I have lunch. |
| one | I have only **one** class with Rob—math. |

**How to Learn a New Word**

- Look at the word.
- Listen to the word.
- Listen to the word in a sentence. What does it mean?
- Say the word.
- Spell the word.
- Say the word again.

## WORD WORK

**Where does each new word fit in the chart? Say the word and spell it.**

Example: 4.
> next
> n-e-x-t

| What to Look For | Word |
|------------------|------|
| 4. starts with **n** | _ _ _ _ |
| 5. ends with **y** | _ _ _ _ |
| 6. starts with **th** | _ _ _ _ _ _ |
| 7. ends with **n** | _ _ _ _ |
| 8. rhymes with **no** | _ _ |

| What to Look For | Word |
|------------------|------|
| 9. starts with **fr** | _ _ _ _ |
| 10. means "1" | _ _ _ |
| 11. is the opposite of **old** | _ _ _ |
| 12. is the opposite of **last** | _ _ _ _ _ |
| 13. means "where you live" | _ _ _ _ |

# Reading and Spelling

**LISTEN AND LEARN**

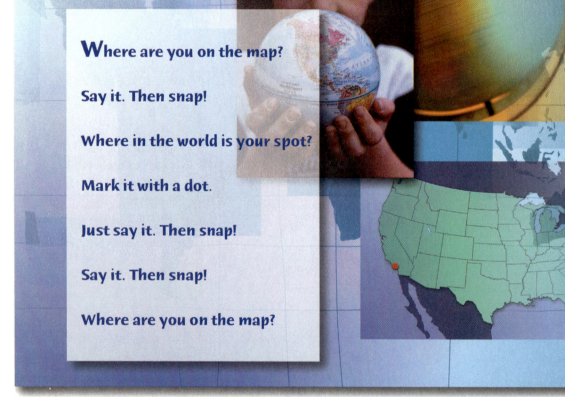

## On the Map

**W**here are you on the map?

Say it. Then snap!

Where in the world is your spot?

Mark it with a dot.

Just say it. Then snap!

Say it. Then snap!

Where are you on the map?

## CONNECT SOUNDS AND LETTERS

What sound does each letter make?

**m**a**p**          **b**a**g**          **j**o**g**          **d**o**t**

## READING STRATEGY

**Follow these steps to read a word.**

**1** Point to the first letter. Say the sound.

**s**ad

**2** Point to the second letter. Say the sound.

s**a**d

**3** Point to the last letter. Say the sound.

sa**d**

**4** Now blend all the sounds together to say the word. Say the word again. What is it?

**s + a + d = sad**

> I blend 3 sounds to say **sad**.

## READING AND SPELLING PRACTICE

**Blend the sounds to read these words.**

**1.** job     **2.** at     **3.** gas     **4.** mom     **5.** mad     **6.** pot

**Use what you learned to read the sentences.**

**7.** What a bad day!
**8.** First I drop a new pot.
**9.** Then my mom is mad at me.
**10.** Next the van has no gas.
**11.** I go to my job.
**12.** At last, I go home!

<u>**13.–16.**</u> **Now write the sentences that your teacher reads.**

## WORD WORK

**Look at the first picture. Then read the word. Use letter cards to make a new word for the next picture. Change just 1 letter each time.**

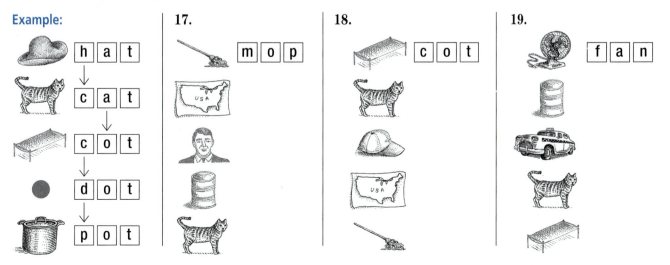

**Example:**

h a t
↓
c a t
↓
c o t
↓
d o t
↓
p o t

**17.** m o p

**18.** c o t

**19.** f a n

# Read on Your Own

# New at School

Lupe is new at Lakeside School.
First she has science lab with Pat and Ron.
Pat helps Lupe.
Next they have P.E. class.
Pat and Lupe go fast. Ron does not go fast.
He has a cold and has to stop!
Then Pat, Lupe, and Ron go to lunch.
They have a lot of hot soup.
At last it is time to go home.
Lupe is glad to have 2 new friends!

## CHECK YOUR UNDERSTANDING

Tell the story to your partner. Use the words and pictures.

First        Next        Then        Last

# She Likes School a Lot!

**Some sentences tell something. Other sentences show a strong feeling.**

This sentence tells something. It ends with a period.

Pizza is a new food for Lupe.

This sentence shows a strong feeling. It ends with an exclamation mark.

She likes it a lot!

All sentences start with a capital letter.

She wants to eat pizza every day.

## STUDY SENTENCES

**Look at the story on page 52. Answer these questions.**

Example: **1.** The first sentence ends with a period.

1. What does the first sentence end with?
2. What does the last sentence end with?
3. How many words are in the fifth sentence?
4. How many words are in the sixth sentence?
5. Does each sentence start with a capital letter?

## WRITE SENTENCES

**Listen to the tape. Write these sentences correctly.**

Example: **6.** Lupe likes science lab.

6. Lupe likes science lab
7. she likes to study
8. the class has a test tomorrow
9. Lupe will do well
10. she also likes P.E. class
11. her teacher is Ms. Sampson
12. they run a lot
13. Lupe is fast
14. she likes soccer and football
15. Lupe likes school a lot

# Learn About Math Problems

| ADDITION | SUBTRACTION | MULTIPLICATION | DIVISION |
|---|---|---|---|

**ADDITION**

plus sign

$17 + 14 = 31$ — sum

equals sign

**Say:**
- Seventeen plus fourteen equals thirty-one.
- Seventeen and fourteen is thirty-one.

**SUBTRACTION**

minus sign

$$\begin{array}{r} 23 \\ -\ 9 \\ \hline 14 \end{array}$$ ← difference

**Say:**
- Twenty-three minus nine is fourteen.
- The difference between nine and twenty-three is fourteen.

**MULTIPLICATION**

times sign or multiplication sign

$$\begin{array}{r} 25 \\ \times\ 3 \\ \hline 75 \end{array}$$ ← product

**Say:**
- Twenty-five times three equals seventy-five.
- Twenty-five multiplied by three is seventy-five.

**DIVISION**

quotient

$39 \div 3 = 13$

division sign

$$\begin{array}{r} 13 \\ 3\overline{)39} \\ -3 \\ \hline 09 \\ -\ 9 \\ \hline 0 \end{array}$$

**Say:**
- Thirty-nine divided by three is thirteen.
- Three into thirty-nine is thirteen.

**Solve each problem. Then read it aloud.**

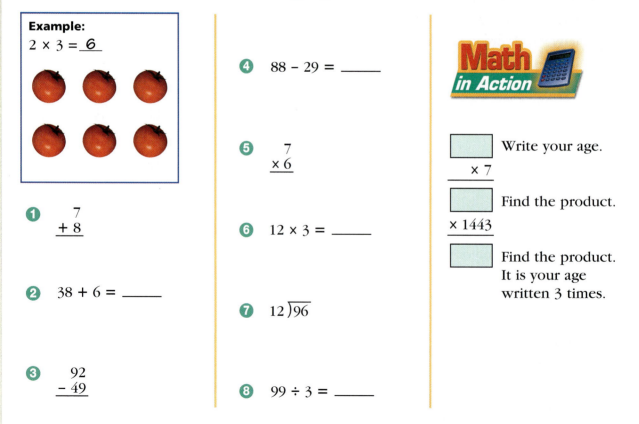

## Add, Subtract, Multiply, and Divide

**Example:**

$2 \times 3 = \underline{6}$

**1** $\quad\begin{array}{r} 7 \\ +\ 8 \\ \hline \end{array}$

**2** $\quad 38 + 6 = \underline{\hphantom{xxx}}$

**3** $\quad\begin{array}{r} 92 \\ -\ 49 \\ \hline \end{array}$

**4** $\quad 88 - 29 = \underline{\hphantom{xxx}}$

**5** $\quad\begin{array}{r} 7 \\ \times\ 6 \\ \hline \end{array}$

**6** $\quad 12 \times 3 = \underline{\hphantom{xxx}}$

**7** $\quad 12\overline{)96}$

**8** $\quad 99 \div 3 = \underline{\hphantom{xxx}}$

**Math in Action**

▢ Write your age.

$\times\ 7$

▢ Find the product.

$\times\ 1443$

▢ Find the product. It is your age written 3 times.

# Writing Project  POSTCARD

**Make a postcard about yourself. Send the postcard to a friend or relative.**

## PLAN WHAT YOU WILL WRITE

Think about what you will write. Make some notes.
Remember: there isn't much room on a postcard!

## WRITE YOUR POSTCARD

Include these parts on your postcard.

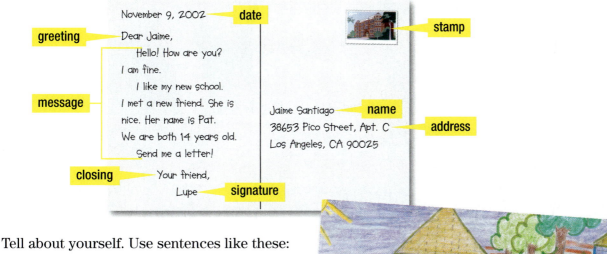

November 9, 2002 — **date**

**greeting** → Dear Jaime,

Hello! How are you?
I am fine.
I like my new school.
I met a new friend. She is
nice. Her name is Pat.
We are both 14 years old.
Send me a letter!

**message**

**stamp**

Jaime Santiago — **name**
38653 Pico Street, Apt. C
Los Angeles, CA 90025

**address**

**closing** → Your friend,
Lupe — **signature**

Tell about yourself. Use sentences like these:

- I am _____.
- We are _____.

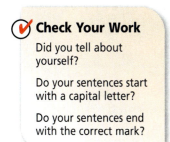

**✔ Check Your Work**

Did you tell about yourself?

Do your sentences start with a capital letter?

Do your sentences end with the correct mark?

Make a picture of your home or town on the other side of the postcard.

## SEND YOUR POSTCARD

Put a stamp on your postcard. Then put it in a mailbox!

# Set the Table

There are many things wrong with this picture!
Tell your partner about them. Then draw a
picture of another funny food. Ask the class
to guess what is wrong with your picture.

## In This Unit

### Vocabulary
• Colors, Shapes, and Sizes
• Foods and Food Groups

### Language Functions
• Express Likes
• Describe

### Patterns and Structures
• Adjectives
• Action Verbs
• Negative Sentences

### Reading
• Phonics: Short *u*, Short *i*,
  Digraph *ch,* and *tch*
• Comprehension:
  Identify Steps in a Process (sequence chain)

### Writing
• Sentences to Describe
• Sentences with *not*
• Exhibit Card

### Content Area Connection
• Science (food pyramid)

# What Foods Do You Like?

**Listen and chant.**

little, red tomatoes

## Tasty Salad

Lettuce, lettuce,
Fresh, green lettuce.
Carrots, carrots,
Long, orange carrots.
Onions, onions,
Large, round onions.
Salad, salad,
Tasty salad.
What a treat!

yellow corn

big, white cauliflower

long, orange carrot

tiny, green peas

purple cabbage

fresh, green lettuce

large, round onion

**Adjectives**
An **adjective** describes a person, place, or thing.

**long, orange** carrots
**large, round** onions

**EXPRESS YOURSELF** ▶ EXPRESS LIKES; DESCRIBE

**1.–6.** Work with a partner. Tell your partner about 6 foods you like. Use an adjective to describe each food.

**Example: 1.** I like yellow corn.

**WRITE LABELS** ✏️

**7.–10.** Draw 4 foods you like. Write a label for each picture. Use adjectives to describe each food.

**Example: 7.**

big, round bagel

# What Is Red and Round? A Tomato!

Look at the picture. Read the words that name a color or shape.

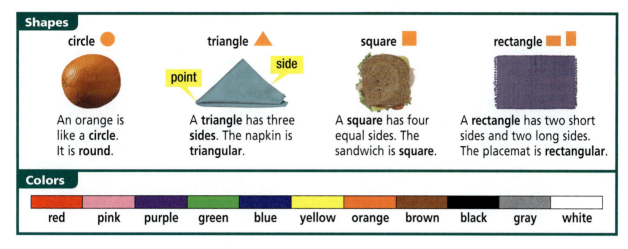

**Shapes**

circle

An orange is like a **circle**. It is **round**.

triangle

point    side

A **triangle** has three **sides**. The napkin is **triangular**.

square

A **square** has four equal sides. The sandwich is **square**.

rectangle

A **rectangle** has two short sides and two long sides. The placemat is **rectangular**.

**Colors**

| red | pink | purple | green | blue | yellow | orange | brown | black | gray | white |

## BUILD SENTENCES

Read each sentence below. Add words to tell the color, size, or shape. Say the new sentence.

**Example: 1.** A blueberry is round.
It is also small.

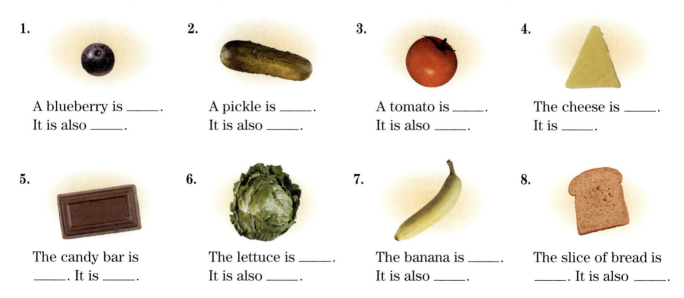

1.
A blueberry is _____.
It is also _____.

2.
A pickle is _____.
It is also _____.

3.
A tomato is _____.
It is also _____.

4.
The cheese is _____.
It is _____.

5.
The candy bar is
_____. It is _____.

6.
The lettuce is _____.
It is also _____.

7.
The banana is _____.
It is also _____.

8.
The slice of bread is
_____. It is also _____.

## WRITE SENTENCES 🖍

**9.–16.** Write a sentence for each picture above. Tell about the shape of the food.

**Example: 9.** A blueberry is like a circle.

# What's for Lunch?

Look at the picture. Say the name of each food.

## WHO'S TALKING? ▶ DESCRIBE

**1.–3.** Listen to each person talk about the lunch.
Point to the correct lunch. Then describe it.

## WRITE A LIST

**4.** What do you want for lunch? Write a list.
Draw a picture of each food. Use adjectives
to describe the food.

**Example: 4.**

TODAY'S LUNCH

a small, green salad
hot pizza
a tall glass of milk
red apple

# How Do You Make a Fruit Drink?

An **action verb** tells what someone does.

I **make** great fruit drinks.

I **cut** bananas.

I **put** them in the blender.

I **add** ice.

## BUILD SENTENCES

Tell how to make a fruit drink. Choose a verb from the box to complete each sentence. Say the new sentence.

**Example:** **1.** I wash the strawberries.

| Action Verbs | | |
|---|---|---|
| put | open | cut |
| get | push | wash |

**1.**

I _____ the strawberries.

**2.**

I _____ the strawberries.

**3.**

I _____ some ice.

**4.**

I _____ the yogurt.

**5.**

I _____ the yogurt in the blender.

**6.**

I _____ the button.

## WRITE SENTENCES 🖊

7.–10. Write 4 sentences to tell how you make a sandwich. Write each sentence on a card. Mix up the cards. Have your partner put the sentences in order.

**Example:** **7.**

I put jam on the bread.

# Read and Think Together

**Make a sequence chain to tell about _I Make Pictures Move!_**
**Follow these steps.**

**1** Think about how Andy makes his drawing.
Draw a box. In it, write what Andy does first.

> Andy draws bread.

**2** Draw 4 more boxes. Tell what else Andy does.

> Andy draws bread.
> ↓
> He draws tomatoes.
> ↓
> [ ]
> ↓
> [ ]
> ↓
> [ ]

**3** Use your sequence chain to tell a partner
how Andy makes his drawing. Then tell
what Dingo does at the end of the story.

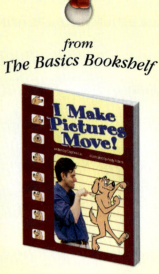

*from*
*The Basics Bookshelf*

**THEME BOOK**

First see how an artist
draws a meal for his dog,
and then flip the pages
to watch the dog eat it!

# Words to Know

## REVIEW WORDS YOU KNOW

**Read the words aloud. Which word goes in the sentence?**

| good | go |
|------|-----|
| like | look |
| who | with |

1. The lunch is _____ .
2. These kids _____ the food.
3. They eat _____ their hands.

## LEARN TO READ

**Learn new words.**

| | |
|---|---|
| **something** | I want **something** to eat. |
| **make** | I can **make** spaghetti! |
| **long** | First, I get a box of **long** noodles. |
| **large** | I put them in a **large** pot of hot water. |
| **move** | I **move** the pot to the back of the stove. |
| **different** | Then, I use a **different** pot for the sauce. |
| **small** | I cut an onion into **small** pieces. |
| **open** | I **open** a can of tomatoes. |
| **same** | I cook the onions and tomatoes in the **same** pot. |
| **eat** | At last, I **eat** my pasta! |

### How to Learn a New Word

- Look at the word.
- Listen to the word.
- Listen to the word in a sentence. What does it mean?
- Say the word.
- Spell the word.
- Say the word again.

## WORD WORK

**Write each new word on a card. Sort the cards into these groups:**

4. These 2 words end in **t**.
5. These 3 words start with an **s**.
6. These 3 words tell about size.
7. These 4 words name actions.
8. This word is made up of 2 smaller words.

**Read the words in each group aloud. Then make up new groups with a partner.**

Example: **4.**

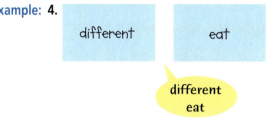

different
eat

# Reading and Spelling

**LISTEN AND LEARN**

# Ice Cream

Fill your cup with ice cream.

Fill it to the brim.

Catch the melted chocolate

Dripping down your chin.


Fill your cup with ice cream.

Add some nuts and then,

Catch the melted chocolate

Dripping down your chin!

## CONNECT SOUNDS AND LETTERS

**How many sounds does each word have?**

**c u p**

**n u t**

**l i d**

**ch i n**

## READING STRATEGY

**Follow these steps to read a word.**

**1** Point to the letters **ch**. Say the sound.

ch i n

**2** Point to the next letter. Say the sound.

ch i n

**3** Point to the last letter. Say the sound.

ch i n

**4** Now blend all the sounds together to say the word. Say the word again. What is it?

**ch + i + n = chin**

The letters **ch** make one sound. I blend 3 sounds to say **chin**.

## READING AND SPELLING PRACTICE

**Blend the sounds to read these words.**

**1.** chin    **2.** cup    **3.** can    **4.** catch    **5.** jumps    **6.** bug

**Use what you learned to read the sentences.**

**7.** There is something in my cup.

**8.** I can see it move.

**9.** It is small and green.

**10.** It jumps up and lands on my hand.

**11.** Now the bug is on my chin!

**12.** Can I catch it? No!

**13.–16.** Now write the sentences that your teacher reads.

## WORD WORK

**Look at the first picture. Then read the word. Use letter cards to make a new word for the next picture.**

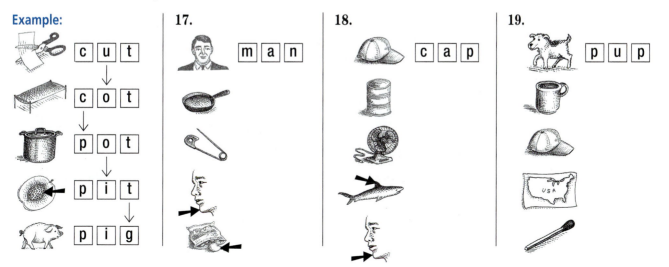

# Read on Your Own

## Something Good for Lunch

Kim likes hot dogs for lunch.
She cooks a batch of hot dogs in a big pot.
Next Kim chops some small onions.
She opens a large bag of buns.
She fills the buns with hot dogs, mustard, and onions.
She opens a bag of chips, too.
She pours a cup of punch.
This is too much food to eat!
Kim calls Mitch.
Then they sit and eat a great lunch!

## CHECK YOUR UNDERSTANDING

Tell the story to your partner. Use the words and pictures.

| Kim makes hot dogs. | She adds chips and punch. | Kim calls Mitch. | They eat lunch! |

# I Am Not a Cook!

> **A negative sentence has a negative word, like _not._**

The cake is **not** right.

The cookies are **not** good.

The kitchen is **not** clean.

I am **not** happy.

## BUILD SENTENCES

Look at each picture below. Add a verb and the word _not_ to complete each sentence. Say the new sentence.

**Example:** **1.** The burrito is not green.

1.

The burrito
____ ____ green.

2.

The limes
____ ____ square.

3.

The watermelon
____ ____ thin.

4.

The crackers
____ ____ blue.

5.

The kiwi ____ ____
triangular.

6.

I ____ ____ a nurse.

## WRITE SENTENCES

<u>7.–12.</u> Work with a partner. For each picture, write a new negative sentence. Use _is not_ or _are not_.

**Example:** **7.** The burrito is not purple.

# Learn About Food Groups

**CLASSIFICATION**

When you **classify**, you put things in **categories**, or **groups**.

category → Vegetables

a list of foods in the category →
1. peas
2. carrots
3. lettuce
4. peppers
5. mushrooms

**Study the food pyramid. Then do the activity.**

## What Kinds of Foods Do You Eat?

**You will need:** a notebook and a pencil

### ACTIVITY STEPS

**1 Make a List**
Write all the foods you ate yesterday.

**2 Put the Foods in Groups**
Classify the foods on your list. Use the 6 food groups you learned about.

**3 Count the Servings**
Draw the food pyramid. Next to each group, write the number of servings you ate.

**THINK IT OVER ?**

1. Look at the food pyramid you drew. From which food group did you eat the most servings?

2. Do you need to eat more from some groups? Which ones?

3. Do you need to eat less from some groups? Which ones?

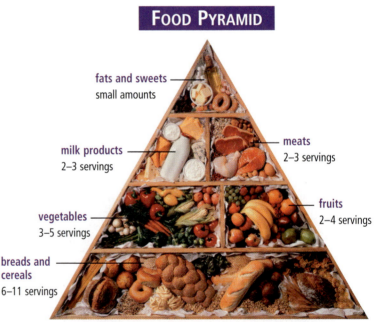

**FOOD PYRAMID**

fats and sweets
small amounts

milk products
2–3 servings

meats
2–3 servings

vegetables
3–5 servings

fruits
2–4 servings

breads and cereals
6–11 servings

This food pyramid shows the number of servings you should eat each day. Eat more of the foods from the bottom of the pyramid. Eat fewer foods from the top.

# Writing Project  EXHIBIT CARD

Use food to make a piece of art. Write a card to tell how
you make it. Then have an art show with your class!

## CHOOSE YOUR DESIGN

Think of art you can make with food. Choose one.

boat made of melon

face made of fruits
and vegetables

octopus made of a banana

## MAKE AND DESCRIBE YOUR ART

**1** Get or draw the food you need.
Build your piece of art.

**2** Write your card. Tell how you make the art.
Use adjectives to describe the foods. Check pages 310–311
of your Handbook for adjectives to use.

**3** Work with a partner to check your work.

> I pick a long, yellow banana. I cut
> the peel into 8 long, thin strips.
> I add little black and white beans
> for eyes.

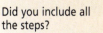 **Check Your Work**

Did you include all
the steps?

Did you use adjectives
to describe the
foods you used?

Does each sentence
begin with a capital letter
and end in a period?

## HAVE AN ART SHOW

Take a tour of the class art show. Read about your
classmates' art. Tell which pieces you like the most.

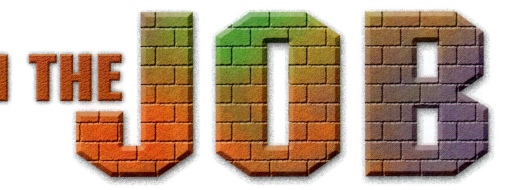

# ON THE JOB

Work with a partner. Look at the picture.
What workers do you see?
Draw tools they use. Trade drawings.
Match the drawings to the correct workers.

## In This Unit

### Vocabulary
- Actions
- Tools and Careers
- Science and Measurement Words

### Language Functions
- Give Information
- Ask and Answer Questions

### Patterns and Structures
- Present Tense Verbs
- Yes-or-No Questions
- Questions with *Who?*, *What?*, *Where?*, and *When?*

### Reading
- Phonics: Short *e*, *sh*, *ck*, and Double Consonants
- Comprehension: Identify Details (concept web)

### Writing
- Sentences
- Questions and Answers
- Job Handbook

### Content Area Connection
- Science (scientific processes) and Mathematics (measurement)

# What Is the Job for Me?

**Listen and sing.**

## JOBS

Artists paint, and artists draw.

Carpenters hammer, and they saw.

Gardeners plant, and gardeners mow.

Farmers harvest, and they sow.

Teachers teach us how to write.

Police protect us through the night.

With so many choices of what to be,

I wonder what job is the one for me.

| Careers | Actions |
| --- | --- |
| artists | draw |
| carpenters | build |
| gardeners | plant |
| teachers | teach |

**EXPRESS YOURSELF** ▶ GIVE INFORMATION

<u>1.–3.</u> **Work with a partner. Choose 3 jobs. Tell what the workers do.**

Example: **1.** Artists paint and draw.

**WRITE LABELS** 🖍

<u>4.</u> **Draw a picture of a worker. Label your drawing.**

Example: **4.**

Cab Driver

# People in Action

To tell what another person or thing does, use a **verb** that ends in **-s**.

The carpenter **builds** a box.

He **uses** glue.

It **holds** the sides together.

His son **helps.**

## BUILD SENTENCES

Say each sentence. Add the correct form of the action verb.     **Example:  1.** He mops the floor.

**1.**

He _____ the floor. (**mop**)

**2.**

She _____ the plants. (**water**)

**3.**

She _____ newspapers. (**sell**)

**4.**

It _____ the clothes. (**clean**)

**5.**

He _____ . (**run**)

**6.**

She _____ the news. (**report**)

## WRITE SENTENCES ✏️

<u>7.–10.</u>  Think of a worker. Act out what the worker does. Have your partner guess the worker and write 4 sentences about his or her job.

**Example:  7.** The gardener pulls the weeds.

# Are They at Work?

A question asks for information. It ends with a **question mark.**

You can answer some questions with *yes* or *no.*

Is this the gym**?** Yes.

When you tell more in your answer, use the correct **pronoun.**

Is this the gym? Yes, **it** is.

Are the girls alone? No, **they** are not.

Can Rob play? Yes, **he** can.

## ANSWER QUESTIONS

Look at each picture below. Read the question. Answer it.

**Example:** **1.** Yes, she can.

**1.**

Can the writer use the computer?

**2.**

Is the photographer in an office?

**3.**

Are Linda and Brian carpenters?

**4.**

Are Dave and Wendy pilots?

**5.**

Can the architect draw?

**6.**

Are Julia and Miguel dancers?

## WRITE QUESTIONS ✏️

**7.–12.** Write a new question for each picture above. Start each question with *Is*, *Are*, or *Can.* Put a question mark at the end.

**Example:** **7.** Is she a writer?

# Tools of the Trade

Look at the pictures. Read the words.

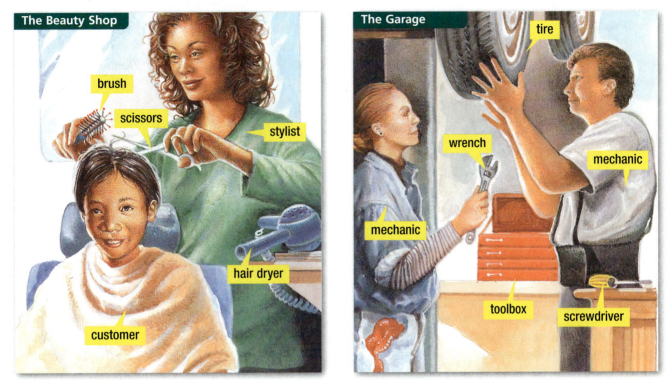

## WHO'S TALKING? ▶ ASK AND ANSWER QUESTIONS

1.–2. Listen.

Who is talking? Point to the correct person.
Then act out the scene with a partner.
Ask and answer questions.

## WRITE ANSWERS

Look at the pictures above. Ask a partner each
question. Write your partner's answer.

**Example: 3.** Can the stylist cut hair?
Yes, she can.

**In the Beauty Shop**

3. Can the stylist cut hair?
4. Is a customer in the chair?
5. Is the hair dryer in her hand?
6. Are they in a cafeteria?

**In the Garage**

7. Are they in a garage?
8. Is she a teacher?
9. Is the wrench in the toolbox?
10. Can they fix the car?

# Read and Think Together

Make a concept web to tell about the people in *What Is It?*
Follow these steps.

**1** Think about the story. Who is in it?

> Who is in the story?

**2** Who is the first person in the story?
Write the name of her job.

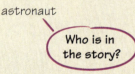

> astronaut
>
> Who is in the story?

**3** Add the other people in the story to the web.

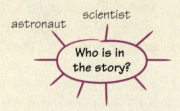

> astronaut    scientist
>
> Who is in the story?

**4** Finish the web. Use it to tell the story
to a partner.

*from*
*The Basics Bookshelf*

**THEME BOOK**

In this fantasy, a visitor
from space has an
adventure on Earth.

# Words to Know

## REVIEW WORDS YOU KNOW

**Read the words aloud. Which word goes in the sentence?**

| what | work |
|------|------|
| many | you |
| There | Then |

1. The photographers _____ at the race.
2. They take _____ pictures.
3. _____ are 25 people in the race.

## LEARN TO READ

**Learn new words.**

| study | I **study** photography in school. |
|-------|-----------------------------------|
| learn | I **learn** how to use a camera. |
| carry | I **carry** a camera in my backpack. |
| find | I always **find** something to photograph. |
| use | I **use** a lot of film. |
| love | I **love** to take pictures of my mom. |
| face | She always has a smile on her **face**. |
| when | My friends run **when** they see me. |
| want | They don't **want** to be photographed. |
| say | They **say**, "Don't take a picture of us!" |

**How to Learn a New Word**

- Look at the word.
- Listen to the word.
- Listen to the word in a sentence. What does it mean?
- Say the word.
- Spell the word.
- Say the word again.

## WORD WORK

**4.–13. Work with a partner. Write each new word on a card. Mix your cards together for the game. Turn them so the words are down. Then:**

- Turn over 2 cards.
- Spell the words. Are they the same?
- If so, keep them. If not, turn them over again.
- The player with more cards at the end wins.

**Example:**

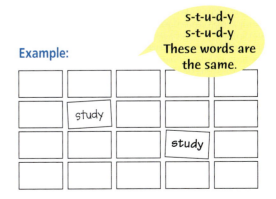

s-t-u-d-y
s-t-u-d-y
These words are the same.

# Reading and Spelling

## LISTEN AND LEARN

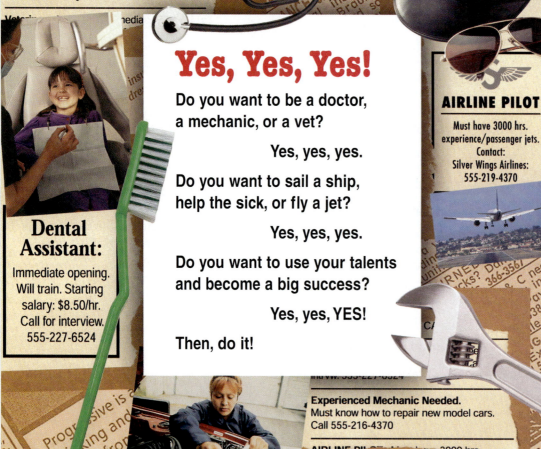

**DOCTOR WANTED!** California town needs doctor for small clinic. Fair salary. Grateful patients. Send resume to Ms. Daisy Milos, PO Box 432, Dry Creek, CA 90992

### Yes, Yes, Yes!

Do you want to be a doctor,
a mechanic, or a vet?

Yes, yes, yes.

Do you want to sail a ship,
help the sick, or fly a jet?

Yes, yes, yes.

Do you want to use your talents
and become a big success?

Yes, yes, YES!

Then, do it!

**AIRLINE PILOT**

Must have 3000 hrs. experience/passenger jets.
Contact:
Silver Wings Airlines:
555-219-4370

**Dental Assistant:**

Immediate opening.
Will train. Starting
salary: $8.50/hr.
Call for interview.
555-227-6524

**Experienced Mechanic Needed.**
Must know how to repair new model cars.
Call 555-216-4370

## CONNECT SOUNDS AND LETTERS

How many sounds does each word have?

**j e t**      **t e n**      **sh e ll**      **ch e ck**

▶ Transparencies 21–25

## READING STRATEGY

**Follow these steps to read a word.**

**1** Point to the first letter. Say the sound.

**be**ll

**2** Point to the second letter. Say the sound.

b**e**ll

**3** Point to the last two letters. Say the sound.

be**ll**

**4** Now blend all the sounds together to say the word. Say the word again. What is it?

**b + e + ll = bell**

These two consonants are the same, so I say just one sound.

## READING AND SPELLING PRACTICE

**Blend the sounds to read these words.**

**1.** shot    **2.** neck    **3.** vet    **4.** black    **5.** kiss    **6.** ten

**Use what you learned to read the sentences.**

**7.** My cat, Fuzz, is sick.

**8.** I carry him to the vet.

**9.** I kiss him on the neck.

**10.** The vet gives my cat a shot.

**11.** He gives me ten black pills for my cat.

**12.** Then I tell Fuzz, "Let's go home."

**13.–16.** Now write the sentences that your teacher reads.

## WORD WORK

**Name each picture. What letters are missing from the names? Use letter cards to make the words.**

Example: **17.** | j | e | t |

**17.** 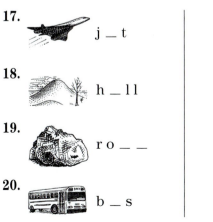 j _ t

**18.** h _ ll

**19.** r o _ _

**20.** b _ s

**21.** 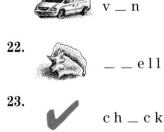 v _ n

**22.** _ _ e l l

**23.**  c h _ c k

**24.** f i _ _

**25.** 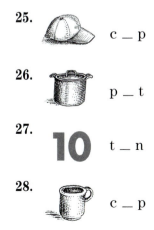 c _ p

**26.** p _ t

**27.** 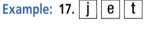 **10** t _ n

**28.** c _ p

# Read on Your Own

# Let Ben Take It

Ben is a bike messenger.
Do you want to send something?
Ben can get it there fast.
Just tell him where it must go.
He gets his map.
He uses it to find a shop.
Then he hops on his bike and . . . zip!
He is off like a jet.
Ben can carry a lot of different things:
food, pictures, letters, flowers.
They fit in the big bag on his back.
Ben loves his job.
When you want to send something,
let Ben take it!

## CHECK YOUR UNDERSTANDING

Copy and complete the map. Then tell a partner about Ben's job.

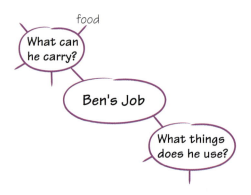

# Questions About Work

You can use the words *Who*, *What*, *Where*, or *When* to start a question.

Use *Who* to ask about a person.
**Who** are you?

Use *What* to ask about a thing.
**What** is in your bag?

Use *Where* to ask about a place.
**Where** is the shop?

Use *When* to ask about a time.
**When** can you deliver the box?

## MATCH QUESTIONS AND ANSWERS

Read each question. Find the sentence that answers it.
Read the questions and answers to a partner.

Example: **1.** Who is the bike messenger?
**E.** Ben is the bike messenger.

| Questions | Answers |
|---|---|
| **1.** Who is the bike messenger? | **A.** His helmet is on his head. |
| **2.** What is in his bag? | **B.** A box is in his bag. |
| **3.** Where is his helmet? | **C.** His next delivery is at 8:30. |
| **4.** When is his next delivery? | **D.** Ben is in the city. |
| **5.** Where is Ben? | **E.** Ben is the bike messenger. |

## WRITE QUESTIONS AND ANSWERS

Make a question to go with each answer.
Then write the question and answer.

Example: **6.** What is in the bag? A box of candy is in the bag.

**6.** What _____? A box of candy is in the bag.

**7.** What _____? It is a birthday present for Mr. Lee.

**8.** Where _____? His office is in that tall building.

**9.** When _____? His birthday is tomorrow.

**10.** Who _____? Ben can deliver the box.

**11.** Where _____? Ben is near the tall building.

**12.** When _____? Ben is ready to deliver the box now!

# Learn About Measurement

## OBSERVE

round

long

big

little

rough

smooth

## MEASURE

scale

The weight of the rock is 8 ounces.

16 ounces = 1 pound
2000 pounds = 1 ton

## COMPARE

heavy

light

**Read the instructions. Then do the activity.**

# ▶ Be a Scientist: Study Rocks

**You will need:** different kinds of rocks, a scale, a notebook, and a pencil

## ACTIVITY STEPS

**1 Observe**
Make an observation log. Assign each rock a letter to identify it. Study the rocks. Take notes in the log about how each rock looks and feels.

**2 Measure**
Weigh each rock. Write the weights in your log.

**3 Compare**
How are the rocks alike? How are they different? Find out which rocks are the lightest. Find out which are the heaviest.

**4 Sort**
Put the rocks in groups, or categories. Is each rock heavy or light? Is it rough or smooth?

### Observation Log

| Rock | Color | Size | Shape | Weight |
|------|-------|------|-------|--------|
| A | gray | big | round | 10 oz. |
|  |  |  |  |  |
|  |  |  |  |  |
|  |  |  |  |  |

### THINK IT OVER ❓

1. Is a big rock always heavier than a small one? Explain what you learned.
2. Where do you see different types of rocks in nature? How are they different?

# Writing Project JOB HANDBOOK

**Interview a worker about his or her job.**
**Make a job handbook to keep in your classroom.**

## INTERVIEW A WORKER

Think of a worker you want to interview. Plan a time you can talk with the person.

**1** Think of questions.

1. What is your name?

2. Where do you work?

3. What is your job?

4. What do you like about your job?

**2** Ask your questions.

Where do you work?

I work at Lakeside School.

**3** Write the answers.

1. What is your name?
   My name is Mrs. Varela.
2. Where do you work?
   Lakeside School
3. What is your job?

4. What do you like about your job?

## MAKE A JOB REPORT

Ask the worker for his or her picture.
Copy your questions and the answers.
At the top of the page, write the worker's job.

> ✔ **Check Your Work**
>
> Did you write all your questions?
>
> Did you end each question with a question mark?
>
> Did you write answers for all the questions?

**Teacher**

What is your name?
   My name is Mrs. Varela.
Where do you work?
   I work at Lakeside School.
What is your job?
   I am a social studies teacher.
What do you like about your job?
   I like the students.
   I like reading about history.

## MAKE A JOB HANDBOOK

Add your report and the picture to a class handbook.

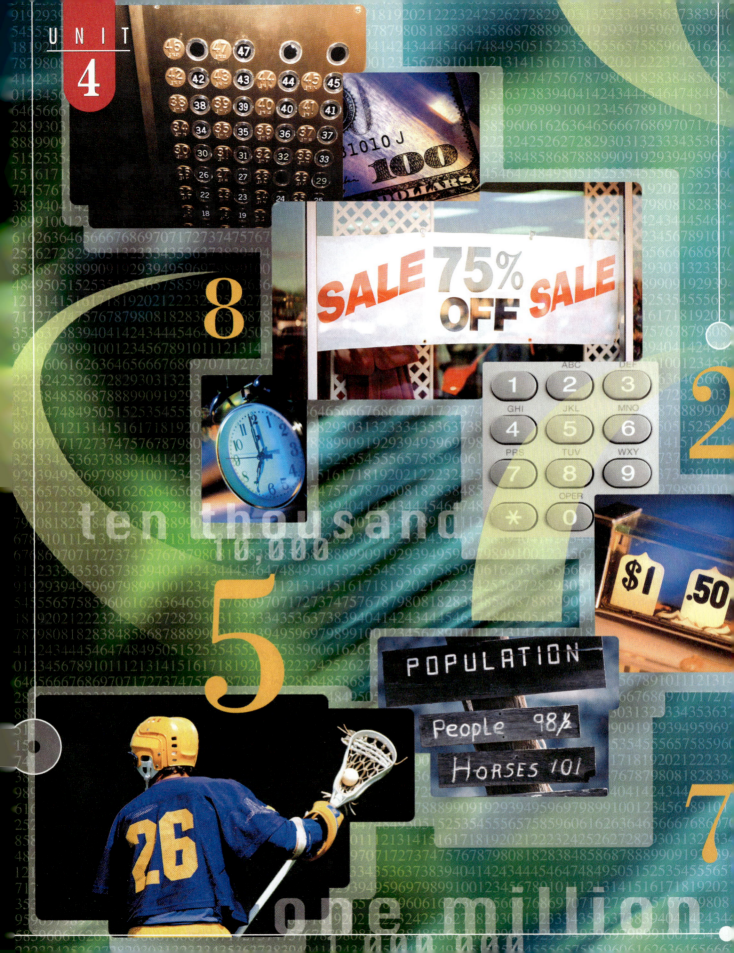

SALE 75% OFF SALE

$100 DOLLARS

8

ten thousand
10,000

5

2

POPULATION

People    98%

Horses 101

$1    .50

26

7

one million

# Numbers Count

Look at the pictures.
What do they show?
Work with a partner to find
more numbers around you.

## In This Unit

### Vocabulary
- Cardinal Numbers
- Ordinal Numbers
- Geography

### Language Functions
- Ask Questions
- Give Information
- Express Needs

### Patterns and Structures
- Questions with *Do* and *Does*
- Negative Sentences
- Contractions with *not*

### Reading
- Phonics: Blends and Digraphs
- Comprehension:
  Identify Problems and Solutions
  (problem-and-solution chart)
  Identify Details

### Writing
- Questions and Answers
- Sentences
- Fact Sheet

### Content Area Connection
- Social Studies (geography/charts)

# Numbers Everywhere!

**Listen and chant.**

## Numbers!

Does it cost ten dollars
To go to the show?
Without numbers
We wouldn't know.

Without numbers
We'd be in a fix.
Does the show start at five?
Or is it at six?

Do we need two tickets?
Or do we need three?
Without numbers,
Where would we be?

> **Questions with *Do* and *Does***
> Use **do** with *I*, *you*, *we*, and *they*.
> **Do you** need two tickets?
> Use **does** with *he*, *she*, and *it*.
> **Does it** cost ten dollars?

## EXPRESS YOURSELF ▶ ASK QUESTIONS

<u>1.–4.</u> **Work with a partner. Ask 4 questions.**
**Choose words from each column.**

| | | |
|---|---|---|
| Do you | have | five cookies? |
| Do they | see | two pencils? |
| Does he | need | seven backpacks? |
| Does she | want | three markers? |

Examples: **1.** Do you need two pencils?
**2.** Does she see five cookies?

## WRITE QUESTIONS AND ANSWERS

<u>5.–8.</u> **Write 4 questions on cards. Use *Do* or *Does*.**
**Trade cards with a partner. Answer the questions you get.**

Example: **5.** Do you have a highlighter?
No, I do not.

# From One to One Million

## Number Words

| | | | | | | | | | |
|---|---|---|---|---|---|---|---|---|---|
| 0 | zero | 11 | eleven | 21 | twenty-one | 40 | forty | 100 | one hundred |
| 1 | one | 12 | twelve | 22 | twenty-two | 50 | fifty | 101 | one hundred one |
| 2 | two | 13 | thirteen | 23 | twenty-three | 60 | sixty | 500 | five hundred |
| 3 | three | 14 | fourteen | 24 | twenty-four | 70 | seventy | 550 | five hundred fifty |
| 4 | four | 15 | fifteen | 25 | twenty-five | 80 | eighty | 1,000 | one thousand |
| 5 | five | 16 | sixteen | 26 | twenty-six | 90 | ninety | 1,151 | one thousand, one hundred fifty-one |
| 6 | six | 17 | seventeen | 27 | twenty-seven | | | 5,000 | five thousand |
| 7 | seven | 18 | eighteen | 28 | twenty-eight | | | 10,000 | ten thousand |
| 8 | eight | 19 | nineteen | 29 | twenty-nine | | | 100,000 | one hundred thousand |
| 9 | nine | 20 | twenty | 30 | thirty | | | 500,000 | five hundred thousand |
| 10 | ten | | | | | | | 1,000,000 | one million |

**Beijing, China:** population 13,800,000

thirteen million, eight hundred thousand

Put commas after the millions place and the thousands place.

## EXPRESS YOURSELF ▶ GIVE INFORMATION

**Work with a partner. Read each fact about China in 2000.**
**Say a sentence with each fact. Begin your sentence with *China has*.**

1. **65,650** kilometers of railways
2. **206** airports
3. **700,000,000** workers
4. **23,400,000** cellular phones
5. **3,240** television stations
6. **400,000,000** televisions

**Example:** 1. China has sixty-five thousand, six hundred fifty kilometers of railways.

## WRITE SENTENCES

<u>7.–10.</u> **Work with a partner to find numbers in your classroom.**
**Write 4 sentences with the numbers you find.**
**Write words for the numbers.**

**Example:** 7. Our classroom has thirty-three desks.

# Flight 400 Is Not Late!

There are different ways to build negative sentences.

**Add *not* after *am*, *is*, or *are*.**

He is happy.
She is not happy.

**Add *do not* or *does not* before other verbs.**

She gets on the flight.
He does not get on the flight.

## BUILD NEGATIVE SENTENCES

**Read each sentence. Add *not* to make it a negative sentence. Say the new sentence.**

1. We are on Flight 400.
2. It is 10:00.
3. We are late.
4. People are in a hurry.

**Example:** 1. We are on Flight 400.
We are not on Flight 400.

**Read each sentence. Add *do not* or *does not* to make it a negative sentence. Say the new sentence.**

5. The plane leaves at 10:30.
6. We walk very fast.
7. We get to Gate 55.
8. A woman talks to us.
9. We miss the plane.
10. The plane leaves without us.

**Example:** 5. The plane leaves at 10:30
The plane does not leave at 10:30.

When you use *does not*, take the *s* off the verb.

## WRITE SENTENCES

**11.–20.** Write the sentences you made in Items 1–10 above.

**Example:** **11.** We are on Flight 400. We are not on Flight 400.

# First, Second, Third...

Look at the picture. In what order are the people?

## WHO'S TALKING? ▶ EXPRESS NEEDS

**1.–6. Listen.** 📼
**Which person in line is talking?**
**Point to the correct person.**
**Tell what the person needs.**

**Example: 1.** This is the fifth person.
She needs a magazine.

## WRITE SENTENCES ✏️

**7.–14. Write about 8 people in the line.**
**Tell what each person needs.**

**Example: 7.** The first person needs water.

# Read and Think Together

Make a problem-and-solution chart for *A Year Without Rain*. Follow these steps.

**1** Think about the story. What is the main problem? Draw a box and write the problem.

> **Problem:** There is no rain. People are hungry.

**2** What happens next? Add boxes. Write one event in each box.

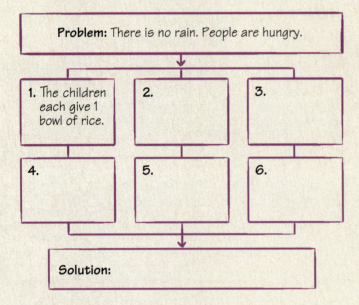

> **Problem:** There is no rain. People are hungry.

> 1. The children each give 1 bowl of rice.
> 2.
> 3.
> 4.
> 5.
> 6.

> Solution:

**3** How is the problem solved? Write the solution in the box at the bottom of your chart.

**4** Use your completed problem-and-solution chart to tell the story to a partner.

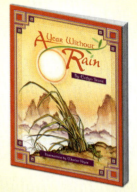

*from*
*The Basics Bookshelf*

**THEME BOOK**

In a time without rain, crops do not grow, but people find a way to feed the hungry.

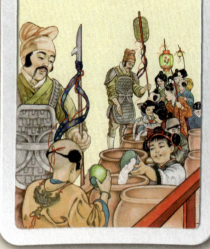

# Words to Know

## REVIEW WORDS YOU KNOW

**Read the words aloud. Which word goes in the sentence?**

| are | say |
|-----|-----|
| year | read |
| find | from |

1. The people _____ in an airport.
2. They _____ the screens.
3. They _____ their flight numbers.

## LEARN TO READ

**Learn new words.**

| | |
|---|---|
| **leave** | Stan and his friend **leave** in June for a vacation. |
| **two** | They go for **two** months: June and July. |
| **out** | They fly in and **out** of many airports. |
| **three** | China, Japan, and Laos are **three** Asian countries. |
| **all** | Stan likes them **all**. |
| **says** | Stan **says**, "Our first stop is in China." |
| **second** | "Our **second** stop is in Japan." |
| **without** | Stan never travels **without** his camera. |
| **enough** | He takes **enough** film to photograph everything. |
| **more** | He brings back **more** pictures of Japan than of China. |

**How to Learn a New Word**

- Look at the word.
- Listen to the word.
- Listen to the word in a sentence. What does it mean?
- Say the word.
- Spell the word.
- Say the word again.

## WORD WORK

**Write each new word on a card. Sort the cards into these groups:**

4. These 2 words have 6 letters.
5. These 5 words have 3 or 4 letters.
6. This word is made up of 2 smaller words.
7. These 2 words name numbers.
8. These 2 words name actions.

**Read the words in each group aloud.**
**Make up new groups with a partner.**

**Example:** 4.

second
enough

# Reading and Spelling

## LISTEN AND LEARN

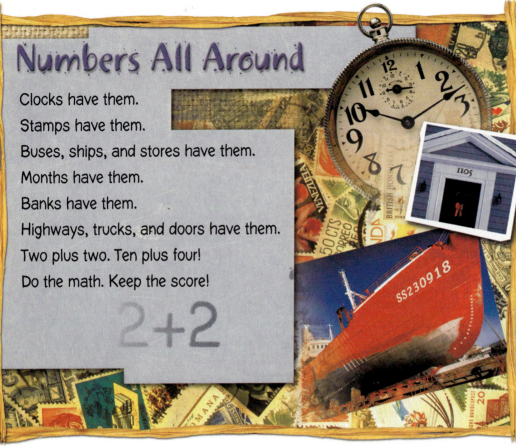

### Numbers All Around

Clocks have them.

Stamps have them.

Buses, ships, and stores have them.

Months have them.

Banks have them.

Highways, trucks, and doors have them.

Two plus two. Ten plus four!

Do the math. Keep the score!

2+2

## CONNECT SOUND AND LETTERS

**How many sounds does each word have?**

1.

clock     band

nest     truck

2.

fish     bath

check     ring

▶ Transparencies 26–30

## READING STRATEGY

Follow these steps to read a word.

**1** Sometimes 2 consonants stand for 1 sound. When you see **sh**, **ch**, **th**, **wh**, or **ng**, say 1 sound. Then blend all the sounds together to say the word.

**sh o p**                                **b a th**

**sh + o + p = shop**          **b + a + th = bath**

> Each word has **3** sounds.

**2** When other consonants are together, each usually makes its own sound. Blend all the sounds together to say the word.

**d r o p**                                **w e n t**

**d + r + o + p = drop**          **w + e + n + t = went**

> Each word has **4** sounds.

## READING AND SPELLING PRACTICE

**Blend the sounds to read these words.**

1. brush      2. bring      3. cash      4. class      5. costs      6. just

**Use what you learned to read the sentences.**

7. Beth needs a brush for art class this spring.
8. She has three dollars in cash.
9. That is enough for a small brush. It costs just $2.39.
10. A big, long brush costs $5.00.
11. Which brush does Beth bring home?

<u>12.–15.</u> **Now write the sentences that your teacher reads.**

## WORD WORK

<u>16.</u> **Write each of these words on a card.**          Example: **16.**

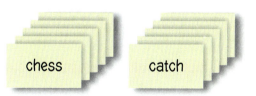

| catch | chess | chin | inch | much |
| match | check | lunch | chat | chop |

**Say each word. Group the words that begin with the same sound.**
**Now group the words that end with the same sound.**
**Look at these words. What do you notice?**

# Read on Your Own

Stan is in a big rush. His plane leaves at 2:00 p.m. The clock says 1:57 p.m. Stan has three minutes to catch his plane. That is not very long! He jumps out of the cab and slams the door. Bang! He drops his bag. All of his things fall out of the bag. Then he drops his ticket! A man helps Stan. He picks up the ticket and asks, "When does your plane leave?"

Stan says, "I think it just left without me."

The man looks at Stan's ticket. He grins and tells Stan, "You have enough time. Your plane leaves tomorrow at two."

## CHECK YOUR UNDERSTANDING

Copy the web. Then complete it. Tell the story to a partner.

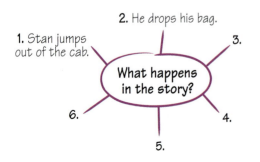

2. He drops his bag.

1. Stan jumps out of the cab.

3.

What happens in the story?

6.

4.

5.

# I Don't Want to Pay $10.00!

When you make a <mark>contraction,</mark> you join two words together.

| | |
|---|---|
| is + not = isn't | do + not = don't |
| are + not = aren't | does + not = doesn't |

<mark>no space</mark>     <mark>Write an apostrophe in place of the *o*.</mark>

**Use these contractions in negative sentences.**

The food at the airport **isn't** very good.
The cookies **aren't** big.
The cake **doesn't** have nuts.
I **don't** want anything to eat.

## READ SENTENCES

**Read the first sentence in each item. Then read the second sentence with the contraction. Listen to how the contraction sounds.**

1. Stan <u>does not</u> want this food. Stan <u>doesn't</u> want this food.
2. The grapes <u>are not</u> green. The grapes <u>aren't</u> green.
3. The sandwich <u>is not</u> fresh. The sandwich <u>isn't</u> fresh.
4. The cookies <u>do not</u> have raisins. The cookies <u>don't</u> have raisins.

**Read each sentence. Change the <u>underlined</u> words to a contraction. Then say the new sentence.**

Example: 5. The salad <u>does not</u> have carrots.
        The salad doesn't have carrots.

5. The salad <u>does not</u> have carrots.
6. The grapes <u>do not</u> taste sweet.
7. The cake <u>is not</u> chocolate.
8. The grapes <u>are not</u> cold.
9. The food <u>is not</u> cheap!
10. Stan <u>is not</u> hungry anymore.

## WRITE SENTENCES

<u>11.–14.</u> **Work with a partner. Write 4 new sentences to tell about the picture above. Use *isn't*, *aren't*, *don't*, and *doesn't*.**

Example: 11. The salad isn't fresh.

# Learn About Geography

## GLOBE

continent

Asia

China

ocean

country

China is a **country** on the **continent** of Asia.

## CHART

Population of China and Japan (July 2000) — title

heading

| COUNTRY | POPULATION |
|---------|------------|
| China | 1,261,832,000 |
| Japan | 126,550,000 |

row

column

Read each **row** to get information about one country.

Each **heading** tells the kind of information in a **column**.

**Listen to the article and study the chart. Then do the Review.**

# Compare Populations

- Why do some places have a large population?

South America is a large **continent**. It has many different kinds of land.

Mountains

Rain Forest

The Coast

Most people live near the coast. Not many people live in the middle of the continent because it has many forests and mountains. Roads and towns are difficult to build in places like that, and it is not easy to ship things.

Compare Colombia and Bolivia, for example. These **countries** are of similar size, but their populations are very different. One reason is the location of each country. Bolivia is an inland country with mountains and rain forests. It has only about 2,000 miles of paved roads, so travel is difficult. Colombia has about 9,000 miles of paved roads. The roads make it easy for people to get there. Colombia also has coasts on both the Caribbean Sea and Pacific Ocean. It is easy to ship things by land or sea. People like to live where it is easy to get the things they need.

### REVIEW

1. **Check Your Understanding** Why do most people in South America live near the coast?
2. **Vocabulary** In what continent are Colombia and Bolivia located?
3. **Use Charts** How many more people live in Colombia than in Bolivia?

Area and Population of Bolivia and Colombia (2000)

| COUNTRY | AREA (in square miles) | POPULATION |
|---------|------------------------|------------|
| Bolivia | 424,164 | 8,153,000 |
| Colombia | 440,831 | 39,686,000 |

# Writing Project  Fact Sheet

**Find number facts about a country. Then write a fact sheet to share with the class.**

## FIND NUMBER FACTS

**1** Choose a country to research. Make a list of questions like these.

**2** Find answers. Get help from your teacher or librarian.

**3** Take notes.

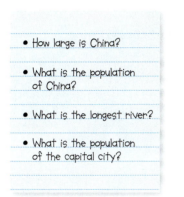

- How large is China?

- What is the population of China?

- What is the longest river?

- What is the population of the capital city?

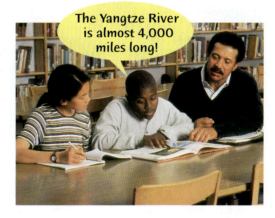

The Yangtze River is almost 4,000 miles long!

- Size: over 3,700,000 square miles

- Population: 1,261,832,000 people

- Yangtze River is almost 4,000 miles long.

- The capital is Beijing. Its population is 13,800,000.

## MAKE A FACT SHEET

Write the name of the country at the top of a piece of paper.
Use your notes to write each question and answer.

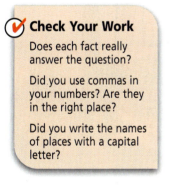

### ✔ Check Your Work

Does each fact really answer the question?

Did you use commas in your numbers? Are they in the right place?

Did you write the names of places with a capital letter?

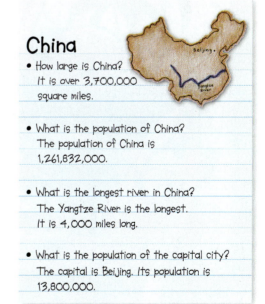

## China
- How large is China? It is over 3,700,000 square miles.

- What is the population of China? The population of China is 1,261,832,000.

- What is the longest river in China? The Yangtze River is the longest. It is 4,000 miles long.

- What is the population of the capital city? The capital is Beijing. Its population is 13,800,000.

## SHARE YOUR FACTS

Point to the country on a world map.
Share your facts with the class.

Welcome to MIAMI

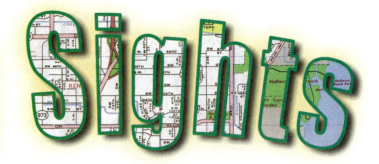

# City Sights

Look at the sign. What does it tell you about this city? Work with a group to make a sign for your city. Describe your sign to the class.

## In This Unit

**Vocabulary**
- Location Words
- Neighborhood
- Maps

**Language Function**
- Ask for and Give Information

**Patterns and Structures**
- Prepositions
- Regular Past Tense Verbs
- Statements with *There is* and *There are*
- Pronoun-Verb Contractions

**Reading**
- Word Patterns and Multisyllabic Words
- Comprehension:
  Identify Details (detail chart)

**Writing**
- Sentences
- Questions and Answers
- Journal Entry

**Content Area Connection**
- Social Studies (maps)

# Out and About in the City

Listen and sing.

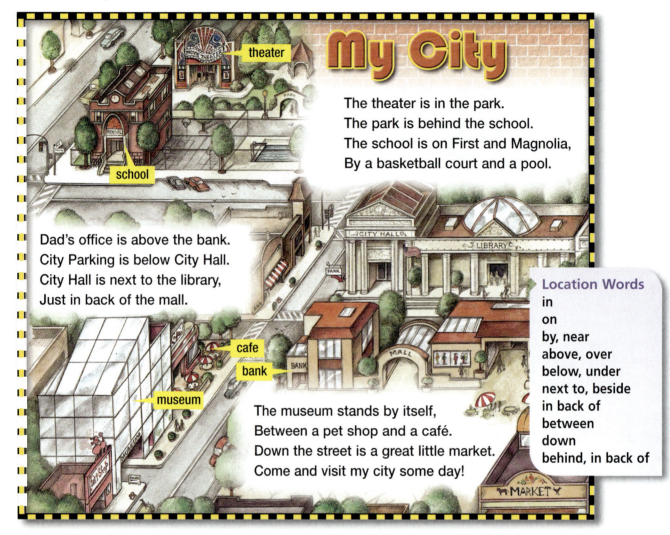

**My City**

The theater is in the park.
The park is behind the school.
The school is on First and Magnolia,
By a basketball court and a pool.

Dad's office is above the bank.
City Parking is below City Hall.
City Hall is next to the library,
Just in back of the mall.

The museum stands by itself,
Between a pet shop and a café.
Down the street is a great little market.
Come and visit my city some day!

**Location Words**
in
on
by, near
above, over
below, under
next to, beside
in back of
between
down
behind, in back of

## EXPRESS YOURSELF ▶ ASK FOR AND GIVE INFORMATION

**Work with a partner. Ask each question about your school.
Answer in a complete sentence. Use a location word.**

**Example:** 1. Where is the library?
It is by the gym.

1. Where is the library?
2. Where is the parking lot?
3. Where is the main office?
4. Where is the cafeteria?
5. Where is the entrance?
6. Where is the gym?

## WRITE SENTENCES

7.–10. **Choose 4 places in your school. Write sentences to tell where they are.**

**Example: 7.** The gym is by the library.

# What Happens Here?

Hardware Store — sign

Bus Station — bus

Hospital — ambulance

Post Office — flag

Library

Fire Station — fire engine

mailbox

Police Station — patrol car

Intersection — stop sign, crosswalk

Gas Station — car, gas pump

Store — parking lot

## EXPRESS YOURSELF ▶ ASK FOR AND GIVE INFORMATION

<u>1.–4.</u> Work with a partner. Ask this question about 4 places in the neighborhood: *What happens at _____?* Answer your partner's questions.

Example: 1. What happens at the bus station?
People wait for the bus.

## WRITE QUESTIONS AND ANSWERS

<u>5.–14.</u> Write a question and answer about each photo above.

Example: 5. What happens at the hardware store?
People buy tools.

# At the Mall

pet shop
bookstore
clothing store
toy store
music store
restaurant
jewelry store
florist
bench
information booth
trash can
escalator

## WHO'S TALKING? ▶ ASK FOR AND GIVE INFORMATION

1.–3. **Listen to the people.**
**Where are they? Point to them in the picture.**
**Act out each scene with a partner. Ask for and give information.**

## WRITE QUESTIONS AND ANSWERS

4.–8. **Write 5 questions about the mall. Then trade**
**papers with a partner and write the answers.**

Example: 4. Where is the bench?
The bench is next to the information booth.

# On My Street

A **verb** changes to show the past tense.

Fred **cleans** the car.

Fred **cleaned** the car.

## BUILD SENTENCES

Look at each picture below. Choose the correct verb to go with each picture. Say the new sentence.

**Example: 1.** She plants the flowers.
She planted the flowers.

**1.**

She ____(plants/planted)____ the flowers.

**2.**

She ____(pulls/pulled)____ the weed.

**3.**

They ____(play/played)____ basketball.

**4.**

He ____(pumps/pumped)____ the tire.

## WRITE SENTENCES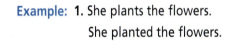

**5.–8.** Write each sentence you made above.

**Example: 5.** She plants the flowers.

# We Played Football in the Park

You can add _-ed_ to many **verbs** to tell about things that happened in the past.

I **wanted** to play football on Saturday.

I **called** my friends.

We **walked** to the park.

## WRITE ABOUT THE PAST

Write each sentence. Add the past tense of the word in dark type.

**Example: 1.** We enjoyed a fun day at the park.

1. **enjoy**    We _____ a fun day at the park.
2. **play**     We _____ football on the grass.
3. **miss**     I _____ the ball.
4. **roll**     It _____ by the picnic table.
5. **turn**     Jessie _____ on the radio.
6. **pick**     She _____ a good station.
7. **enjoy**    I _____ it.
8. **want**     Emilio _____ to hear his new CD.
9. **ask**      Jessie _____ to hear it, too.
10. **listen**  We _____ to the CD.
11. **jump**    Alvin _____ to the beat.
12. **laugh**   We all _____.
13. **learn**   Everyone _____ his funny dance.
14. **talk**    We _____ about school.
15. **pass**    The time _____ quickly.

## READ ALOUD

<u>16.–30.</u>  Work with your teacher. Read aloud each sentence you wrote.

# What Is in Our City?

> You can start a sentence with *There is* or *There are*.

Use *There is* to talk about one person or thing.

**There is** a bike trail near the park.

Use *There are* to talk about two or more persons or things.

**There are** two girls on the trail.

## BUILD SENTENCES

Say each sentence. Add *There is* or *There are*.    **Example: 1.** There are 2 lions.

1. _____ 2 lions.
2. _____ a U.S. flag.
3. _____ some steps.

4. _____ a bus stop.
5. _____ a trash can.
6. _____ people.

## WRITE SENTENCES 🖊

**7.–10.** Work with a partner. Write 4 more sentences to tell about the photos above. Add location words.

**Example: 7.** There are 2 lions in front of the museum.

# Read and Think Together

**Make a detail chart to tell about *More Than a Meal*.
Follow these steps.**

**1** Think about what Carlos did each day in the story. Draw a chart like the one below. Write what Carlos did on Monday.

| Day | Events |
|---|---|
| Monday | delivered meals, took out trash, and fixed a light |
| Tuesday | |
| Wednesday | |
| Thursday | |
| Friday | |

**2** What did Carlos do the rest of the week? Complete the chart with more details. Use words from the book.

**3** Use your detail chart to tell the story to a friend.

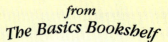

*from*
*The Basics Bookshelf*

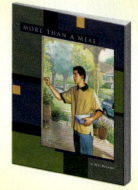

**THEME BOOK**

Meet Carlos in this story about city neighbors helping each other.

# Words to Know

## REVIEW WORDS YOU KNOW

**Read the words aloud. Which word goes in the sentence?**

| Here | Have |
|------|------|
| where | want |
| take | things |

1. _____ is the bus.
2. This is the bus they all _____ .
3. They _____ this bus every day.

## LEARN TO READ

**Learn new words.**

| | |
|------|------|
| city | Padma lives in the **city** of Chicago. |
| above | She lives in an apartment high **above** the street. |
| by | It is on Belmont Street, **by** a Mexican restaurant. |
| sometimes | **Sometimes** she jogs to Lake Michigan. |
| her | **Her** dog, Bandit, likes to run, too. |
| come | Padma's mom says, "**Come** home before dinner." |
| animals | There is a park for dogs and other **animals**. |
| people | **People** call it "Bark Park." |
| down | Bandit runs up and **down** the hill there. |
| under | Then Padma and Bandit rest **under** a tree. |

**How to Learn a New Word**

- Look at the word.
- Listen to the word.
- Listen to the word in a sentence. What does it mean?
- Say the word.
- Spell the word.
- Say the word again.

## WORD WORK

**Where does each new word fit in the chart? Say the word and spell it.**

**Example: 4.** people p-e-o-p-l-e

| What to Look For | Word |
|------------------|------|
| 4. starts with **p** | _ _ _ _ _ _ |
| 5. ends with **y** | _ _ _ _ |
| 6. is the opposite of **over** | _ _ _ _ _ |
| 7. starts with **a** | _ _ _ _ _ _ |
| 8. ends with **er** | _ _ _ |

| What to Look For | Word |
|------------------|------|
| 9. has 3 syllables | _ _ _ _ _ _ _ |
| 10. means "next to" | _ _ |
| 11. rhymes with **some** | _ _ _ _ |
| 12. means the opposite of **up** | _ _ _ _ |
| 13. has 2 smaller words in it | _ _ _ _ _ _ _ _ _ |

# Reading and Spelling

## LISTEN AND LEARN 🎵

## New Friend

I met you,
you met me,
at a picnic in the park.
I said, "Hi!"
You said, "Hey!"
We played soccer until dark.

I met you,
you met me,
at the park again.
I said, "Hi!"
You said, "Hey!"
I'm glad you're my new friend.

## LOOK FOR WORD PATTERNS

| Some words have only one vowel at the end. The vowel is usually long. | Some words have one vowel and then one or more consonants. The vowel is usually short. |
|---|---|
| no    hi    me | on    him    melt |

## READING STRATEGY

**Follow these steps to read a word.**

**1** Look for a pattern in the word. Find the vowel.
How many consonants come after the vowel?
Use the pattern to figure out the vowel sound.

**go** → The vowel **o** is at the end, so it is long.

**got** → A consonant comes after the vowel **o**, so the vowel is short.

**2** Start at the beginning. Blend the sounds together
to say the word.

**go**    g + o = go

**got**    g + o + t = got

**Reading Help**

Look for patterns in a long word, too.

First divide the word into parts. Then look for a pattern in each part.

basket        napkin
bas ket       nap kin

What pattern do you see in each part? Is the vowel long or short?

## READING AND SPELLING PRACTICE

**Use what you learned to read the sentences.**

1. Meg is lost. She has to be in the city soon.
2. Meg stops to get gas. She asks for help.
3. A man by the pump gives her a map.
4. He tells her, "Take the tunnel at Elm Canyon."
5. "Then go down the hill to First Street, and go left."
6. "Thank you so much!" Meg answers.

<u>7.–10.</u> **Now write the sentences that your teacher reads.**

## WORD WORK

<u>11.–18.</u> **Copy the chart. Then read these words:**

| me | sock | be | bed |
|----|------|----|-----|
| no | men  | so | not |

**Write each word in the chart. Put it under
the word that has the same vowel sound.**

| go | got | we | web |
|----|-----|----|-----|
| 11. | 13. | 15. | 17. |
| 12. | 14. | 16. | 18. |

Example: 11.

| go |
|----|
| 11. no |

# Read on Your Own

**CITY PEOPLE**
Tom Santos

# Meet Jo

**Jo works at the City Animal Hospital. I asked her to tell me about what she does at her job.**

This is Samson. Samson has a bad rash. He has this thing around his neck so he can't bite his skin. Sometimes we play catch. He needs to run a lot.

I have a great job. I love to help the animals. Look. This cat got hit in traffic. It is so sad when that happens. I had to make her a special bed.

This rabbit is Velvet. I like to brush him. He is so soft! Velvet had to get his shots. He needs to rest for a day or two. Then he will go home.

So, that is my job. I help hundreds of animals. It is great to see them get well. I miss them when they go home.

## CHECK YOUR UNDERSTANDING

**Copy and complete the chart.
Show what Jo does for each animal.
Then tell a partner about Jo's job.**

| Animal | How Jo Helps |
|---|---|
| a cat that got hit | Jo makes a special bed. |
| | |
| | |

# They're at the Museum!

**You can put a pronoun and a verb together to form a <mark>contraction.</mark>**

falcon

| Contraction | Example |
|---|---|
| I + am = I'm | **I'm** Mrs. Patch. |
| you + are = you're | **You're** at the Natural History Museum. |
| he + is = he's<br>she + is = she's<br>it + is = it's | Look at this bird. **It's** a falcon. |
| we + are = we're | **We're** happy to have birds like this. |
| they + are = they're | **They're** wonderful animals. |

## BUILD SENTENCES

**Look at the <u>underlined</u> words in each sentence. Use a contraction in their place. Say the new sentence.**

Example: **1.** Mrs. Patch holds a falcon. It's a big bird.

1. Mrs. Patch holds a falcon. <u>It is</u> a big bird.
2. The children listen to Mrs. Patch. <u>They are</u> very interested.
3. One boy raises his hand. <u>He is</u> afraid of the bird.
4. "<u>You are</u> brave, Mrs. Patch. Does that falcon hurt people?"
5. <u>She is</u> happy to answer his question.
6. "No, falcons are afraid of humans. <u>We are</u> so big."

## WRITE SENTENCES

**Replace the <u>underlined</u> words with pronouns. Then combine the pronoun and the word *is* or *are*. Write the new sentence.**

Example: **7.** She's helpful.

7. <u>Mrs. Patch</u> is helpful.
8. <u>The boy</u> is not afraid anymore.
9. <u>The visit</u> is over too soon.
10. <u>The students</u> are sad to go.
11. <u>A girl</u> is at the door.
12. <u>Her parents</u> are glad to see her.

# Learn About Cities

**MAP**

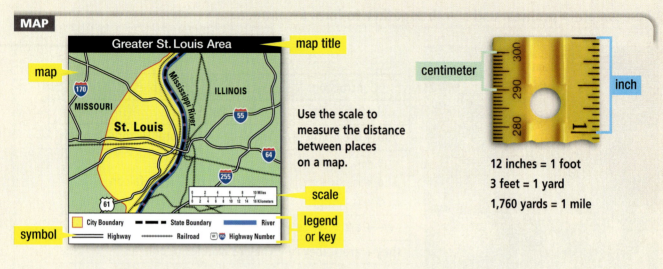

map title

map

Greater St. Louis Area

ILLINOIS

MISSOURI

St. Louis

Mississippi River

Use the scale to measure the distance between places on a map.

scale

symbol

City Boundary — State Boundary — River
Highway ·········· Railroad ⬡ ⬡ Highway Number

legend or key

centimeter

inch

12 inches = 1 foot
3 feet = 1 yard
1,760 yards = 1 mile

**Listen to the article and study the maps. Then do the Review.**

# Saint Louis, Gateway to the West

• How and why has St. Louis changed over the years?

Saint Louis, Missouri, is located near where the Mississippi and Missouri Rivers meet. Fur traders settled in the area in 1764 because boats could easily travel there. Soon the town became the starting point for explorers, fur trappers, and settlers traveling west.

**Rivers Connected to the Mississippi**

The Great Lakes

Mississippi

Missouri

ST. LOUIS

Mississippi

• City
— River

In the 1850s, the railroads joined St. Louis with other large cities like Chicago. Companies could easily ship goods in and out of the city. From 1840 to 1870, St. Louis' population increased by almost 300,000 people!

ST. LOUIS

St. Louis Highways

Mississippi River

Highways and bridges across the Mississippi River made it even easier to get to St. Louis. Today St. Louis is one of the leading railway and trucking centers in the United States.

**REVIEW**

1. **Check Your Understanding** Why did the fur traders choose to settle in the St. Louis area?
2. **Vocabulary** Name some highways that go to St. Louis.
3. **Use Maps** What does the dot symbol on the map of rivers mean?

# Writing Project  JOURNAL ENTRY

**Write a journal entry for each day last week. Tell what you did each day.**

## THINK ABOUT LAST WEEK

Make a detail chart. Tell what you did last week and where you did it.

| Day | Events | Place |
|-----|--------|-------|
| Monday | walked the dog | in the park |
| Tuesday | played basketball | on the court at the Youth Center |
| Wednesday | skated | behind the school |
| Thursday | walked | near the library |
| Friday | cooked soup | in the kitchen |
| Saturday | washed cars | at the gas station |
| Sunday | painted a picture | in my bedroom |

## WRITE YOUR JOURNAL ENTRY

Use your detail chart to write your journal entry. Check pages 314–318 in your Handbook for verbs to use. Check and correct your work.

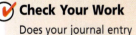 **Check Your Work**

Does your journal entry explain what you did last week?

Did you use the correct past tense verbs?

Do all your sentences start with a capital letter and end with the correct mark?

Write your journal entry on a clean sheet of paper. Add drawings or photos.

Last Monday, I walked the dog in the park.

On Tuesday, I played basketball on the court at the Youth Center.

On Wednesday, I skated behind the school.

On Thursday, I walked near the library.

On Friday, I cooked soup in the kitchen.

On Saturday, I washed cars at the gas station.

On Sunday, I painted a picture in my bedroom.

*Empanadas/Tío Beto y Tía Paz*, Carmen Lomas Garza, acrylic. Copyright © 1996.

# Welcome Home!

Look at the picture. What does each person say? What does each person do? Act out the scene with a partner or a group.

## In This Unit

### Vocabulary
- Family
- Rooms in a House
- Household Objects
- Mathematics

### Language Functions
- Give Information
- Ask and Answer Questions

### Patterns and Structures
- Present Tense Verbs (*have, has*)
- Plural Nouns

### Reading
- Phonics: Long Vowels
- Comprehension: Relate Main Idea and Details (main-idea diagram)

### Writing
- Sentences
- Questions
- Family Album

### Content Area Connection
- Mathematics (fractions, decimals, and percents)

# Meet My Family

**Listen and sing.**

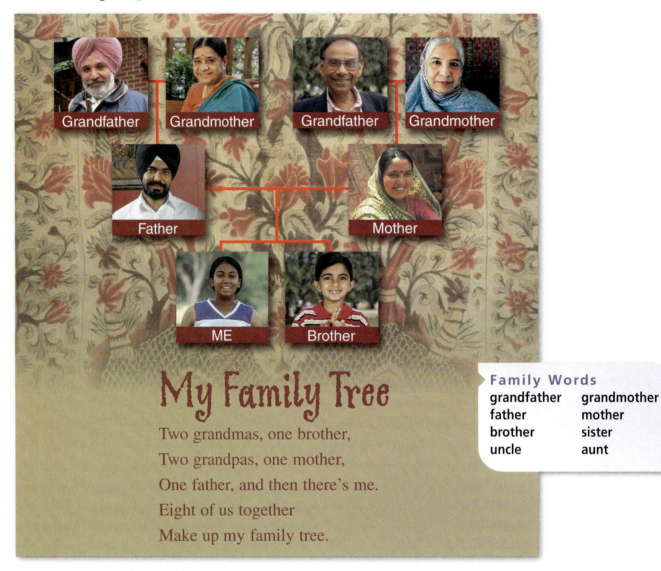

Grandfather | Grandmother | Grandfather | Grandmother

Father | Mother

ME | Brother

## My Family Tree

Two grandmas, one brother,

Two grandpas, one mother,

One father, and then there's me.

Eight of us together

Make up my family tree.

**Family Words**

| | |
|---|---|
| grandfather | grandmother |
| father | mother |
| brother | sister |
| uncle | aunt |

**EXPRESS YOURSELF** ▶ GIVE INFORMATION

1. **Change the song to tell about another family. Sing it to a partner.**

Example: 1. One grandma, two brothers,

One sister, one mother,

One uncle, and then there's me.

Seven of us together

Make up our family tree.

**WRITE LABELS FOR A FAMILY TREE**

2.–3. **Cut pictures of people out of magazines. Use them to make a family tree. Trade papers with a partner. Write labels for the family tree.**

# I Have a Great Family

Use *have* with *I*, *you*, *we*, and *they*. Use *has* with *he*, *she*, or *it*.

Hi, I'm Robert. I **have** a sister. I **don't have** any brothers. We **have** a big house. It **has** four bedrooms. My dad **has** an office in our house.

## BUILD SENTENCES

Read each sentence. Add *have* or *has*. Then say the sentence.

**Example: 1.** She has a brother.

**1.**

She _____ a brother.

**2.**

They _____ two children.

**3.**

He _____ an aunt.

**4.**

"I _____ a wonderful grandmother!"

**5.**

The house _____ two bedrooms.

**6.**

The sisters _____ a new brother.

## WRITE SENTENCES ✏️

<u>7.–10.</u> Write 4 sentences about people in your family. Use *have* or *has*.

**Example: 7.** I have a brother.

# Let Me Show You My House!

## WHO'S TALKING? ▶ GIVE INFORMATION

<u>1.–3.</u> **Listen.** 📼

Who is talking? Point to the correct person.
Then tell where each person is in the house.

## WRITE SENTENCES 🖊

<u>4.–7.</u> **Work in a group of 4. Each person acts out a scene from above. Tell where each person is and what each person has. Then write the sentences.**

**Example: 4.** Pablo is in the bedroom.
He has a guitar.

# What Is in Each Room?

**In the Bedroom**
- door
- bed
- dresser

**In the Bathroom**
- shower
- toilet
- bathtub
- sink

**In the Living Room**
- lamp
- bookcase
- chair
- floor
- table

**In the Kitchen**
- curtains
- refrigerator
- stove
- oven
- cabinets

## EXPRESS YOURSELF ▶ ASK AND ANSWER QUESTIONS

**Work with a partner. Ask each question. Answer in a complete sentence.**

Example: **1.** Where is the bed? The bed is in the bedroom.

**1.** Where is the bed?

**2.** Where is the refrigerator?

**3.** Where is the shower?

**4.** Where is the table?

**5.** Where are the curtains?

**6.** Where is the sofa?

## WRITE SENTENCES

<u>7.–10.</u>  **What kind of house do you want? Draw it.
Then write 4 sentences to tell about your house.**

Example: **7.** My house has three bedrooms.

# Read and Think Together

**Make two diagrams to tell about the main ideas of**
*Families.* **Follow these steps.**

**1** Think about pages 4–19 in the book. What are the
pages mainly about? Write a sentence in a box.

> Families do a lot of things together.

**2** Think of details from the book that tell about this
main idea. Add them to your diagram.

> Families do a lot of things together.
>
> They love and care for one another.

**3** Make a new main idea diagram for pages 20–26 of
the book.

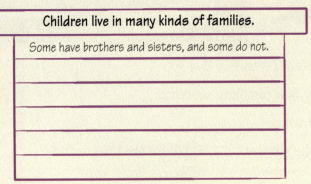

> Children live in many kinds of families.
>
> Some have brothers and sisters, and some do not.

**4** Use your main idea diagrams to tell a partner
about *Families.*

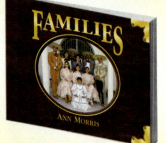

*from*
*The Basics Bookshelf*

**THEME BOOK**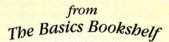

This photo essay shows
how family members
everywhere love and care
for each other.

# Words to Know

## REVIEW WORDS YOU KNOW

**Read the words aloud. Which word goes in the sentence?**

| | |
|---|---|
| down | day |
| small | same |
| city | see |

1. It's a good _____ to ride bikes.
2. The boy rides a _____ bike.
3. They can _____ a bridge.

## LEARN TO READ

**Learn new words.**

| | |
|---|---|
| family | There are six people in my **family**. |
| together | We ride bicycles **together**. |
| other | We like to do **other** things, too. |
| really | We **really** like to hike in the woods. |
| father | My **father** carries a heavy backpack. |
| mother | My **mother** walks fast. Everyone follows her. |
| our | She is **our** leader! |
| watch | We sometimes stop to **watch** the birds. |
| eyes | Once I saw an eagle with my own **eyes**. |
| head | It was flying in circles over my **head**! |

**How to Learn a New Word**

- Look at the word.
- Listen to the word.
- Listen to the word in a sentence. What does it mean?
- Say the word.
- Spell the word.
- Say the word again.

## WORD WORK

**4.–13. Work with a partner. Write each new word on a card. Mix your cards together for the game. Turn them so the words are down. Then:**

- Turn over 2 cards.
- Spell the words. Are they the same?
- If so, keep them. If not, turn them over again.
- The player with more cards at the end wins.

**Example:**

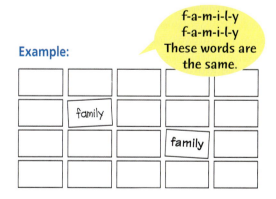

f-a-m-i-l-y
f-a-m-i-l-y
These words are the same.

# Reading and Spelling

## LISTEN AND LEARN

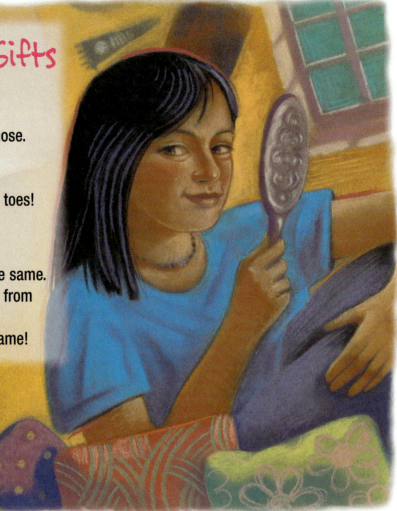

### Family Gifts

Mom's smile,
Dad's chin,
And Grandpa's nose.
Mom's eyes,
Dad's hair,
Even Grandma's toes!

Mom's hands,
Dad's ears.
Mine are just the same.
I like these gifts from
My family,
Especially my name!

## LOOK FOR WORD PATTERNS

How are the words alike? Is the vowel sound short or long?

c**a**k**e**        b**i**k**e**        gl**o**b**e**        fl**u**t**e**s

## READING STRATEGY

**Follow these steps to read a word.**

**1** Look for a pattern. The **e** makes the other vowel say its name: **a**.

l **a** k **e**

> **Reading Help**
>
> A few words that end in **e** do <u>not</u> have a long vowel sound.
>
> give     some     have

**2** Start at the beginning. Blend the sounds together in your head. Then say the word.

l **a** k **e**      l + a + k + ~~e~~ = **lake**

> The **e** at the end of a word has no sound. It tells me that the **a** is long.

## READING AND SPELLING PRACTICE

**Use what you learned to read the sentences.**

1. My mother likes to make cakes.
2. She says to use pure butter.
3. She melts the butter on the stove.
4. I taste the cake mix. Yum!
5. It's fun to bake a cake at home!

<u>6.–9.</u> **Now write the sentences that your teacher reads.**

## WORD WORK

<u>10.–21.</u> **Copy the chart. Then read these words:**

| back | can | made | mad |
|------|-----|------|-----|
| hop | robe | cane | rob |
| note | hope | not | bake |

**Write each word in the chart. Put it under the word that has the same vowel sound.**

| map | cake | dot | rope |
|-----|------|-----|------|
| 10. | 13. | 16. | 19. |
| 11. | 14. | 17. | 20. |
| 12. | 15. | 18. | 21. |

**Example: 10.**

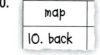

| map |
|-----|
| 10. back |

# Read on Your Own

# When We Came to Wisconsin

La Gigantona can come in different colors and shapes. Here is one in a parade.

Hi. My name is Pablo Soto. My mother's name is Sandra. We are from Nicaragua.

In Nicaragua, my family made big puppets to sell. The name of one puppet that we made is *La Gigantona*. We made the head of this puppet with paper and paste. We made the eyes of the puppet really big, with long, thick lashes. We made the arms from long tubes. They swing from side to side. We put a white robe and a cute hat on the puppet. People like to watch this big puppet in parades.

My mother and I left Nicaragua and came to Wisconsin. Here, we make piñatas. We make a piñata with paper and paste, just like we made the head of *La Gigantona*. One day, a man came to our store. He asked us to make a big puppet for a parade in Wisconsin. At last, *La Gigantona* is back in our family!

## CHECK YOUR UNDERSTANDING

Copy and complete this diagram. Add details that support the main idea. Then tell your partner how the family made the big puppet.

| We made a big puppet. |
|---|
| We made the head with paper and paste. |
|  |
|  |
|  |

# Boxes and Boxes—We're Moving!

**A noun names a person, place, or thing.**

A **singular noun** names one thing.

box

A **plural noun** names more than one thing.

boxes

**Study these rules for forming plurals.**

| To make most nouns plural, just add -s. | boy boys | girl girls | book books | truck trucks |
|---|---|---|---|---|
| If the noun ends in x, ch, sh, s, or z, add -es. | box boxes | dish dishes | glass glasses | lunch lunches |
| Some nouns change in different ways to show the plural. | man men | woman women | child children | foot feet |

## BUILD SENTENCES

**Say each sentence. Use the plural form of the missing words.**

**Example:** **1.** The women drink from glasses.

**1.**

glass
woman

The _____ drink from _____.

**2.**

child

The _____ read on the sofa.

**3.**

man
sandwich

The _____ eat _____.

**4.**

boy
book

The _____ pack _____.

**5.**

box
mover

The _____ carry the _____.

**6.**

friend

Their _____ wave good-bye.

## WRITE QUESTIONS

**7.–10.** Choose 4 pictures from above. Write a question about each picture. Ask a partner your questions.

**Example:** **7.** What do the men eat?

# Learn About Fractions, Decimals, and Percents

| FRACTION | DECIMAL | PERCENT |
|---|---|---|

**My Family**
1. Mama
2. Grandma
3. Sabina, my sister
4. Alex, my brother
5. Tom—me!

numerator

$$\frac{3}{5}$$

denominator

**Say:** three-fifths
**Example:** Three-fifths of my family are kids.

0.6

decimal point

**Say:** six-tenths
**Example:** Six-tenths of my family are kids.

60%

percent symbol

**Say:** sixty percent
**Example:** Sixty percent of my family are kids.

**Study the lesson. Then do the Exercises.**

## Family Math

### Think and Discuss

You can use fractions, decimals, or percents to describe the family in the picture.

**1 Write a fraction:**

Ask yourself how many of the people are kids. This is the numerator. How many people are there in the whole family? This is the denominator.

kids $\dfrac{3}{5}$ whole family

**2 Write a decimal:**

Divide the numerator by the denominator.

$$5\overline{)3.0}$$
0.6

Show the decimal point in the answer.

Add a decimal point and a zero.

**3 Write a percent:**

Multiply the decimal by 100. Add the percent symbol.

$$0.6 \times 100 = 60$$

60% percent symbol

Three-fifths of my family are kids. Six-tenths of my family are kids. Sixty percent of my family are kids.

### Exercises

Write a fraction, a decimal, and a percent for each answer.

**1**

Sabina ate 2 slices of pizza. How much of the pizza is left?

**2**

How many candles are red?

# Writing Project  FAMILY ALBUM

**Make an album with information about the people in your family.**

## PLAN YOUR FAMILY ALBUM

What will you show for each person: a photo, an object, or a drawing? What will you say? Make a chart.

| Who? | What the Person Likes | What the Person Has | Where? |
|------|------------------------|----------------------|--------|
| sister | fish | fish bowl | in her bedroom |
| mother | flowers | flower press | in the kitchen |

## MAKE AND SHARE YOUR FAMILY ALBUM

Write 2 sentences to go with each photo, object, or drawing. Then check and correct your work.

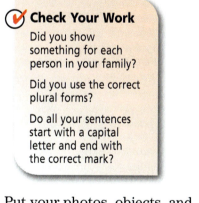

### ✔ Check Your Work

Did you show something for each person in your family?

Did you use the correct plural forms?

Do all your sentences start with a capital letter and end with the correct mark?

Put your photos, objects, and drawings into a book. Copy your sentences. Display the book in your classroom.

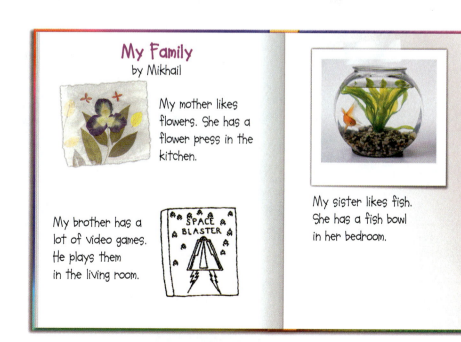

**My Family**
by Mikhail

My mother likes flowers. She has a flower press in the kitchen.

My brother has a lot of video games. He plays them in the living room.

SPACE BLASTER

My sister likes fish. She has a fish bowl in her bedroom.

# PACK YOUR BAGS!

Look at the picture of the rain forest.

What do you see? Listen to the tape.

What sounds do you hear?

# Come Along!

**Listen and chant.**

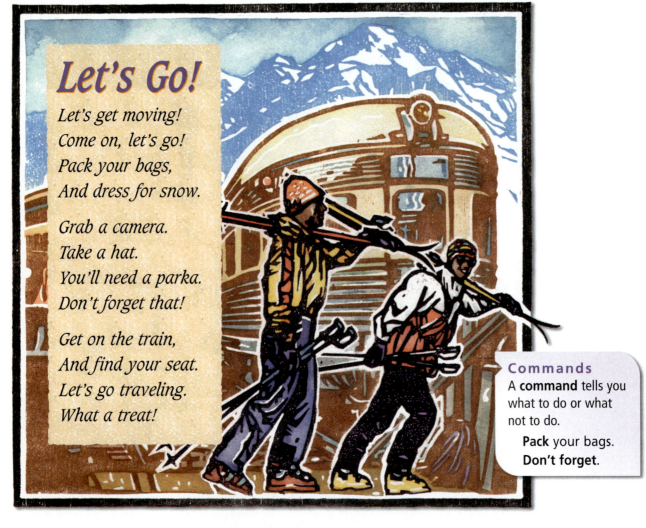

## Let's Go!

Let's get moving!
Come on, let's go!
Pack your bags,
And dress for snow.

Grab a camera.
Take a hat.
You'll need a parka.
Don't forget that!

Get on the train,
And find your seat.
Let's go traveling.
What a treat!

**Commands**

A **command** tells you what to do or what not to do.

**Pack** your bags.
**Don't forget**.

**EXPRESS YOURSELF** ▶ GIVE AND CARRY OUT COMMANDS

**Work with a partner. Read the commands from the chant. Act them out.**

1. Pack your bags.
2. Grab a camera.
3. Dress for snow.
4. Take a hat.
5. Get on the train.
6. Find your seat.

**WRITE COMMANDS**

**7.–10. Your partner wants to take a trip. Write 4 commands to tell your partner what to do on the trip.**

**Example: 7.** Dress for rain.

# What Places Can You Explore?

The Seashore — airplane, beach, island, ocean, sailboat

The Mountains — mountain, valley, forest, lake, raft

The Canyon — canyon, river

The Desert — cactus, bicycle, sand

## EXPRESS YOURSELF  ▶ DESCRIBE PLACES

**1.–4.** **Work with a partner. Describe each picture above. Use adjectives.**

Example: **1.** There are tall trees in the green forest.
The blue lake is large. The raft is slow.

### Adjectives

| blue | tiny | slow | short | hot |
|------|------|------|-------|------|
| green | small | fast | tall | cold |
| brown | big | | long | wet |
| white | large | | | dry |

## WRITE A POSTCARD

**5.** **Choose a place to explore. Describe it in a postcard.**

Example: **5.**

Dear Lin,

I am in the mountains.
There is a big lake here.
A lot of tall trees grow
around the lake.

Your friend,
Sanjana

Lin Yang
8362 Hoover Street
New York, NY 10165

# How Is the Weather There?

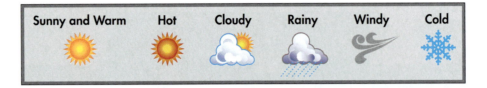

| Sunny and Warm | Hot | Cloudy | Rainy | Windy | Cold |
|---|---|---|---|---|---|

bathing suit

sandal

sneaker

It is **sunny and warm** at the seashore.

scarf

parka

glove

It is **cold** in the mountains.

coat

skirt

shoe

It is **windy** in the city.

## WHO'S TALKING? ▶ GIVE INFORMATION

**1.–3. Listen.**

Which person is talking? Point to the correct picture.
Tell what the weather is like there.

## WRITE ABOUT THE WEATHER

Write each sentence. Add words to tell about the weather.

**Example: 4.** I wear a parka when it is cold.

**4.** I wear a parka when it is _____.

**5.** I wear sandals when it is _____ and _____.

**6.** I wear a coat when it is _____.

**7.** I wear a raincoat when it is _____.

**8.** I wear gloves when it is _____.

umbrella

raincoat

boot

It is **rainy** in the forest.

# We Can Explore All Year Long

Use **can** before another **verb** to tell what people are able to do.

> can + hike = can hike

In this park, we **can hike** up the mountain.

I **can see** some pretty trees.

My friend **can take** a lot of pictures.

Never add *-s* to *can*.

## BUILD SENTENCES

Look at each picture below. Make a sentence to go with the picture.
Choose words from each column. Say the sentence.

| In the winter,<br>In the spring,<br>In the summer,<br>In the fall, | I can<br>you can<br>he can<br>she can<br>we can<br>they can | sail a boat.<br>hike.<br>ride a bike.<br>ice-skate. |
|---|---|---|

**Example:** **1.** In the winter, you can ice-skate.

**1.** winter
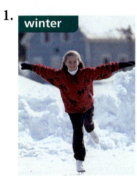

**2.** spring

**3.** summer

**4.** fall

## WRITE SENTENCES ✏️

<u>5.–8.</u> Draw a picture for each season. Show what people
can do then. Write a sentence to go with the picture.
Use words from the box.

| | |
|---|---|
| swim in a lake | plant a garden |
| ski in the mountains | eat outside |
| play soccer | read a book |

**Example:** **5.** In the spring, we can swim in a lake.

# Read and Think Together

**Make a concept map to tell about *Explore!***
**Follow these steps.**

**1** Think about the book. What is it mainly about?

**2** What places does the book describe? Add sections
to the map. Write the name of a place inside
each section.

**3** Write words around each place.
Tell what you can find there.

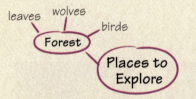

**4** Use your completed map to tell a partner
about the book.

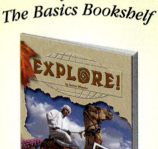

*from*
*The Basics Bookshelf*

**THEME BOOK**

Enjoy sights around
the world as you read
this book about travel.

# Words to Know

## REVIEW WORDS YOU KNOW

**Read the words aloud. Which word goes in the sentence?**

| family | first |
|--------|-------|
| says | she |
| letters | learn |

1. The _____ hikes together.
2. Father _____ the names of plants.
3. The children _____ about trees.

## LEARN TO READ

**Learn new words.**

| | |
|---|---|
| **places** | Jean likes to explore unusual **places**. |
| **important** | Travel is very **important** to her. |
| **world** | She travels all around the **world**. |
| **always** | She **always** plans her trips carefully. |
| **or** | She travels either by plane **or** by boat. |
| **river** | She sails up the Amazon **River** in a boat. |
| **through** | She hikes **through** the Amazon rain forest, too. |
| **once** | She goes to Tahiti not **once**, but twice a year. |
| **water** | She loves swimming in the clear **water**. |
| **below** | She can see hundreds of fish **below** her! |

### How to Learn a New Word

- Look at the word.
- Listen to the word.
- Listen to the word in a sentence. What does it mean?
- Say the word.
- Spell the word.
- Say the word again.

## WORD WORK

**Work with a partner. Answer each question. Then use each word in a sentence.**

4. Which word has 9 letters?
5. Which word begins with 3 consonants?
6. Which words have 1 syllable?
7. Which words have 2 syllables?
8. Which word means "one time"?
9. Which word means "all the time"?

**Example: 4.** important

My family is <u>important</u> to me.

# Reading and Spelling

**LISTEN AND LEARN**

## On the Beach

Sailboats sail along the bay
As the sunset ends the day.
Little crabs and starfish play
In the pools along the shore.
Seaweed gathers on the beach.
As the seagulls dive and soar,
Endless waves will sweep the sand
With a whisper or a roar.
The high tide and the low tide
Bring sea gifts to my door.

## LOOK FOR WORD PATTERNS

**How are the words alike? Are the vowel sounds long or short?**

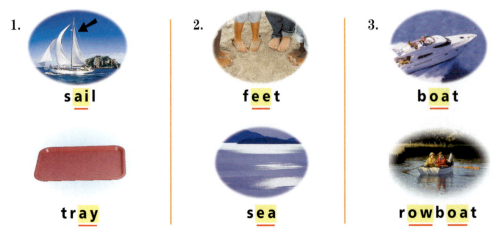

1. s**ai**l

   tr**ay**

2. f**ee**t

   s**ea**

3. b**oa**t

   r**ow**b**oa**t

## READING STRATEGY

**Follow these steps to read a word.**

**1** Look for a pattern. Do you see two vowels together?

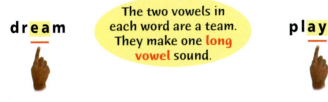

**d r e a m**

The two vowels in each word are a team. They make one **long vowel** sound.

**p l a y**

**Reading Help**

Some long words are made up of two small words.

day + dream = daydream

sail + boat = sailboat

sea + shell = seashell

To read these words, find the two small words. Then sound them out and say the two words together.

**2** Start at the beginning of the word. Blend the sounds in your head. Then say the word.

**dream**      d + r + e~~a~~ + m = **dream**      **play**      p + l + a~~y~~ = **play**

## READING AND SPELLING PRACTICE

**Use what you learned to read the sentences.**

1. Joan and her family spend weekends at the seashore.
2. They keep a rowboat by the beach.
3. Joan likes to swim in the water or row the boat.
4. When it rains, she always stays inside.
5. A good book and hot tea are all she needs.
6. She just sits and reads all day!

**7.–10.** **Now write the sentences that your teacher reads.**

## WORD WORK

**11.** Write each word on a card.

| rain | coast | sail | leaf | play | paint |
| stay | snow | deep | show | grow | road |
| beach | bee | sweet | read | feet | boat |

Then say each word. **Sort the words by vowel sound. Make 3 groups.**

**12.** Now make 6 new groups. Put the words with the same vowel sound *and* spelling together. What do you notice?

**Example: 12.**

rain

stay

You can spell **long a** more than one way.

# Read on Your Own

EXPLORE A WETLAND

**W**elcome to Black Creek Wetland. What a great way to spend a Sunday afternoon! My name is Jean Clay. I am your guide. Step into the rowboat. Stay in your seat while we move through the water.

Canada has many wetlands. Black Creek Wetland is one of them. A wetland is a low, wet place. Rainwater and many streams keep it wet. Black Creek is on the shore of Lake Ontario. Plants such as reeds and cattails grow here. This is an important place for animals, too. Ducks and geese lay their eggs here in May.

Sometimes, people drain the water from wetlands. Then they use the land to grow wheat or other crops. Not here. We plan to keep this wetland for the ducks, geese, and other animals.

Canada

United States

Black Creek
Wetland

Lake Ontario

## CHECK YOUR UNDERSTANDING

Copy and complete the map. Tell a partner what you learned about Black Creek Wetland.

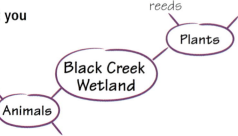

reeds

Plants

Black Creek
Wetland

Animals

# Special Places, Special People

**A proper noun names one particular person, place, or thing.**

**A proper noun begins with a capital letter.**

| name of a person | Jorge is a scientist. |
|---|---|
| name of a special place, a city, or a country | He will go to El Yunque near San Juan, Puerto Rico, to study the birds. |
| name of a month or a day | He will leave Monday, July 15. |

## STUDY CAPITALIZATION

**Look at the story on page 138. Answer these questions.**

**Example:** **1.** Jean Clay is the name of a person. Joyce Hsu is another person's name.

1. Which 2 words are the name of a person? Tell another person's name.
2. Which word names a country? Name another country.
3. Which word names a month? Name another month.
4. Which word names a day of the week? Name another day of the week.
5. Which words name a special place? Name another special place.

## WRITE SENTENCES

**Write each sentence correctly. Add the capital letters.**

**Example:** **6.** Jorge will take a trip to Puerto Rico.

6. Jorge will take a trip to puerto rico.
7. On Monday, july 15, he flies into San Juan.
8. On tuesday, July 16, Jorge takes a bus to the rain forest.
9. The rain forest is called el yunque.
10. It is 40 kilometers from san juan.
11. He will stay there until thursday, july 18.
12. On Sunday, July 21, Jorge flies back to the united states.
13. He goes to his home in miami, Florida.

Jorge studies the birds in the rain forest.

# Learn About Cycles

**DIAGRAMS**

A **cycle** is a series of events that happen again and again.

A **diagram** is a drawing. It can show how a cycle works.

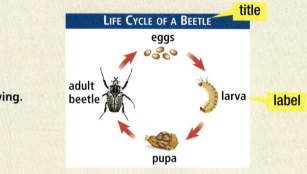

LIFE CYCLE OF A BEETLE — title

eggs

adult beetle

larva — label

pupa

Study the diagram and listen to the article. Then do the Review.

# Earth's Amazing Water Cycle

• How does the water cycle work?

The Earth's water can take many forms. It can be a **liquid**, like rainwater, or a **solid**, like ice.

rain

ice

It can even take the form of **vapor**. You cannot see vapor. When water boils, it turns to water vapor.

The Earth's water is recycled. Heat from the sun turns water on the Earth into water vapor. This process is called **evaporation**. The water vapor is carried up by the air. Air that is full of water vapor can cool off. When this happens, clouds form and the water vapor turns into water again. The water falls from the clouds as rain or snow, for example, and becomes part of the water on Earth. Some of this water—in rivers and lakes, for example—evaporates, and the cycle begins again.

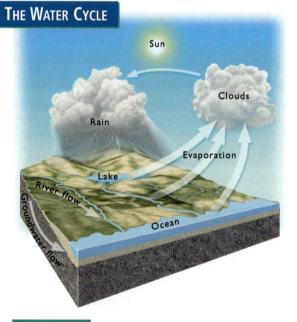

THE WATER CYCLE

Sun

Clouds

Rain

Evaporation

Lake

River flow

Groundwater flow

Ocean

**REVIEW**

1. **Check Your Understanding** Tell in your own words how the water cycle works. Use the diagram.
2. **Vocabulary** Give an example of another cycle.
3. **Use Diagrams** Draw a diagram to show how another cycle works.

# Writing Project

CLASS TRAVEL BOOK

Create a travel book like *Explore!* Each person can make one page. Describe where you want to go. Tell how you can get there. Tell what you can see and do.

## CHOOSE A PLACE

**1** Where do you want to go? Look in books, magazines, or newspapers for information. Take notes. Start a concept map.

**2** Collect or draw pictures.

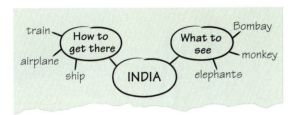

## PLAN YOUR PAGE

What will you show on your page? Use your notes to complete these sentences:

1. Take _____.
2. Explore _____.
3. You can _____. You can _____.

## MAKE AND SHARE YOUR PAGE

Put your pictures on construction paper.
Write your sentences on another piece of paper.
Check and correct your work.

> ✔ **Check Your Work**
>
> Does your page describe a place and how to get there?
>
> Did you tell what you can see and do?
>
> Did you use capital letters correctly?

Then put your sentences on the construction paper. Put everyone's pages together to make a class travel book. Read the book aloud.

# Friend to Friend

Look at the pictures.

Act out the scenes with a partner.

Talk about how each character feels.

## In This Unit

**Vocabulary**
- Feelings
- Graphs

**Language Functions**
- Describe Actions
- Express Feelings

**Patterns and Structures**
- Regular Past Tense Verbs
- Irregular Past Tense Verbs *(was, were)*
- Negative Sentences and Contractions with *not*
- Possessive Nouns

**Reading**
- Verb Ending: *-ed*
- Comprehension: Identify Cause and Effect (cause-and-effect chart)

**Writing**
- Sentences
- Friendship Book

**Content Area Connection**
- Mathematics (bar graphs)

# Together We Dreamed

**Listen and sing.**

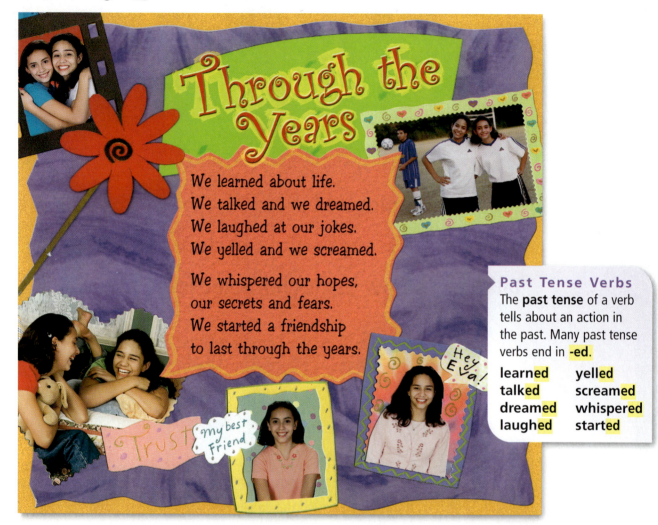

**Through the Years**

We learned about life.
We talked and we dreamed.
We laughed at our jokes.
We yelled and we screamed.

We whispered our hopes,
our secrets and fears.
We started a friendship
to last through the years.

> **Past Tense Verbs**
> The **past tense** of a verb tells about an action in the past. Many past tense verbs end in **-ed.**
>
> | | |
> |---|---|
> | learn**ed** | yell**ed** |
> | talk**ed** | scream**ed** |
> | dream**ed** | whisper**ed** |
> | laugh**ed** | start**ed** |

*Hey Eva!*

*Trust* my best Friend

## EXPRESS YOURSELF  ▶ DESCRIBE ACTIONS

**Complete each sentence. Tell what your friends did. You can use a verb from the box above.**

Example: **1.** I finished the race. My friends yelled.

**1.** I finished the race. My friends _____.

**2.** I danced a funny dance. My friends _____.

**3.** I learned a sport. My friends _____ it, too.

**4.** I shared my dreams. My friends _____, too.

## WRITE SENTENCES

**5.–8. Write about 4 things you did. Then tell what your friends did.**

Example: **5.** I talked about my idea. My friends listened.

# How Do the Friends Feel?

Len has lots of friends. Like all people, Len and his friends feel different at different times.

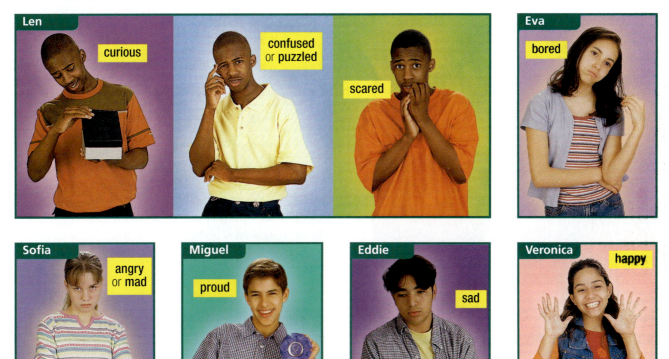

## WHO'S TALKING? ▶ EXPRESS FEELINGS

1.–4. Listen.
Who is talking? Point to the correct person.
Act out the scene. Tell how you feel. Use your face and body
to show your feelings, too.

## WRITE ABOUT FEELINGS

5.–8. Work in a group of 4. Write each feeling word on a card. Mix up
the cards. Each person chooses a card and acts out the feeling. Write a
sentence to tell how each person feels.

Example: **5.** Nora is bored.

# Were the Friends Happy?

**Use *was* and *were* to tell about the past.**

| Pronoun | Verb | Example |
|---|---|---|
| I | was | I **was** happy. |
| you | were | You **were** excited. |
| he, she, it | was | He **was** proud. |
| we | were | We **were** the winning team! |
| they | were | They **were** good losers, though. |

Use *There was* for one person or thing.
Use *There were* for two or more.

> **There was** one girl on their team.
> **There were** two girls on our team.

## BUILD SENTENCES

**Read each sentence. Change the <u>underlined</u> verb to the past tense. Say the new sentence.**

**Example:** **1.** We were at my house.

| Present | Past |
|---|---|
| is | was |
| are | were |

1. We <u>are</u> at my house.
2. We <u>are</u> on the sofa.
3. The sofa <u>is</u> too small for all of us.
4. Len <u>is</u> on the floor.
5. Veronica <u>is</u> on the floor, too.
6. There <u>are</u> no pillows to sit on.
7. Len and Veronica <u>are</u> mad.
8. Finally, there <u>is</u> food to eat!
9. We <u>are</u> all happy again.

## WRITE SENTENCES ✏️

**<u>10.–14.</u> Write 5 sentences about the past. Tell about a day with your friends. Use *was* and *were*.**

**Examples:** **10.** Yesterday I was at the library.

**11.** A lot of my friends were there, too.

# The Friends Didn't Scare Len!

**There are different ways to build negative sentences in the past tense.**

**Add the word *not* after *was* and *were*.**

Len **was not** scared.
Eddie and Miguel **were not** happy.

**With other verbs, add *did not* before the verb.**

The trick workdid noted.

When you add *did not* to a sentence, take the *-ed* off the main verb.

## BUILD SENTENCES

**Read the sentences in number 1. Then answer the questions in number 2. Say your answer in a complete sentence. Use *did not*, *was not*, or *were not*.**

**Example:** **2.** They did not trick Sofia.

**1.** The friends tricked Veronica.
   They were proud!
   The snake jumped out.
   Veronica was afraid.
   She screamed.

**2.** Did the friends trick Sofia?
   Were they proud?
   Did the snake jump out?
   Was Sofia afraid?
   Did she scream?

## WRITE SENTENCES ✏️

**3.–7.** **Write each sentence you made above. Then write it again. Use contractions to replace *did not*, *was not*, and *were not*.**

**Example:** **3.** They did not trick Sofia.
          They didn't trick Sofia.

> **Contractions**
> did + not = **didn't**
> was + not = **wasn't**
> were + not = **weren't**

# Read and Think Together

**Make a cause-and-effect chart for *Friends Are Like That*. Follow these steps.**

**1** Copy the following cause-and-effect chart. Think about the story. Write the effect next to each cause.

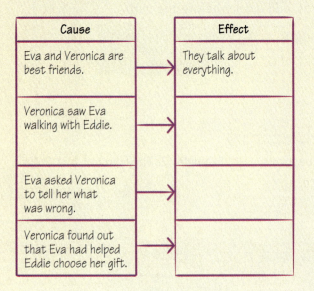

| Cause | Effect |
|---|---|
| Eva and Veronica are best friends. | They talk about everything. |
| Veronica saw Eva walking with Eddie. | |
| Eva asked Veronica to tell her what was wrong. | |
| Veronica found out that Eva had helped Eddie choose her gift. | |

**2** Use your completed chart to retell the story to a partner.

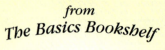

*from*
*The Basics Bookshelf*

**THEME BOOK**

Veronica invites you to read her diary. Find out how she learned to trust her best friend.

# Words to Know

## REVIEW WORDS YOU KNOW

**Read the words aloud. Which word goes in the sentence?**

| | |
|---|---|
| which | watch |
| around | always |
| Sometimes | Something |

1. The boys will _____ a movie.
2. They _____ buy popcorn at the movies.
3. _____ they get cold drinks, too.

## LEARN TO READ

**Learn new words.**

| | |
|---|---|
| saw | Last week I **saw** a movie. |
| was | I **was** sitting in the first row. |
| were | A lot of kids from school **were** there. |
| their | Some kids came with **their** mothers and fathers. |
| said | "Look, there's Sofia," I **said** to my dad. |
| began | They shut off the lights, and the movie **began**. |
| about | The movie was **about** some kids in the 1950s. |
| dance | I watched them **dance** to old music. |
| thought | My dad **thought** the music was great. |
| again | We want to see that movie **again** next week. |

### How to Learn a New Word

- Look at the word.
- Listen to the word.
- Listen to the word in a sentence. What does it mean?
- Say the word.
- Spell the word.
- Say the word again.

## WORD WORK

**Write each sentence. Add the missing word.**  **Example:  4.** My friends were at school the next day.

4. My friends _ _ _ _ at school the next day.
5. I asked them what they _ _ _ _ _ _ _ of the movie.
6. "It _ _ _ good!" Sofia _ _ _ _. "My mom and dad can _ _ _ _ _ like that."
7. "All _ _ _ _ _ friends dance like that, too."
8. Math class _ _ _ _ _, and we sat down.
9. Then Ms. Jong said something _ _ _ _ _ the movie.
10. She said, "I _ _ _ that movie when I was in sixth grade!"
11. "It will be fun to see it _ _ _ _ _ with my children!"

# Reading and Spelling

## LISTEN AND LEARN 📼

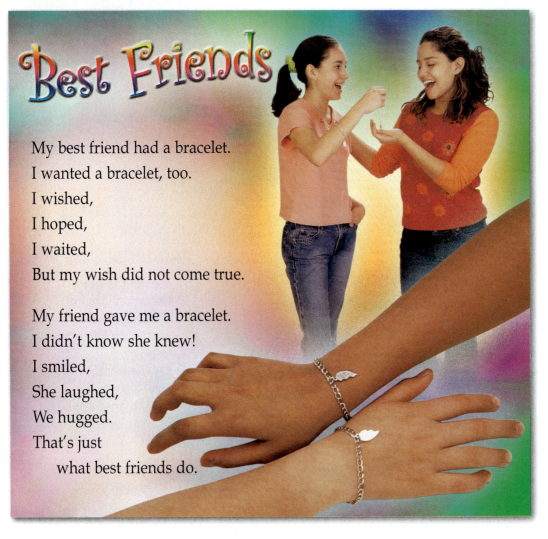

**Best Friends**

My best friend had a bracelet.
I wanted a bracelet, too.
I wished,
I hoped,
I waited,
But my wish did not come true.

My friend gave me a bracelet.
I didn't know she knew!
I smiled,
She laughed,
We hugged.
That's just
        what best friends do.

## STUDY VERB ENDINGS

| | | |
|---|---|---|
| For some verbs, you can just add **-ed**.<br><br>**wish + ed = wished**<br><br>**need + ed = needed** | This verb ends in silent **e**.<br>   **smile**<br>When you add **-ed**, drop the **e**.<br><br>   **smil~~e~~ + ed = smiled** | This verb ends in one vowel and one consonant.<br><br>   **hug**<br>When you add **-ed**, double the consonant.<br><br>   **hug**g**ed** |

## READING STRATEGY

**Follow these steps to read a word with -ed.**

**1** Look for the ending you know. Cover it.

**lift*ed***

**lift**

**2** Look for vowel and consonant patterns to sound out the root word.

**lift**         **l + i + f + t = lift**

> I see two consonants after the vowel **i**, so the **i** is short.

**3** Look at the entire word again. Blend the root word and the ending to read the word.

**lift + ed = lifted**

> Blend **lift** and **ed** to say the word **lifted**.

### Reading Help

There are three different sounds for **-ed**.

**1. The sound for *d***

| | |
|---|---|
| waved | hugged |
| smiled | rained |

**2. The sound for *t***

| | |
|---|---|
| picked | liked |
| wished | hoped |

**3. The sounds for *ed***

| | |
|---|---|
| waited | ended |
| needed | melted |

Say each word. Which group has words with two syllables?

## READING AND SPELLING PRACTICE

**Use what you learned to read the sentences.**

1. Eddie hated to be sick. He was so bored!
2. He needed something to do.
3. He picked a book to read and flipped through it.
4. Just then, Eddie saw Len at his window.
5. Eddie waved.  "I'm so glad you stopped by!" he said.

**6.–9.** Now write the sentences that your teacher reads.

## WORD WORK

**10.–15.**  Read these words. Then write each word on a card.
**Match the 6 pairs that go together. What do you notice?**

| | | |
|---|---|---|
| waited | need | wait |
| rub | hope | liked |
| hoped | like | needed |
| rip | rubbed | ripped |

**Example:**

**10.**

rub          rubbed

> I double the **b** when I add **-ed**.

# Read on Your Own

# EVA'S LESSON

Eva was mad. She tapped her foot. She looked at the clock above the stove. "Veronica has ten more seconds to get here," she said. Eva waited and waited. Veronica was always late. They had planned to work on their dance for the school show. Eva thought Veronica was not very good. She thought Veronica needed a lot of help.

While she waited, Eva played the CD for their dance. She clapped her hands and kicked to the beat. She began to sing. She kicked again. This time, she kicked too high. She slipped and landed on the rug! Just then, Veronica peeked in the kitchen window. She saw Eva and rushed to help her. Eva smiled and rubbed her leg. "Now I know I was the one who needed help," she joked.

## CHECK YOUR UNDERSTANDING

Copy and complete this chart. Write what happened as a result of each cause. Use the finished chart to tell the story to your partner.

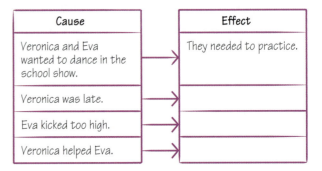

| Cause | Effect |
|-------|--------|
| Veronica and Eva wanted to dance in the school show. | They needed to practice. |
| Veronica was late. | |
| Eva kicked too high. | |
| Veronica helped Eva. | |

# Eddie's Friends Do Well

**Some nouns show ownership. They end in 's.**

Eva and Veronica picked costumes for their show. Eva's costume was purple and green. Veronica's costume was red and blue. Sofia's mom gave them matching caps to wear.

## BUILD SENTENCES

**Say each sentence. Add 's to the word in dark print.**

**Example: 1.** Eva's mom and dad came to the show.

**1. Eva** _____ mom and dad came to the show.

**2. Veronica** _____ mom came, too.

**3. friend** She borrowed her _____ camera to record the show.

**4. show** Eva and Veronica were the _____ final act.

**5. crowd** The _____ cheers made them feel good.

**6. Eddie** Veronica was very proud when she saw _____ big smile.

## WRITE SENTENCES

**7.–9.** Work with a partner. Look at the picture. Write 3 sentences about the picture. Use possessive nouns.

**Example: 7.** Miguel's shirt is orange.

# Learn About Bar Graphs

## BAR GRAPHS

A **bar graph** compares numbers. It is a good way to see information quickly.

This bar graph shows how many students have birthdays in January, February, March, and April.

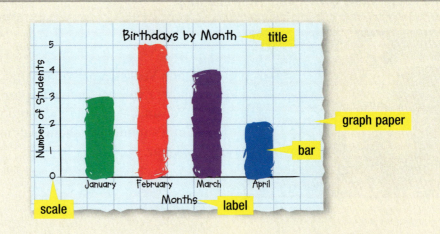

Read the instructions. Then do the activity.

# Make a Survey and Graph the Results

**You will need:** a data chart, a calculator, graph paper

### ACTIVITY STEPS

#### 1 Make a Survey

Interview three students in each age group. Ask: "How many minutes do you talk on the phone each day?" Record the results in a chart.

**Minutes on the Phone**

| Age | Student 1 | Student 2 | Student 3 | Total | Average |
|-----|-----------|-----------|-----------|-------|---------|
| 12  |           |           |           |       |         |
| 13  |           |           |           |       |         |
| 14  |           |           |           |       |         |

#### 2 Find Averages

• Add the minutes for each age group. Write the total.

• Divide each total by 3 to get the average number of minutes on the phone.

#### 3 Make a Bar Graph

• Label the bottom line of your graph: **Ages**.

• Label the scale: **Minutes on the Phone**.

• Draw the bars to make the graph.

• Write a title.

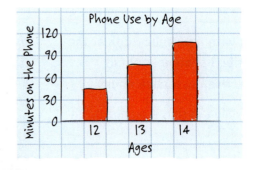

### THINK IT OVER

1. Look at your chart. What do the numbers tell you?
2. Why might there be differences among age groups?
3. Why is a bar graph a good way to see the results of your survey?

# Writing Project  FRIENDSHIP BOOK

**Make a page for a friendship book. Tell about a day with a good friend. Tell how you felt.**

## THINK ABOUT A SPECIAL TIME

Make a chart like this. What do you remember? Add your notes to the chart.

| What We Did | Where | My Feelings |
|---|---|---|
| shopped | at the mall | excited |
| talked and laughed | at the mall | happy |
| had ice cream | at a restaurant | happy |
| watched a movie | in the theater | surprised |

## PLAN YOUR PAGE

What will you show? Draw pictures or use photographs. What words will you use? Check page 312 of your Handbook for feeling words.

## MAKE AND SHARE YOUR PAGE

Write sentences for your book. Use your notes. Check and correct your work.

> ✔ **Check Your Work**
>
> Did you tell about a day with a friend?
>
> Did you tell your feelings?
>
> Do your verbs tell about the past?

Copy your sentences. Put them and your artwork on construction paper. Add your page to a class friendship book.

### A Day at the Mall
by Rosa Arias

Maura and I shopped at the mall last weekend.

I was excited to get new clothes.

We talked and laughed for hours!

I was so happy to be with Maura.

We had ice cream at a restaurant. I liked that!

Then we watched a movie in the theater.

I was surprised at the end of the movie.

# Dance!

1.  Jump high,

2.  jump low,

3.  turn,

4.  hop, hop.

5.  Step forward,

6.  step back,

7.  turn,

8.  kick, kick.

9.  Reach up,

10.  reach down,

11.  wiggle,

12.  spin.

Now you try the dance. Come on! Jump in!

# Let's Celebrate!

Learn the dance. Try it!
Then use some of the moves to
make up a new dance.

## In This Unit

### Vocabulary
- Actions
- Country Words
- Geography

### Language Functions
- Ask and Answer Questions
- Describe People

### Patterns and Structures
- Adverbs
- Present Progressive Verbs
- Phrases with *like to* and *want to*

### Reading
- Verb Ending: *-ing*
- Comprehension:
  Classify (concept map)
  Identify Details

### Writing
- Sentences
- Description
- Celebration Poster

### Content Area Connection
- Social Studies (maps)

# How Do You Dance?

**Listen and chant.**

# You Can Dance!

Can you dance?
  No, I can't dance.
You can't dance?
  No! I just can't dance.
Can you jump high?
  I can jump high.
Can you jump low?
  I can jump low.
Can you step forward?
  I can step forward.
Can you step back?
  I can step back.
Can you turn quickly?
  I can turn quickly.
Then you can dance.
Now you can dance!

> **Adverbs**
> Many **adverbs** end in **-ly**.
> They tell how:
> > turn **quickly**
> > dance **wildly**
>
> Other adverbs tell when
> or where:
> > dance **now**
> > step **back**

## EXPRESS YOURSELF  ▶ASK AND ANSWER QUESTIONS

**Work with a partner. Ask these questions.**
**Answer in a complete sentence. Then act it out.**

**Example: 1.** Can you jump high?
    Yes, I can jump high.

1. Can you jump high?
2. Can you jump low?
3. Can you step forward?
4. How do you jump?
5. Where do you step?
6. How do you turn?

## WRITE ANSWERS TO QUESTIONS

<u>7.–10.</u> **How do you dance? Write 4 sentences to answer the question. Use adverbs to tell how you dance.**

**Example: 7.** I dance fast.

# What Are They Doing?

These **verbs** tell what is happening now.

The man **is jumping**.

The women **are standing**.

They **are dancing**.

## BUILD SENTENCES

Look at the pictures below. Say sentences to go with each picture.
Choose words from each column.

| The boy<br>The girl<br>The people<br>He<br>She<br>They | is<br>are | jumping.<br>playing the drums.<br>turning around.<br>kicking.<br>dancing.<br>marching. |
|---|---|---|

**Example:** **1.** The girl is turning around.

**1.**    **2.**    **3.**    **4.**

## WRITE SENTENCES

**5.–8.** Write 2 sentences for each picture. Tell how
the people are moving. Use an adverb in each sentence.

**Example:** **5.** The girl is turning around quickly.

She is dancing happily.

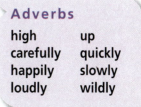

**Adverbs**

| high | up |
|---|---|
| carefully | quickly |
| happily | slowly |
| loudly | wildly |

# People Celebrate Around the World

**Look at the pictures. Read about the people.**

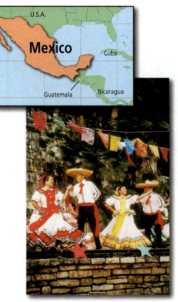

This dragon dance is from **China.** People do the dragon dance to celebrate the **Chinese** New Year.

These dancers are from **Mexico.** They are doing a **Mexican** dance.

These dancers are **English.** They are doing an old dance from **England.**

## WHO'S TALKING? ▶DESCRIBE PEOPLE

**1.–3. Listen.**
Who is talking? Point to the correct picture.
Then describe the dancers.
Tell what they look like. Tell what they are doing.

## WRITE A DESCRIPTION

**4.–8.** Interview 5 people from different countries.
Write 2 sentences to describe each person.

**Example:** 4. Juan is from Cuba.
He is Cuban.

| Country | A Person from the Country |
|---------|---------------------------|
| India | Indian |
| Mongolia | Mongolian |
| Japan | Japanese |
| Vietnam | Vietnamese |
| Cuba | Cuban |
| Guatemala | Guatemalan |
| Nicaragua | Nicaraguan |
| Ireland | Irish |

# Everyone Likes to Dance

**Use a verb to complete a phrase with *like to* or *want to*.**

| like to | + | verb |

They **like to dance**.

She **likes to perform**.

| want to | + | verb |

They **want to celebrate**.

She **wants to keep** a tradition.

Add an -*s* when you use *he*, *she*, or *it*.

## BUILD SENTENCES

Read each sentence. Add the correct form of *like to* or *want to*. Say the new sentence.

Example: **1.** The dancers like to march.

**1.** China

The dancers _____ march.

**2.** Mexico

He _____ perform.

**3.** England

The men _____ jump.

**4.** Turkey

The dancers _____ move.

**5.** Korea

She _____ turn.

**6.** Japan

She _____ celebrate.

## WRITE SENTENCES

**7.–12.** Write 2 sentences for each picture above. Use *like to* or *want to* and a country word.

Example: **7.** The dancers from China want to celebrate.
The Chinese dancers like to march.

# Read and Think Together

Make a concept map to tell about *Let's Dance!*
Follow these steps.

**1** Think about the book. What is it mostly about?

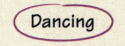

**2** Who dances? Add a section to the map.
Write **Who?** inside. Write the people who dance.

**3** What else does the book tell you? Add more sections
with **Why?**, **How?**, and **Where?**

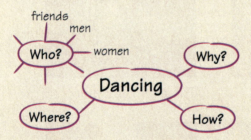

**4** Add a few words from the book for each section.
Then use your map to tell a partner about the book.

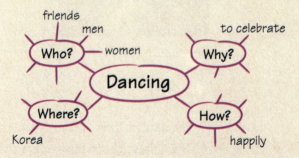

*from*
*The Basics Bookshelf*

**THEME BOOK**

This photo essay shows
how people around
the world celebrate
through dance.

# Words to Know

## REVIEW WORDS YOU KNOW

**Read the words aloud. Which word goes in the sentence?**

| | |
|---|---|
| enough | through |
| really | world |
| above | on |

1. The parade goes _____ the streets.
2. The floats are _____ big.
3. This parade is _____ Thanksgiving Day.

## LEARN TO READ

**Learn new words.**

| | |
|---|---|
| celebrate | We like to **celebrate**. Today is my sister's birthday. |
| most | **Most** of her friends are here, but not all of them. |
| young | Her friends are **young** kids from school. |
| children | There are about 10 **children** in our yard. |
| started | The party **started** at 3:00. |
| beginning | It is now 4:00, and it is **beginning** to rain. |
| change | My mother says, "We need to **change** our plans!" |
| another | "Let's move the party to **another** place!" |
| only | The house is the **only** place to go. |
| following | The kids are quickly **following** me inside. This is fun! |

### How to Learn a New Word

- Look at the word.
- Listen to the word.
- Listen to the word in a sentence. What does it mean?
- Say the word.
- Spell the word.
- Say the word again.

## WORD WORK

**Write each sentence. Add the missing word.**   **Example:** 4. In my family, we dance when we celebrate.

4. In my family, we dance when we _ _ _ _ _ _ _ _ _ _ .
5. I learned the waltz when I was very _ _ _ _ _ _ .
6. I _ _ _ _ _ _ _ to learn it when I was five.
7. The basic dance steps never _ _ _ _ _ _ _ .
8. The waltz is not the _ _ _ _ dance I know.
9. My father is teaching me _ _ _ _ _ _ _ dance called the cha-cha.
10. He wants all his _ _ _ _ _ _ _ _ to know how to dance.
11. My house is _ _ _ _ _ _ _ _ _ _ to look like a dance club!

# Reading and Spelling

**LISTEN AND LEARN**

## Invitation

Tap your foot. Tap your foot.

You are really tapping.

Jump around. Jump around.

You are really jumping.

Leap high. Leap high.

You are really leaping.

Smile for me. Smile for me.

You are really smiling!

## STUDY VERB ENDINGS

For some verbs, you can just add **-ing**.

> **leap** + **ing** = **leaping**
>
> **jump** + **ing** = **jumping**

This verb ends in silent **e**.

> **smile**

When you add **-ing**, drop the **e**.

> **smil** + **ing** = **smiling**

This verb ends in one vowel and one consonant.

> **tap**

When you add **-ing**, double the consonant.

> **tap<u>p</u>ing**

## READING STRATEGY

Follow these steps to read a word with *-ing*.

**1** Look for the ending you know. Cover it.

    **leaping**

    **leap**

**2** Look for vowel and consonant patterns to sound out the root word.

    **leap**

    **l + eă + p = leap**

> Remember that **ea** makes one vowel sound. Blend three sounds to say **leap**.

**3** Uncover the ending. Blend the syllables to read the entire word.

    **leap + ing = leaping**

> Blend **leap** and **ing** to say the word **leaping**.

**Reading Help**

Some words end in silent **e**. They have a long vowel sound.

    **shake**

Look at this word and cover the **-ing**.

    **shaking**

You do not see the **e** in the root word, but the vowel is still long.

## READING AND SPELLING PRACTICE

Use what you learned to read the sentences.

1. The first grade class is getting ready for a show.
2. I am helping with the costumes and taking care of the children.
3. Most of the children are running around. Some are screaming!
4. The music is playing. The show is beginning.
5. Two kids are waving at me. They dance very well!

<u>6.–9.</u> Now write the sentences that your teacher reads.

## WORD WORK

<u>10.–15.</u> Read these words. Then write each word on a card. Match the 6 pairs that go together. What do you notice?

| | | |
|---|---|---|
| jumping | reach | jump |
| hop | smile | waving |
| smiling | wave | reaching |
| make | hopping | making |

Example:

10.

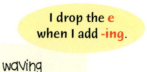

> I drop the **e** when I add **-ing**.

# Read on Your Own

Chinese New Year

# Dance to Celebrate!

People dance to celebrate a holiday. These people are beginning the Chinese New Year with a dance. They are greeting the Chinese dragon, which brings good luck. Nine men inside the costume are lifting the dragon with long poles. Another man is beating a drum. He is following the dragon.

Jewish Wedding

People dance to celebrate an important day in the family. This bride is having fun at her wedding. Three men are lifting her in her seat while her husband watches. The family is dancing around them. They are smiling and clapping.

English Maypole Dance

People dance to celebrate the seasons. May Day is the time to welcome spring. These children are skipping around a maypole. They are weaving ribbons over and under, making a braid around the maypole.

All around the world, people dance to celebrate the special times in their lives!

## CHECK YOUR UNDERSTANDING

**Write each sentence. Label it *T* for *True* or *F* for *False*.**
**If it is false, write the sentence again to make it true.**

Example:   **1.** There are six men inside the dragon costume.   **F**

There are nine men inside the dragon costume.

**Chinese New Year**

**1.** There are six men inside the dragon costume.

**2.** People dance to celebrate a holiday.

**3.** The Chinese dragon brings bad luck.

**Jewish Wedding**

**4.** A wedding is an important day.

**5.** The bride is standing.

**6.** The bride is sad.

**7.** The family is dancing.

**English Maypole Dance**

**8.** The children are skipping around the maypole.

**9.** The children are celebrating summer.

**10.** The children are weaving ribbons.

## EXPAND YOUR VOCABULARY

<u>11.–13.</u> **Tell about each picture on page 166. Use some of these words and phrases.**

| | | | | |
|---|---|---|---|---|
| wedding | bride | around the maypole | May | dancing |
| spring | dragon | having fun | costume | in the family |

Example:   **11.** People are lifting the dragon.

They are inside the costume.

## WRITE ABOUT CELEBRATIONS ✏️

<u>14.</u> **Choose a celebration from page 166. Write sentences to describe it.**

Example:   **14.** Children are dancing around a maypole.

They are celebrating spring.

# Learn About Maps

**MAPS**

Thailand is
a **country**.

On a map, a dot
shows a **city**.

A star on a map shows the
**capital**. The government
of a country is located in
the capital city.

A **border** divides one
country from another.
The black lines on this
map show borders.

Listen to the article and study the map below. Then do the Review.

# New Year Celebrations in Southeast Asia

• How do people in Southeast Asia celebrate the new year?

People in Southeast Asia celebrate the new year at different times and in different ways. Some countries celebrate in winter after the shortest day of the year. In Vietnam, people celebrate for an entire week in January or early February. During this time, the Vietnamese people of Ho Chi Minh City decorate their homes with small fruit trees full of orange-colored fruit.

Other countries celebrate the new year at the beginning of spring. In Thailand, people celebrate the new year from April 13 to April 15. All over Thailand, especially in the city of Chiang Mai, people splash water on each other to wash away bad luck.

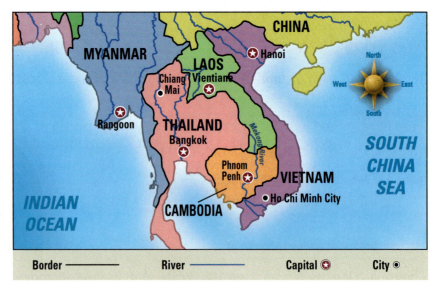

Border ——— River ——— Capital ⭐ City ◉

## REVIEW

1. **Check Your Understanding** How do people in Thailand and Vietnam celebrate the new year?
2. **Vocabulary** Name a country that has a border with Thailand.
3. **Use Maps** List the capitals shown on the map.

# Writing Project 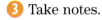 CELEBRATION POSTER

Make a poster about a family celebration. Describe the celebration.
Tell what you do. Tell what you wear and what you eat.

## INTERVIEW SOMEONE IN YOUR FAMILY

**1** Brainstorm questions.   **2** Ask your questions.   **3** Take notes.

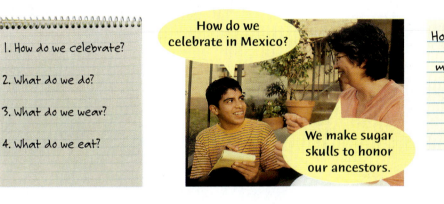

1. How do we celebrate?

2. What do we do?

3. What do we wear?

4. What do we eat?

How do we celebrate in Mexico?

We make sugar skulls to honor our ancestors.

How do we celebrate in Mexico?

make sugar skulls

## PLAN YOUR POSTER

What will you show? Draw or find pictures. What words
will you use? Be sure to spell them correctly.

## MAKE AND SHARE YOUR POSTER

Put your pictures on your poster. Write sentences
on another piece of paper. Tell what is happening
in your pictures. Then check and correct your work.

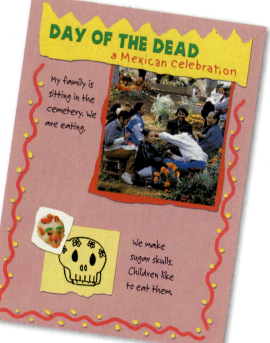

DAY OF THE DEAD
a Mexican celebration

My family is sitting in the cemetery. We are eating.

We make sugar skulls. Children like to eat them.

✔ **Check Your Work**

Do your sentences describe the picture?

Did you use a verb with *-ing* to tell what is happening?

Did you use capital letters correctly?

Write your sentences on the poster.
Read your sentences aloud.
Tell your class about your poster.

# Here to Help

Look at the pictures. These women work as a team to get people what they need. Tell what is happening in each picture. Then work in a small group. Think of 3 other workers who depend on one another to get people what they need. Draw a picture to show how they work together.

## In This Unit

### Vocabulary
• Time
• Local Government

### Language Function
• Tell What May Happen

### Patterns and Structures
• Verbs (*may, might, could*)
• Phrases with *have to* and *need to*
• Possessive Pronouns

### Reading
• Long Vowels: *ie, igh; ui, ue*
• Comprehension:
  Identify Cause and Effect
  (cause-and-effect chart)

### Writing
• Sentences
• Captions
• Job Advertisement

### Content Area Connection
• Social Studies (local government)

# I Could Help

**Listen and chant.**

## I Could Be a Paramedic

I think I'll be a paramedic
In the town of West McCheswick.
Someone may fall.
A man might call,
And I could get there quick.

If I could be a paramedic
In the town of West McCheswick,
I might save lives.
I'd get to drive
A big, white mobile clinic.

> **Verbs**
> Sometimes you aren't sure if something will happen. Use *may, might,* or *could* with another verb to tell about it.
>
> Someone **may fall**.
> A man **might call**.
> I **could be** a paramedic.

---

**EXPRESS YOURSELF** ▶TELL WHAT MAY HAPPEN

**Work with a partner. Read each question. Answer with** *may, might,* **or** *could.*

**Example: 1.** What kind of job could you have?
I could be a police officer.

1. What kind of job could you have?
2. What might you do in your work?
3. Where might you work?
4. How may you help your community?

---

**WRITE SENTENCES**

<u>5.–7.</u> **Interview a partner. What might he or she be? Write 3 sentences about what you learn. Use** *may, might,* **and** *could.*

**Example: 5.** Jasmine may be a firefighter.

# They All Work in Our City

7:00 a.m.

It's seven o'clock.

9:30 a.m.

It's nine thirty.
It's half past nine.

12:00 p.m.

It's noon.
It's twelve o'clock.

4:15 p.m.

It's four fifteen.
It's a quarter after four.
It's fifteen after four.

5:50 p.m.

It's five fifty.
It's ten to six.
It's ten of six.

12:00 a.m.

It's midnight.
It's twelve o'clock.

## WHO'S TALKING? ▶ TELL WHAT MAY HAPPEN

1.–3. Listen. 🎞️
Who is talking? Point to the correct person.
Say what time it is. Tell what the person may do.

## WRITE SENTENCES ✏️

Read each clock. Write a sentence. Tell something
that you might do at that time.

Example: 4. At seven thirty, I may call you.

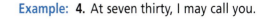

4. 7:30 (a.m.)   5. (p.m.)   6. 4:45 (p.m.)   7. (p.m.)   8. 12:00 (a.m.)   9. (a.m.)

# We Have to Help!

**Use a verb to complete a phrase with *have to* or *need to*.**

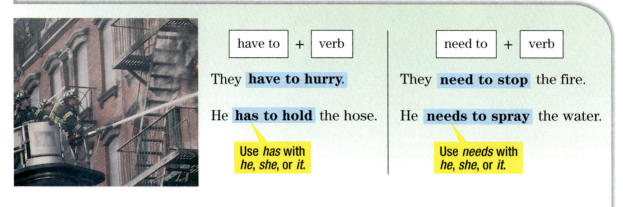

| have to | + | verb |

They **have to hurry**.

He **has to hold** the hose.

> Use *has* with *he*, *she*, or *it*.

| need to | + | verb |

They **need to stop** the fire.

He **needs to spray** the water.

> Use *needs* with *he*, *she*, or *it*.

## BUILD SENTENCES

Look at each picture. Read the sentence. Add the correct form of *have to* or *need to*. Say the new sentence.

Example: **1.** He needs to recycle the trash.

**1.**

He _____ recycle the trash.

**2.**

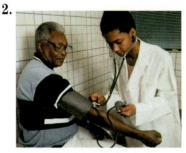

She _____ help the sick.

**3.**

They _____ fight the fire.

**4.**

They _____ fix the road.

**5.**

They _____ work on the wires.

**6.**

He _____ deliver the mail.

## WRITE ABOUT JOBS ✏️

**7.–9.** Work with a partner. Act out 3 jobs. Your partner guesses what you *need to* or *have to* do. Write the sentence.

Example: **7.** You need to drive the bus.

# What Is Your Job?

> These **pronouns** tell who or what owns something.

| Pronoun | Example |
|---------|---------|
| my | I am in this picture. **My** hand is on Malcolm's chin. |
| your | You can see Mark. He is on **your** left. |
| his | He has **his** hand on Malcolm's shoulder. |
| her | Sally's lifting Malcolm's legs on **her** shoulder. |
| its | The ocean is rough. **Its** waves almost knocked us down. |
| our | We are practicing **our** rescue plan. |
| your | Did your team practice **your** rescue plan, too? |
| their | Our supervisors are watching from **their** towers on the beach. |

## BUILD SENTENCES

**Read each sentence. Add the missing pronoun. Say the new sentence.**

Example: **1.** This young man fell and hurt his arm.

1. This young man fell and hurt _____ **(his / your)** _____ arm.
2. We called his parents. They are waiting for _____ **(its / their)** _____ son at the hospital.
3. We need to get this man into _____ **(our / its)** _____ ambulance.
4. I have tightened all the straps around _____ **(his / her)** _____ body.
5. Are you ready to lift the stretcher, Tom?
   Are you holding _____ **(their / your)** _____ side?
6. Is Joanne ready? Does she have _____ **(his / her)** _____ equipment?
7. One, two, three lift! Do you all still have
   _____ **(your / my)** _____ sides of the stretcher?
8. OK. The ambulance is ready to go. It has _____ **(my / its)** _____ sirens on. Everything will be all right!

## WRITE CAPTIONS ✏️

**9.–12.** Talk with a group. List some things people own. Draw 4 things and write captions. Use the correct pronoun.

Example: **9.**

his flashlight

# Read and Think Together

**Make a cause-and-effect chart for _Power Out!_**
**Follow these steps.**

**1** Draw a box like the one below. What important event happens in the beginning of the story? Write it in the box.

> **Cause:** The power goes out.

**2** What happens because the power goes out? Draw 4 boxes. Draw a picture of the effect in each box. Write about it, too.

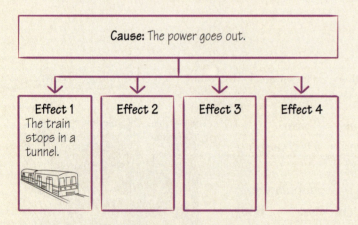

> **Cause:** The power goes out.

| Effect 1 | Effect 2 | Effect 3 | Effect 4 |
|---|---|---|---|
| The train stops in a tunnel. | | | |

**3** Compare your chart with a partner. Did you choose the same effects?

**4** Use your finished chart to retell the story to your partner.

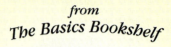

*from*
### The Basics Bookshelf

## THEME BOOK

Learn how people help each other get through an emergency in a big city.

# Words to Know

## REVIEW WORDS YOU KNOW

**Read the words aloud. Which word goes in the sentence?**

| | |
|---|---|
| river | picture |
| only | important |
| were | water |

1. The _____ is rising fast.
2. It is _____ to work together.
3. The sandbags will hold back the _____.

## LEARN TO READ

**Learn new words.**

| | |
|---|---|
| **been** | Mina has **been** in India since 1992. |
| **four** | **Four** years ago, there was an earthquake. |
| **sound** | Mina heard a loud **sound**. |
| **caused** | The earthquake **caused** her house to fall down. |
| **between** | Mina was trapped **between** a wall and a table. |
| **could** | She **could** not move. |
| **almost** | She **almost** didn't get out, but she did. |
| **life** | A rescue team saved her **life**. |
| **often** | Mina **often** tells that story. |
| **never** | We **never** get tired of hearing it. |

### How to Learn a New Word

- Look at the word.
- Listen to the word.
- Listen to the word in a sentence. What does it mean?
- Say the word.
- Spell the word.
- Say the word again.

## WORD WORK

**Where does each new word fit in the chart? Say the word and spell it.**

**Example:** 4. caused
c-a-u-s-e-d

| What to Look For | Word |
|---|---|
| 4. ends in **ed** | _ _ _ _ _ _ |
| 5. ends in **nd** | _ _ _ _ _ |
| 6. is a number | _ _ _ _ |
| 7. begins with **al** | _ _ _ _ _ _ |
| 8. means "many times" | _ _ _ _ _ |

| What to Look For | Word |
|---|---|
| 9. has one syllable and **ee** | _ _ _ _ |
| 10. has **tw** | _ _ _ _ _ _ _ |
| 11. has a long **i** sound | _ _ _ _ |
| 12. rhymes with **good** | _ _ _ _ _ |
| 13. is the opposite of **always** | _ _ _ _ _ |

# Reading and Spelling

## LISTEN AND LEARN

# Night Watch

The night watchman at the museum
wears a suit of blue,
a bright red tie, a badge, a belt,
and shiny leather shoes.

The night watchman at the museum
works the whole night through.
He checks the lights, the doors, the locks,
each painting, and the statues.

## CONNECT SOUNDS AND LETTERS

What letters stand for the vowel sound in each word?

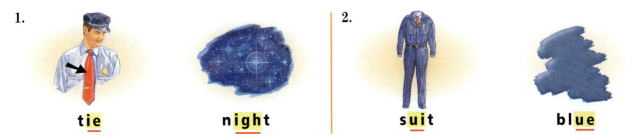

1.
t**ie**   n**igh**t

2.
s**ui**t   bl**ue**

## READING STRATEGY

**Follow these steps to read a word.**

**1** Look for a pattern of letters.

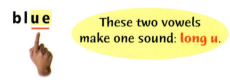

bl**ue**

These two vowels make one sound: **long u**.

h**igh**

These three letters make one sound: **long i**.

**2** Start at the beginning. Blend the sounds in your head. Then say the word.

**b l u e**     b + l + u~~e~~ = **blue**

**h i g h**     h + i~~gh~~ = **high**

## READING AND SPELLING PRACTICE

**Look for a pattern to read these words.**

**1.** lights     **2.** suit     **3.** blue     **4.** tie     **5.** Sue     **6.** high

**Use what you learned to read the sentences.**

**7.** Sue fixes street lights between 6 and 9 at night.

**8.** One night she did not tie her safety belt.

**9.** The belt opened. Sue almost fell from a high pole!

**10.** Her blue suit got stuck on the pole. That saved her life.

**11.** "I might die if I don't tie my belt right," Sue said.

**12.–16.** Now write the sentences that your teacher reads.

## WORD WORK

**17.** Write each of these words on a card.

| tie | high | true | sight | fried | right | clue |
|-----|------|------|-------|-------|-------|------|
| pie | fruit | blue | die | sigh | suit | glue |

**Say each word. Sort the words by vowel sound. Make 2 groups.**

**18.** Then put the words with the same vowel sound *and* spelling together. Make 4 groups. What do you notice?

Example: **18.**

You can spell **long i** more than one way.

tie     high

# Read on Your Own

# Hot Crumbs Cause Fire

TOKYO, JAPAN — A fire woke Kenji Yamada at 4 a.m. last night. He called the fire station. Fire trucks soon came to the rescue.

"The flames were so high and so bright!" Yamada said. "It's true! I almost died!" When he tried to throw water on the fire, he burned his right hand. Paramedics treated him.

Firefighters asked what caused the fire. At first, Yamada didn't have a clue. He said he went to bed. Then he smelled smoke. It came from his kitchen. "I think it was something in my trash," he sighed.

Yamada had some fruit at 9 p.m. At 9:30 he made tempura. He put the fried crumbs in his trash can.

When you cook tempura, the oil gets very hot.

Those crumbs can be as hot as 100°C. After a while, the crumbs might start a fire. They did last night at Yamada's home. In fact, hot crumbs caused six fires in Tokyo this year.

## CHECK YOUR UNDERSTANDING

**Write sentences that tell what happened in the article. Use a sentence starter from column 1 and a sentence ending from column 2.**

**Example:**  **1.** Yamada made tempura, and the crumbs caused a fire.

**Column 1**
1. Yamada made tempura,
2. Yamada called the fire station
3. The fire trucks came
4. Yamada burned his hand
5. Hot crumbs caused

**Column 2**
A. six fires in Tokyo this year.
B. after Yamada called the fire station.
C. and the crumbs caused a fire.
D. because he smelled smoke.
E. when he tried to throw water on the fire.

## EXPAND YOUR VOCABULARY

<u>6.</u> **Copy the concept map. Work with a group to add community workers. Add words to tell what each worker does.**

**Use the concept map to tell your group about community workers who help in emergencies.**

**Example:** Firefighters are community workers. They put out fires.

## WRITE ABOUT COMMUNITY WORKERS

<u>7.</u> **Write 3 clues about a community worker and then ask, "Who is it?" Trade clues with a partner. Try to guess your partner's community worker.**

**Example:**  **7.** He uses a ladder.
He rescues people.
He puts out fires.
Who is it?

# Learn About Local Government

## LOCAL GOVERNMENT

state

TEXAS

county

Harris County
Houston

A **city** is usually part of a **county**. There are many counties in a **state**.

mayor

city council member

Many cities have a **mayor** and a **city council**. Together, they **govern** the city.

People pay **taxes** to the city where they live. The city makes a **budget**, or plan, for how to spend the money.

The budget provides for important **services** such as fire protection.

Listen to the article. Then do the Review.

# Your Local Government in Action

• How do the mayor and city council help the city?

City governments can be organized in different ways. Some cities have a mayor and a city council. They are elected by the voters to govern the city.

The mayor and the city council run the city. They decide how to spend the city's money. They make a budget to pay for important services like these:

buses

roads

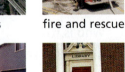

fire and rescue

police

trash collection

library

The mayor may hire city workers such as the Fire Chief or Police Chief. The mayor represents the city at special meetings and events.

The mayor runs the meetings of the city council. The mayor and the council work together to make important decisions that meet the needs of people in their city. For example, they may decide to spend money on a new park. They may have to set limits on how much water people use. Their leadership can affect the lives of the people in the city for many years.

## REVIEW

1. **Check Your Understanding** Tell three things the mayor does.
2. **Vocabulary** Name three services that might be in a city's budget.
3. **Vocabulary** Order the following from largest to smallest: county, city, state.

# Writing Project  JOB ADVERTISEMENT

**You depend on many community services. Think of a service you would like to have at your school. Work with a partner and write an ad for the job.**

## CHOOSE A JOB

**1** Brainstorm jobs. They can be real or funny jobs. Check page 305 of your Handbook for job names.

skateboard coach

homework helper

School Jobs

clothes advisor

computer game teacher

**2** Write questions.

- What is the job?
- Where is the job?
- When does the worker need to work?
- What does the worker have to do?

**3** Answer the questions.

- What is the job? The job is for a computer game teacher.
- Where is the job? at Lakeside School
- When does the worker need to work? from 8:30 to noon
- What does the worker have to do? The worker has to teach fun games and help kids.

## PLAN YOUR AD

What words will you use? Use your notes.

## MAKE AND SHARE YOUR AD

Use poster paper. Make drawings or find magazine pictures for the poster. Write your sentences. Check and correct your work.

> ✔ **Check Your Work**
>
> Does your ad describe the job?
>
> Did you write what the worker has to do?
>
> Did you check your spelling?

Display your job ad in the classroom.
Read the ads that your classmates made.
Can you suggest someone for one of the jobs?

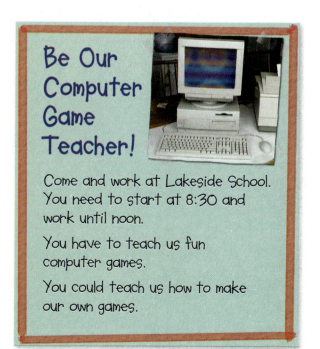

Be Our Computer Game Teacher!

Come and work at Lakeside School. You need to start at 8:30 and work until noon.

You have to teach us fun computer games.

You could teach us how to make our own games.

These kids are working together to make their community look better.

# Make a Difference!

How can you make the world a better place?
Draw a picture to show your idea. Get into a
group with students who have ideas like yours.
Make a list of the steps you can take to make
your idea happen.

## In This Unit

### Vocabulary
• Direction Words
• Civil Rights
• Data Displays

### Language Functions
• Give Information
• Give Directions
• Express Wants and Feelings

### Patterns and Structures
• Irregular Past Tense Verbs
• Prepositions

### Reading
• R-Controlled Vowels
• Comprehension:
  Identify Sequence (time line)
  Classify Information

### Writing
• Directions
• Charts
• Personal Narrative in a Mandala

### Content Area Connection
• Mathematics (table and circle graph)

# You Made a Difference!

**Listen and sing.**

## A Better Place

When I came to school,
I was alone and new.
I felt lonely and scared,
but then I met you.

You spoke to me
with a smile on your face.
You made my world
a better place.

### Verbs

Some verbs have a special form to tell about the past.

| PRESENT | PAST |
| --- | --- |
| am | was |
| are | were |
| come | came |
| feel | felt |
| meet | met |
| speak | spoke |
| make | made |

## EXPRESS YOURSELF ▶ GIVE INFORMATION

1. Work with a partner. Talk about someone who made a difference your first day at school. Use some of the past tense verbs that you learned.

Example: **1.** I met Sokha. She made me feel happy at my new school.

## WRITE SENTENCES

Write each sentence. Change the underlined verb to the past tense.

Example: **2.** I came to my new school.

**2.** I come to my new school.

**3.** I feel worried and nervous.

**4.** I meet my new teacher.

**5.** I am curious about my classmates.

**6.** The students are friendly.

**7.** I make a new friend.

# How Do Kids Help at the Senior Center?

Luisa pushes Mrs. Adams **around the pond**.

Lee and Mr. Roberts walk **into the room**.

Shabbir goes **up the ladder.**

Jared and his grandfather walk **down the ramp**.

Jim and his grandfather go **across the bridge**.

## EXPRESS YOURSELF ▶ GIVE DIRECTIONS

**Work with a partner. Give directions to get:**

1. from the rose bushes to the couch
2. from the piano to the bridge
3. from the television to the bench
4. from the fish pond to the card table
5. from the card table to the bench

Example: 1. Go around the fish pond.
Go up the ramp. Go into the
room. There is the couch!

## WRITE DIRECTIONS ✏️

6. Choose two places in your school. Write directions from one place to the other. Then help your partner follow the directions.

Example: 6. Start in our classroom. Go into the hallway. Turn right. Go down the stairs.
Walk across the hallway to the first door. Open the door.
Go into the room. You are in the band room!

# Use Your Rights to Change the World

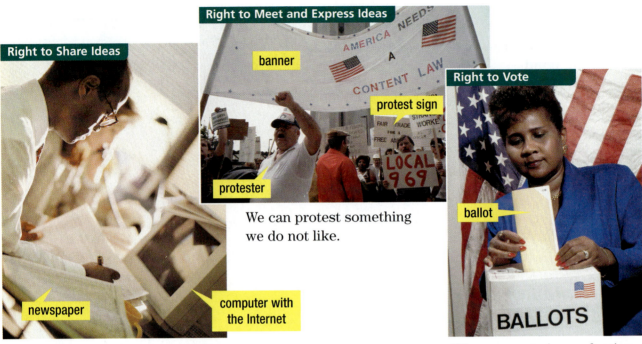

**Right to Share Ideas**

newspaper

computer with the Internet

**Right to Meet and Express Ideas**

banner

protest sign

protester

We can protest something we do not like.

**Right to Vote**

ballot

BALLOTS

We can print our ideas in a newspaper or publish them over the Internet.

When we vote in an election, we choose our leaders.

## WHO'S TALKING? ▶ EXPRESS WANTS AND FEELINGS

**1.–3. Listen.**

Who is talking? Point to the correct picture.

Talk to a partner about what each person wants and feels.

## WRITE ABOUT SOMETHING YOU WANT TO CHANGE

**4.** What do you want to change at your school? How can you make those changes?
Work with your class to make a chart like this.

Example: **4.**

| What to Change | Who Makes the Decision | What Strategies to Use |
|---|---|---|
| have art class for everyone | school board | go to school board meetings, write letters |

# Some People Who Led America

**These verbs have special forms to tell about the past.**

| Present | Past | Example |
|---------|------|---------|
| think | thought | Susan B. Anthony and Elizabeth Cady Stanton **thought** women should have the right to vote. |
| lead | led | Together, they **led** a movement to get more rights for women. |
| go | went | They **went** to cities around the country. |
| give | gave | They **gave** speeches to try to change the law. |
| speak | spoke | They **spoke** at many meetings. |
| see | saw | Many people **saw** them. In 1920, Congress passed a law that gave women the right to vote. |

## BUILD SENTENCES

**Read each sentence. Change the <u>underlined</u> verb to tell about the past.
Say the new sentence to a partner.**

Example:  **1.** In 1965, César Chávez led a protest to get better treatment for farmworkers.

**1.** In 1965, César Chávez <u>leads</u> a protest to get better treatment for farmworkers.

**2.** He <u>goes</u> to farms throughout California.

**3.** He <u>speaks</u> to many farmworkers. By 1970, many growers agreed to fair treatment for the farmworkers.

**4.** Martin Luther King, Jr., <u>thinks</u> African Americans should have equal rights.

**5.** He <u>gives</u> many speeches.

**6.** Thousands of people <u>see</u> him. A new law was passed in 1964 to give all Americans equal rights.

## WRITE ABOUT EVENTS IN YOUR HISTORY 🖊

<u>7.–10.</u>  **Write 4 sentences to tell about when you came to the United States. What did you think? What did you do?**

Example:  **7.** I thought everyone looked so different.

# Read and Think Together

Work with a group to make a time line for *Who Was Martin Luther King, Jr.?* Follow these steps.

**1** What happened first? Draw a dot. Write the year that Martin was born. Then write a sentence that tells what happened in that year.

**1929**
Martin was born in Atlanta, Georgia.

**2** What happened next? Draw a line. Add another dot for each important date and event. Tell what happened. Use words from the story to write the sentence.

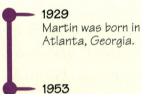

**1929**
Martin was born in Atlanta, Georgia.

**1953**
Martin married Coretta Scott.

**3** Use your finished time line to tell the class about the life of Martin Luther King, Jr. Each student in your group can tell about one of the events.

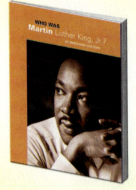

*from*
## The Basics Bookshelf

## THEME BOOK

Read this biography of Martin Luther King, Jr., to learn why he was one of America's great leaders.

# Words to Know

## REVIEW WORDS YOU KNOW

**Read the words aloud. Which word goes in the sentence?**

| | |
|---|---|
| play | places |
| their | to |
| of | other |

1. This woman goes to different _____.
2. She teaches people _____ read.
3. A lot _____ people thank her.

## LEARN TO READ

**Learn new words.**

| | |
|---|---|
| country | Indra was born in a **country** in Asia. |
| called | The country is **called** Indonesia. |
| lived | He **lived** there as a child. |
| house | He grew up in a **house** built on long posts. |
| now | Indra came to the U.S. **Now** he lives in California. |
| American | Last year, Indra became an **American** citizen. |
| would | He **would** like to help people in Indonesia. |
| know | He **knows** how they could grow more food. |
| should | He thinks they **should** plant different crops each year. |
| also | Indra **also** wants to help the farmers sell their crops. |

**How to Learn a New Word**

- Look at the word.
- Listen to the word.
- Listen to the word in a sentence. What does it mean?
- Say the word.
- Spell the word.
- Say the word again.

## WORD WORK

**4.–13. Make a map for each new word. Write the word in the center. Complete the other boxes. Then use the word in a sentence of your own.**

Example: 4.

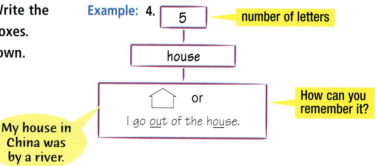

My house in China was by a river.

# Reading and Spelling

## LISTEN AND LEARN

### Let Hope Burn Bright

Let hope burn bright,
bright as a star,
for everyone.

Let hope sing sweet,
sweet as a song,
for everyone.

Let hope fly high,
high as a bird,
for everyone.

Let hope be strong,
strong as a bear,
for everyone.

## CONNECT SOUNDS AND LETTERS

**What is the vowel sound in each word?**

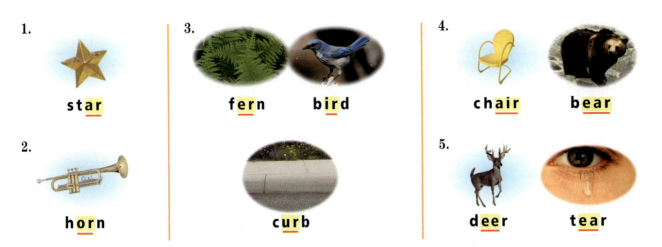

1. st**ar**

2. h**or**n

3. f**er**n     b**ir**d

   c**ur**b

4. ch**air**     b**ear**

5. d**ee**r     t**ea**r

▶ Transparencies 57–61

## READING STRATEGY

**Follow these steps to read a word.**

**1** Look for a pattern in the word. Do you see a **vowel + r**?

y<mark>ar</mark>d

b<mark>ir</mark>d

**2** Start at the beginning. Blend the sounds in your head.
Then say the word.

<u>y</u>ard    y + ar + d = yard

**b**ird    b + ir + d = bird

*A **vowel + r** makes one sound.*

## READING AND SPELLING PRACTICE

**Blend the sounds to read these words.**

   **1.** hair       **2.** skirts       **3.** forms       **4.** art       **5.** wear       **6.** year

**Use what you learned to read the sentences.**

   **7.** Carmen is part of a group that helps women in Latin America.

   **8.** The women make shirts and skirts to wear.

   **9.** They also make hair clips and other crafts to sell.

   **10.** Carmen thinks that these crafts are forms of art.

   **11.** Next year, the group would like to sell the crafts in the U.S.

   <u>**12.–16.**</u> **Now write the sentences that your teacher reads.**

## WORD WORK

<u>**17.–24.**</u> **Read these words. Then write each word on a card.**
**Match the two words that start with the same sound.**
**What do you notice about the vowel sound?**

| | | | | | |
|---|---|---|---|---|---|
| cat | porch | jar | bun | deep | car |
| deer | heat | fat | hear | pond | jam |
| burn | chirp | chip | far | | |

**Example:**

**17.**

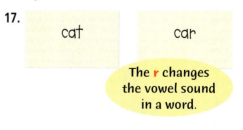

*The **r** changes the vowel sound in a word.*

# Read on Your Own

Nadja Halilbegovich is from Bosnia.

# Kids Are Helping Kids

Kids can help other kids in important ways. Nadja, Hafsat, and Craig show us how.

Nadja helped kids in Bosnia. When Nadja was a girl, ethnic groups in Bosnia started a war. Kids lived in fear. A lot of them were hurt. Nadja started a radio show. She sang on the air to give children courage. She also published two books. They tell how hard it is to live through a war. She hopes her books will help end fighting in the world.

Hafsat helps kids in Nigeria. She formed a group called KIND. The group teaches children their rights. It shows kids how to be leaders. KIND also helps women and children get fair treatment.

Craig was 12 years old when he read that many kids were made to work in hard jobs for no pay. People treated them very badly. He had to help these kids. He formed a group called Free the Children. Now, his group speaks out for children's rights in 27 countries.

Hafsat Abiola is from Nigeria.

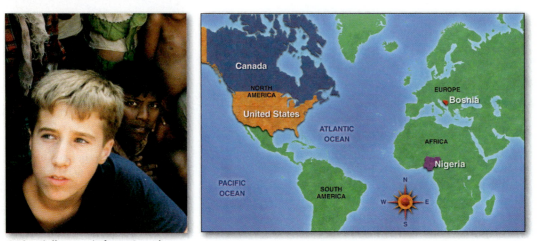

Craig Kielburger is from Canada.

1.–3. Copy the chart and then complete it.

| Who Helped Others? | Where? | What Group of People Did He or She Help? | How? |
|---|---|---|---|
| 1. Nadja Halilbegovich | Bosnia | children | She published two books. She started a radio show. |
|  |  |  |  |
|  |  |  |  |

## EXPAND YOUR VOCABULARY

4.–6. Tell a partner about each person on page 194. Use information from your chart and some of these words and phrases.

| | | |
|---|---|---|
| brings hope | fair treatment | hard jobs |
| sang on the air | rights | formed a group |
| war | published | Free the Children |

Example: 4. Nadja published two books.
 The books tell about the war in Bosnia.

## WRITE ABOUT PEOPLE 

7. Choose one of the kids from page 194 or another person you know.
Tell how the person makes a difference.

Example: 7. Craig helps kids who were made to work in hard jobs.
 He formed a group called Free the Children.

# Learn How to Represent Data

**Data** is information. You can **represent**, or show, data in different ways.

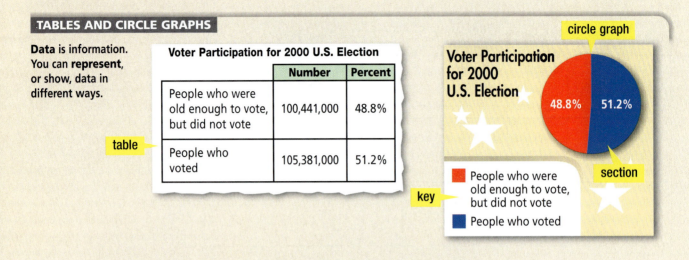

circle graph

**Voter Participation for 2000 U.S. Election**

| | Number | Percent |
|---|---|---|
| People who were old enough to vote, but did not vote | 100,441,000 | 48.8% |
| People who voted | 105,381,000 | 51.2% |

table

key

**Voter Participation for 2000 U.S. Election**

48.8%    51.2%

section

■ People who were old enough to vote, but did not vote
■ People who voted

**Listen to the article. Study the circle graph below. Then do the Review.**

# Voting Patterns in U.S. Elections

• Do Americans make good use of their right to vote?

In the United States today, you can vote if you are a citizen and if you are 18 years old or older. You also have to register, or sign a paper saying that you want to vote.

It hasn't always been so easy to vote. In the Revolutionary War of 1776, Americans fought the British for the right to vote. For almost a hundred years after the war, only white men could vote. Over the years, several amendments to the United States Constitution have expanded the right to vote:

• In 1870, after the Civil War, the 15th Amendment gave all men of any race the right to vote.
• In 1920, the 19th Amendment gave women the right to vote.
• In 1971, the 26th Amendment lowered the voting age to 18.

Some citizens who are 18 or older do not take the time to register to vote. Others register, but do not vote. Study the circle graph to see data for a typical year.

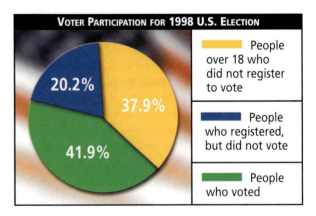

**VOTER PARTICIPATION FOR 1998 U.S. ELECTION**

20.2%    37.9%    41.9%

■ People over 18 who did not register to vote
■ People who registered, but did not vote
■ People who voted

### REVIEW

1. **Check Your Understanding** Who can vote in the United States today? Do Americans use their right to vote? Explain your answer.
2. **Vocabulary** How does a circle graph help you to compare data?
3. **Use Circle Graphs** Compare the data for the 1998 election and the 2000 election. In which year did a higher percentage of people vote? How can you tell?

# Writing Project — MANDALA

**When did you make a difference in the world?**
**Make a mandala to show your class what you did. A mandala is a design in the shape of a circle. You can use it to tell a story with pictures.**

## GATHER YOUR IDEAS

Think of ways you have helped. Maybe you helped someone at school, someone younger than you, or even a stranger. Maybe you helped a little. Maybe you helped a lot. Gather your ideas in a chart like this. Then choose an idea.

| What I Saw | What I Did and How I Felt |
|---|---|
| My sister didn't know math. | I taught her subtraction. I felt proud. |
| Mom wanted to speak to the clerk at the grocery store. She didn't know the English words to use. | I spoke to the clerk for my mom. I felt happy to help. |

## MAKE YOUR MANDALA

Draw a circle. Think about your idea. In the top half of the circle, draw what you saw. In the bottom half of the circle, draw what you did. Write a sentence about each picture.

**✔ Check Your Work**

Did you tell how you helped someone?

Did you describe how you felt?

Did you use the correct form of each verb?

Write your sentences next to each picture on the mandala. Decorate the mandala. Display it in your classroom.

butterfly

zebra

killer whale

tree frog

tiger

python snake

baboon

toucan

polar bear

# ur Living Planet

Play this game with a partner. Toss two coins onto the page at left. Make them land on two different animals. Tell one way the animals are the same. Your partner should tell another way the animals are alike. See who can think of the most ways.

## In This Unit

### Vocabulary
- Opinion Words
- Animals, Plants, and Habitats
- Graphs

### Language Functions
- Give Opinions
- Describe Places
- Make a Suggestion

### Patterns and Structures
- Sensory Adjectives
- Verbs (*must, should*)

### Reading
- Multisyllabic Words
- Comprehension:
  Identify Sequence (data chart, time line)
  Identify Details, Cause and Effect

### Writing
- Opinions
- Description
- Fact-and-Opinion Poster

### Content Area Connection
- Science and Mathematics (line graphs)

# We Must Care for Our Earth!

**Listen and sing.**

## Our Earth

We must keep the air clean
for the eagle to fly.
We must clean up our oceans
so the whales can swim by.
I think we should fight
for our water and sky.
We must help our Earth.
I believe we must try!

**Opinion Words**
People use these words
to give an opinion.

| | |
|---|---|
| must | should |
| think | believe |

## EXPRESS YOURSELF ▶ GIVE YOUR OPINION

How should we protect plants and animals? Work with your class to think of ideas. Finish each sentence below.

**Example: 1.** We should pick up trash.

1. We should _____.     3. I believe that _____.
2. We must _____.       4. I think that _____.

## WRITE OPINIONS

<u>5.–8.</u> What should we do to help the Earth? Work with a group to write 4 ideas. Use opinion words.

**Example: 5.** We should keep the rivers clean.

# What Lives Around the Water?

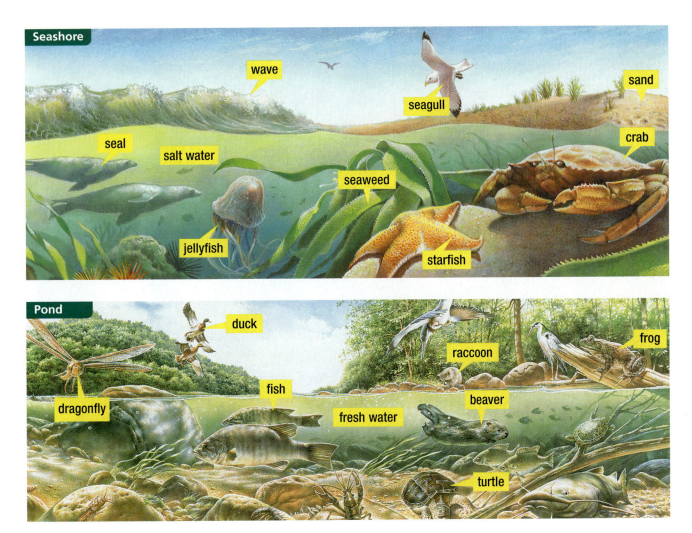

**Seashore** — wave, seagull, sand, seal, salt water, crab, seaweed, jellyfish, starfish

**Pond** — duck, raccoon, frog, fish, dragonfly, beaver, fresh water, turtle

## EXPRESS YOURSELF ▶ Describe Places

**1.–2.** Work with a group. Describe each place. Tell what you can see there.

**Example: 1.** There are big waves at the seashore. There is white sand.

## WRITE A DESCRIPTION

**3.–8.** Write 3 sentences about each picture above. Use adjectives to describe the animals you see.

**Example: 3.** I see a brown beaver and a very big frog at the pond.

### Adjectives

| | |
|---|---|
| green | large |
| brown | small |
| orange | big |
| white | little |

# Life in the Forest

## WHO'S TALKING? ▶ MAKE A SUGGESTION

<u>1.</u> Listen.

Who is making suggestions? Point to the correct person.
Then act out the scene with a partner.

## WRITE SUGGESTIONS

<u>2.–4.</u> **How can we take good care of nature?**
**Write 3 sentences with suggestions.**

Example: **2.** Let's be sure we put out campfires.

> **Suggestions**
> Let's _____.
> Why don't we _____?
> We could _____.
> Can we _____?
> Would you like to _____?

# Describe the Earth

**Adjectives** can tell what something is like.

An adjective can tell how something looks.
The tree is **tall**.

An adjective can tell how something sounds.
A **loud** bird lives in the tree.

An adjective can tell how something feels.
The tree trunk feels **rough**.

## BUILD SENTENCES

Look at each picture below. Add an adjective to tell how each thing looks, sounds, or feels. See Handbook pages 310–311. Say each sentence.

**Example:** 1. The desert is hot and dry.

1. The desert is _____.
2. A _____ cactus grows there.
3. The snake makes a _____ sound.

4. The mountain is _____.
5. A _____ deer lives there.
6. The squirrel makes a _____ sound.

## WRITE A DESCRIPTION ✏

<u>7.</u> Draw a picture of a scene in nature. Write a description of your drawing. Use adjectives.

**Example:** 7. The brown owl is in the tall tree.
The forest is quiet and cool.

# Read and Think Together

Make a data chart and time line for *Rachel Carson*.
Follow these steps.

**1** Copy the chart below. Read the book again.
Collect these facts about Rachel's life.

| Page | Event | Year | Age |
|------|-------|------|-----|
| 9 | Rachel was born. | 1907 | baby |
| 11 | | | |
| 13 | | | |
| 14 | | | |
| 22 | | | |

**2** Use the data chart to make a time line. Draw the
line. Add a dot for the first event. Write the year
above the dot. Below the dot, write a sentence to
tell what happened in that year.

1907

●————————————————

Rachel was born.

**3** Finish the time line. Add 4 more dots, each
with a date and a sentence.

**4** Use your finished time line to tell a group
about Rachel Carson's life.

*from*
## The Basics Bookshelf

**THEME BOOK**

This biography tells how
Rachel Carson changed
the way people treat
our natural world.

# Words to Know

## REVIEW WORDS YOU KNOW

**Read the words aloud. Which word goes in the sentence?**

| | |
|---|---|
| house | head |
| Another | Answer |
| New | Now |

1. One person holds the bird's _____.
2. _____ person holds its body.
3. _____ they can help the bird.

## LEARN TO READ

**Learn new words.**

| | |
|---|---|
| mountains | Alaska has beautiful beaches and tall **mountains**. |
| oil | In 1989, a ship spilled **oil** into a bay in Alaska. |
| found | People **found** sick birds on the beach. |
| because | The birds got sick **because** they ate the oil when they cleaned their feathers. |
| few | Many people, not just a **few**, came to help. |
| try | The people wanted to **try** to save the birds. |
| over | When their work was **over**, many birds were saved. |
| away | The people went **away**, but they did not forget. |
| why | Everyone asked **why** the spill happened. |
| story | Newspapers around the world told the **story**. |

### How to Learn a New Word

- Look at the word.
- Listen to the word.
- Listen to the word in a sentence. What does it mean?
- Say the word.
- Spell the word.
- Say the word again.

## WORD WORK

**Write each sentence. Add the missing word.**   **Example: 1.** Why did the oil spill happen?

4. _ _ _ did the oil spill happen?
5. It happened _ _ _ _ _ _ _ the ship ran aground.
6. The ship started to leak _ _ _.
7. In just a _ _ _ days, the oil was everywhere.
8. Before the spill was _ _ _ _, the oil had coated 1,300 miles of the Alaska shoreline.
9. Ten years later, people still _ _ _ _ _ oil on the beaches.
10. The _ _ _ _ _ of the Alaska oil spill is a sad one.

# Reading and Spelling

**LISTEN AND LEARN**

## Under the Moon

The silent spider
spins her web.
See the fine silver thread,
under the moon.

The silent turtle
swims in the sea.
Feel the swish of flippers,
under the moon.

The silent owl
hunts his supper.
Hear the whisper of wings,
under the moon.

Listen!

## LOOK FOR SYLLABLES IN LONG WORDS

Read the words in each group. Which syllable is the same?

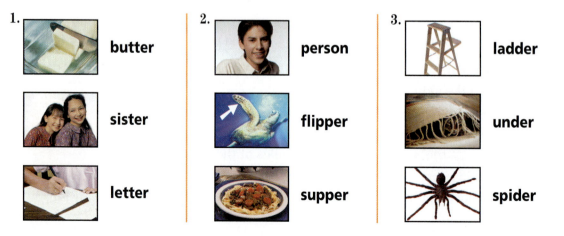

1.
butter

sister

letter

2.
person

flipper

supper

3.
ladder

under

spider

## READING STRATEGY

Follow these steps to read a word.

**1** In a long word, look for a syllable you know.

**garden**                    **after**

**2** Divide the word. Keep the syllable together.

**gar den**                    **af ter**

**3** Blend the two syllables together to read the word.

**gar** + **den** = **garden**        **af** + **ter** = **after**

### Reading Help

Look for these syllables in long words:

| mar | cor | ber | mer |
|-----|-----|-----|-----|
| gar | nor | ter | der |
| par | tor | ner | per |

## READING AND SPELLING PRACTICE

**Use what you learned to read the sentences.**

**1.** Garter snakes are small members of the reptile family.

**2.** In summer, garters can be found in forests, farms, and open lands.

**3.** A few may make a home in wet corners of a garden.

**4.** In winter, garters may be hard to find because they stay under the ground.

**5.** Garters don't bite, so some people keep them as pets!

**6.–10.** Now write the sentences that your teacher reads.

## WORD WORK

**11.–18. Copy the chart. Then read these words:**

| hammer | winter | sister | ladder |
|--------|--------|--------|--------|
| pepper | under | perfume | summer |

| merchant | person | letter | spider |
|----------|--------|--------|--------|
| 11. | 13. | 15. | 17. |
| 12. | 14. | 16. | 18. |

Write each word in the chart. Put it under the word that has the same syllable.

**Example: 11.**

| merchant |
|----------|
| 11. hammer |

# Read on Your Own

Bighorn Sheep

# Animals in the Wild

The bighorn sheep is a mountain animal. It is also found in the desert. It can live above the timberline, where trees don't grow. Bighorn sheep have large, curled horns and a short tail. They can go up steep trails. Because they have thick fur, they can live through winter storms.

White-Tailed Deer

The white-tailed deer is a forest animal with a short tail. It has brown fur in the summer. In the winter, when there is snow, it has gray-white fur. That is why it is so hard to see a white-tailed deer.

The male deer has antlers that drop off in the winter and grow again in the spring. These new antlers soon grow hard and sharp.

Coyote

The coyote is a desert animal. It is also found in mountains and on flat plains. It has long fur and a long tail. The coyote is a member of the dog family. It hunts after dark. At night, you may hear a few coyotes howl. From far away, their sound is like a sad song.

## CHECK YOUR UNDERSTANDING

**Write the correct answer to each item.**

Example: **1.** The bighorn sheep has large, curled horns.

1. The bighorn sheep has _____.
   A. a long tail
   B. short, sharp antlers
   C. large, curled horns

2. The bighorn sheep can live through winter storms because it has _____.
   F. thick fur
   G. gray-white fur
   H. large, curled horns

3. The deer's antlers grow again in the _____.
   A. spring
   B. winter
   C. summer

4. Why is it hard to see the white-tailed deer in the winter?
   F. It stays in its burrow.
   G. Its fur turns gray-white.
   H. There are a lot of winter storms.

5. The coyote and the _____ are in the same family.
   A. deer
   B. dog
   C. bear

6. What does the coyote do at night?
   F. It howls.
   G. It sleeps.
   H. It turns gray-white.

## EXPAND YOUR VOCABULARY

<u>7.</u> **Work with a partner. Copy this chart. Put a ✓ in the correct box.**

| Animal | Has fur | Howls at night | Has a short tail |
|---|---|---|---|
| Bighorn Sheep | ✓ | | |
| White-Tailed deer | | | |
| Coyote | | | |

**Use the chart and the article on page 208 to tell your partner about the animals.**

Example: **7.** All the animals have fur. The bighorn sheep and the white-tailed deer have short tails.

## WRITE ABOUT ANIMALS

<u>8.</u> **Choose a wild animal. Write sentences to describe it.**

Example: **8.** The coyote looks like a dog. It hunts at night.

# Learn About Line Graphs

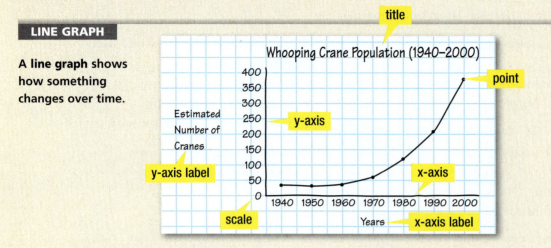

**LINE GRAPH**

A **line graph** shows how something changes over time.

Labels on graph: title, point, y-axis, y-axis label, x-axis, scale, x-axis label

Whooping Crane Population (1940–2000)

Estimated Number of Cranes

Years

**Listen to the article. Study the picture and the graph below. Then do the Review.**

# The Whooping Crane: An Endangered Bird

• Can the whooping crane be saved?

In the 1800s, there were hundreds of whooping cranes in North America. Then the cranes became endangered. Many were hunted. Many of the wetlands where they lived were drained and turned into farms. By the 1940s, only a few whooping cranes were left.

Scientists are working hard to save these cranes. Each spring, whooping cranes lay two eggs and raise only one chick. Some scientists take the extra egg and hatch the chick. Then they release the chick into the wild. This work has helped increase the number of whooping cranes. By 2000, there were about 400 whooping cranes in North America.

The whooping crane is beautiful. It is white with red and black on its head. It has long, thin legs and a long beak.

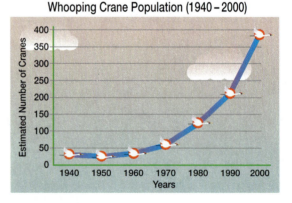

Whooping Crane Population (1940 – 2000)

Estimated Number of Cranes

Years

## REVIEW

1. **Check Your Understanding** Why did whooping cranes become endangered?
2. **Vocabulary** Name the parts of a line graph.
3. **Use Line Graphs** About how many whooping cranes were counted in 1950? In 1990? In what year were there about 125 whooping cranes?

# Writing Project  FACT-AND-OPINION POSTER

**Make a poster to give facts and opinions about an animal.
Then share your poster with the class.**

## RESEARCH AN ANIMAL

**1** Choose an animal. Find out information
about it. Ask your teacher or librarian for
help. Write facts about the animal in a chart.

**2** What do you think or believe about the
animal? Add your opinions to the chart.

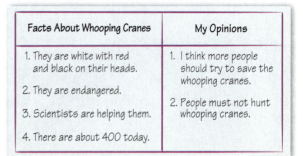

| Facts About Whooping Cranes | My Opinions |
|---|---|
| 1. They are white with red and black on their heads. | 1. I think more people should try to save the whooping cranes. |
| 2. They are endangered. | |
| 3. Scientists are helping them. | 2. People must not hunt whooping cranes. |
| 4. There are about 400 today. | |

## MAKE AND SHARE YOUR POSTER

Draw or find a picture of the animal. Write a caption to
describe your animal. Check pages 310–311 of your Handbook
for adjectives you can use. Write your facts and opinions.
Work with a partner to check your work.

### ✔ Check Your Work

Did you write facts
and opinions about
the animal?

Did you use adjectives
to describe the animal?

Did you use opinion
words like *think* or
*should*?

Use heavy paper. Fold it into 3 sections.
Put your picture and caption in the
middle section. Write your sentences
on the outside sections.

Present your poster to the class. Look
at the other posters. Talk about what
you learned.

### The Whooping Crane

**Facts:**

1. Whooping
   cranes are
   endangered.
2. Scientists are
   working to
   save them.
3. There are
   about 400
   whooping
   cranes
   today.

**My Opinions:**

1. I think more
   people should
   try to save
   whooping
   cranes.
2. People must
   not hunt
   whooping
   cranes.

The whooping crane
is beautiful. It is
white with red and
black on its head. It
has long, thin legs
and a long beak.

1920   1930   1940   1950   1960   1970   1980   1990   2000   2010

1943

1925

1963

2000

# PAST AND PRESENT

Look at the time line of this woman's life.
What can you tell about her?
Make a time line of your life.
Draw pictures to show important events.
Label the years. Tell the class about
your past and present.

## In This Unit

### Vocabulary
- History and Historical Records
- U.S. Government

### Language Functions
- Have a Discussion
- Make Comparisons

### Patterns and Structures
- Nouns
- Present and Past Tense Verbs
- Object Pronouns

### Reading
- Phonics: Words with y
- Comprehension:
  Make Comparisons (comparison chart)

### Writing
- Comparisons
- Letter
- Comparison Poster

### Content Area Connection
- Social Studies (U.S. government)

# What Is History?

**Listen and sing.**

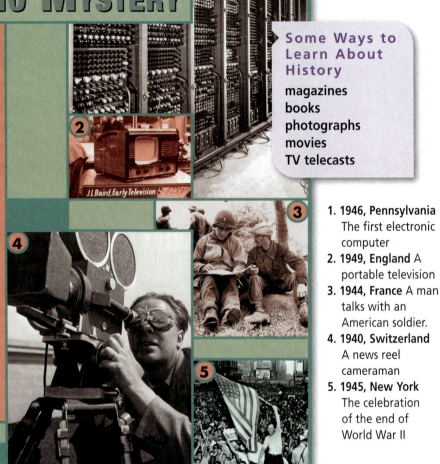

## HISTORY'S NO MYSTERY

History's no mystery.
It's all about the past.
Get the facts from magazines
and books with photographs.

History's no mystery.
It's all about the past.
See it all in movies
and TV telecasts.

Find out for yourself
how life used to be.
You will learn a lot of things
when you study history.

J.L Baird. Early Television

**Some Ways to Learn About History**
magazines
books
photographs
movies
TV telecasts

1. **1946, Pennsylvania** The first electronic computer
2. **1949, England** A portable television
3. **1944, France** A man talks with an American soldier.
4. **1940, Switzerland** A news reel cameraman
5. **1945, New York** The celebration of the end of World War II

## EXPRESS YOURSELF ▶ HAVE A DISCUSSION

**Meet with a group. Use the questions below to start a discussion.**

**Example: 1.** I like to read books to learn about the past.

1. How do you like to learn about the past?
2. Why is it important to learn about history?
3. Have you seen a movie about the past? Tell about it. What did you learn from the movie?

## WRITE SENTENCES

<u>4.</u> **Write a sentence. Tell one important thing you learned in the discussion.**

**Example: 4.** You can get movies about the past at the library.

# How We Learn About the Past

We call the early 1940s "The War Years" because the U.S. fought in World War II from 1941–1945. Here are some ways you can learn about the 1940s.

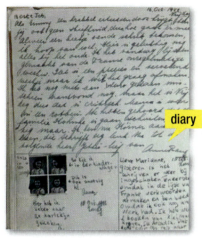
diary

newspaper
photograph

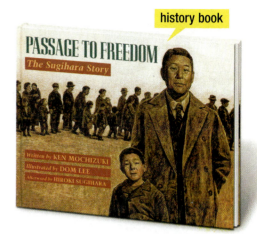
history book

Some people wrote about their lives in **diaries** or **journals**. You can read them to see what people's lives were like in the past.

You can read old **newspapers**. They reported the daily events as they happened. **Photographs** made the news come alive.

Look in books written later by **historians**. A historian reads many **sources** and tells the story of the past.

## WHO'S TALKING? ▶ MAKE COMPARISONS

**1.–3. Listen.**

Three students are talking about their research. Which record of history is each student talking about? Point to the correct picture. Then work with a partner. Compare two of the records shown above.

## WRITE COMPARISONS

**4.–6.** Write 3 comparisons. In each, compare 2 other kinds of records, like movies or magazines. Use words from the box.

**Example: 4.** A magazine and a movie both give us information. A magazine tells about the past with words and pictures, but a movie shows action with pictures that move.

> **Words That Compare**
> | | |
> |---|---|
> | alike | unalike |
> | same | different |
> | and | but |
> | both | |

# The 1940s: Who? What? Where?

A **noun** names a person, place, or thing.

Margaret Bourke-White

<u>World War II</u> began in 1939.
thing

<u>Margaret Bourke-White</u> took <u>photographs</u> of the <u>war</u> in <u>Europe</u>.
person      things      thing      place

<u>Magazines</u> printed her amazing <u>pictures.</u>
things      things

<u>Americans</u> could see what their <u>soldiers</u> were doing.
people      people

## READ SENTENCES

**Say each sentence. Tell if each <u>underlined</u> noun is a person, a place, or a thing.**

**Example:** **1.** Bill Mauldin is the name of a person.

1. <u>Bill Mauldin</u> also recorded the <u>events</u> of <u>World War II</u>.

2. While he was in the <u>army</u> in <u>Italy</u>, he drew <u>cartoons</u> of American <u>soldiers</u>.

3. His <u>pictures</u> were often published in the <u>newspaper</u> *Stars and Stripes.*

Bill Mauldin

4. <u>Ollie Stewart</u> was a <u>reporter</u>.

5. He was the first <u>journalist</u> from the <u>newspaper</u> *Afro-American* to go to the frontline in <u>North Africa</u>.

6. He was also in <u>France</u> when the <u>war</u> ended there.

Ollie Stewart

## WRITE A PARAGRAPH 🖍

**Write the paragraph.**
**Add the missing words.**

| award | newspapers | soldiers |
|-------|-----------|----------|
| Japan | photographs | |

The photographer Joe Rosenthal took ___(7)___ during World War II. He was on an island in ___(8)___ when he took a famous picture of six American ___(9)___ lifting a flag. Many magazines and ___(10)___ printed the picture. Joe won an ___(11)___ for the picture.

Joe Rosenthal took this photo in Iwo Jima, Japan, in 1945.

# The 1940s: What We Did

A **verb** changes to show when an action happens.

Use a present tense verb to tell what happens now.

Today we **listen** to songs on the radio.

Use a past tense verb to tell what happened in the past. To form the past tense, you usually add *-ed*.

In the 1940s, families **listened** to war news on the radio.

Study the verbs in the box. They have a special form to show the past tense.

| Present | Past |
|---------|------|
| are | were |
| build | built |
| eat | ate |
| is | was |
| leave | left |
| say | said |
| wear | wore |

## BUILD SENTENCES

Say each sentence. Add the past tense of the verb in dark type.

Example: **1.** In the United States, people's lives changed a lot during World War II.

1. **change**     In the United States, people's lives _____ a lot during World War II.
2. **are**     There _____ not many things to buy.
3. **print**     The government _____ special stamps.
4. **use**     Everyone _____ the stamps to get things like sugar and cheese.
5. **plant**     Families _____ gardens to grow food.
6. **wear**     Women _____ simple dresses and shoes.
7. **collect**     Children _____ old rubber, paper, and aluminum.
8. **build**     Factories _____ bombs and airplanes from them.
9. **eat**     People _____ food like powdered eggs and potatoes.
10. **is**     There _____ not much gasoline either.
11. **say**     Everyone _____ that life was hard.
12. **leave**     The hardest part was when someone _____ to go to war.

People used ration stamps like these.

## WRITE SENTENCES ✏️

**13.–15.** Choose 3 present tense verbs from the box at the top of the page. Write a sentence for each verb. Trade papers with a partner. Write the sentences again. Put the verb in the past tense.

Example: **13.** Factories build airplanes.

Factories built airplanes.

Women worked in airplane factories for the first time during World War II.

# World War II: A Tragic Time

A **pronoun** can refer to a **noun**.

Anne Frank was a teenager in 1940.

Use these pronouns after an action verb and after words like *to*, *in*, or *with*.

| Pronoun | Use for: | Examples |
|---------|----------|----------|
| him | a boy or a man | **Adolf Hitler** was Germany's leader in World War II. The Nazi Party was loyal to **him**. |
| her | a girl or a woman | **Anne Frank** was Jewish. The Nazis made **her** wear a yellow star. |
| it | a thing | Anne wrote about her life in a **diary**. You can read **it** today. |
| them | two or more people or things | The **Franks** had to hide during the war. A few friends helped **them**. |

## BUILD SENTENCES

Look at the **noun** in the first sentence. Say both sentences. Add the pronoun that refers to, or goes with, the noun.

Example: **1.** Otto Frank, Anne's father, had an office. The family hid above it.

1. Otto Frank, Anne's father, had an **office**. The family hid above _____.
2. A **boy** named Peter also hid there. Anne became good friends with _____.
3. One horrible morning, the Nazis found the **family**. The soldiers took _____ to prison camps.
4. Anne left her **diary** in the hiding place. A friend found _____.
5. **Anne** died in the prison camps. After the war, Mr. Frank published her diary.
   He wanted people to remember _____.

## WRITE A PARAGRAPH ✏️

Work with a partner. Write this paragraph.
Add the word *him*, *her*, *it*, or *them* in each blank.

Example: **6.** Many people have read it.

You can read Anne's diary in many languages. Many people have read ___(6)___. Nelson Mandela, a leader in South Africa, said the story encouraged ___(7)___. Several writers have been interested in Anne. They wrote books about ___(8)___. Many people feel Anne's diary helped ___(9)___ to understand what happened in World War II.

# Things Changed for Us

When you use a **pronoun,** be sure to tell about the right person.

Use these pronouns after an action verb and after words like *to*, *in*, or *with*.

| Pronoun | Use: | Example |
|---------|------|---------|
| me | for yourself | My sister sent this photo to **me** in 1942. |
| you | to talk to another person or persons | "I will write to **you** every day," she promised. |
| us | for yourself and another person | My sister sent letters to **us** from all over the world. |
| him, her, it, or them | to tell about other people or things | We still read **them** often. |

## BUILD SENTENCES

**Read each sentence. Choose the correct pronoun. Say the complete sentence.**

**Example: 1.** During the war, things changed for us.

1. During the war, things changed for _____**(us / it)**_____ .
2. Dad planted a garden. I helped _____**(him / us)**_____ take care of it.
3. Mom asked _____**(me / you)**_____ to put up some special curtains.
4. We called _____**(it / them)**_____ "blackout curtains."
5. At night, airplanes couldn't see _____**(us / him)**_____ or our lights through the curtains.
6. I wanted new shoes. Dad said, "We can't buy shoes for _____**(them / you)**_____ now."
7. There wasn't much rubber. Factories used _____**(it / us)**_____ for the war.
8. We missed my sister. We talked about _____**(her / him)**_____ a lot.
9. She wrote some letters just to _____**(me / her)**_____ .
10. I still have all of _____**(you / them)**_____ .

## WRITE A LETTER

<u>11.</u> **Imagine that you are the boy above.**
**Write a letter to your sister.**
**Tell what you are doing.**
**Use** *me*, *you*, *him*, *her*, *it*, *us*, **and** *them*.

**Example: 11.**

> May 1944
>
> Dear Sister,
> Dad planted a garden. I help him water it and pull the weeds. We grew tomatoes. I wish you could be with us, but we are so proud of you!
> Love,
> Jim

# Read and Think Together

**Make a comparison chart to tell about**
*The Children We Remember.* **Follow these steps.**

**1** Think about the story. What was life like for Jewish children before the Nazis took control? What was life like for them after the Nazis took control?

**2** Show the changes in a chart. In the first column, write details about what things were like before the Nazis came. Use pages 4–5 from the book.

| Before the Nazis | After the Nazis |
|---|---|
| Some Jewish children lived in towns. | |
| | |
| | |
| | |

**3** Read pages 7–18 again. Tell how life changed after the Nazis came. Write the information in the second column.

| Before the Nazis | After the Nazis |
|---|---|
| Some Jewish children lived in towns. | The Nazis took away their homes. |

**4** Work with a partner. Compare the children's lives before and after the Nazis. Use your completed chart.

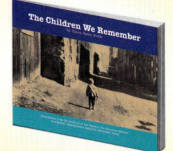

*from*
## The Basics Bookshelf

### THEME BOOK

This historical account tells what happened to many Jewish children during World War II.

# Words to Know

## REVIEW WORDS YOU KNOW

**Read the words aloud. Which word goes in the sentence?**

| some | come |
|------|------|
| celebrate | country |
| children | American |

1. Where did all these people _____ from?
2. They _____ the end of the war.
3. They wave the _____ flag.

**1945, New York City** People were happy when Germany surrendered.

## LEARN TO READ

**Learn new words.**

| | |
|------|------|
| news | People here shout the great **news**: The war is over! |
| words | I cannot find the **words** to say how happy I am. |
| much | There is so **much** excitement everywhere. |
| along | I am an army nurse. I work **along** with 10 other nurses. |
| question | We all have the same **question**: When can we go home? |
| before | I hope to be home **before** the end of May. |
| miss | I will **miss** the nurses in my group. |
| example | Our group is a good **example** of a successful team. |
| ever | These nurses are the best friends I **ever** had. |
| back | Still, it will be so good to get **back** to my family. |

### How to Learn a New Word

- Look at the word.
- Listen to the word.
- Listen to the word in a sentence. What does it mean?
- Say the word.
- Spell the word.
- Say the word again.

## WORD WORK

**4.–13. Work with a partner. Write each new word on a card. Mix your cards together for the game. Turn them so the words are down. Then:**

- Turn over 2 cards.
- Spell the words. Are they the same?
- If so, use the word in a sentence and keep the cards. If not, turn them over again.
- The player with more cards at the end wins.

**Example:**

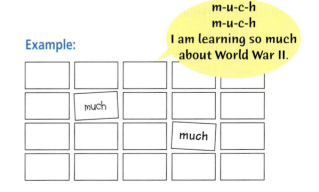

m-u-c-h m-u-c-h I am learning so much about World War II.

# Reading and Spelling

**LISTEN AND LEARN**

## take a look at TODAY

Everything around you, everything you see

Will soon be part of our history.

The dance you do.

The "look" that's new.

The funny hair.

The clothes you wear.

The number one song on the latest Top Ten.

Everything will change and change again.

So, let the years go by,

Then you'll say with a sigh,

"I remember when . . .!"

And "That's how it was way back then!"

## CONNECT SOUNDS AND LETTERS

The letter *y* can have 3 sounds.

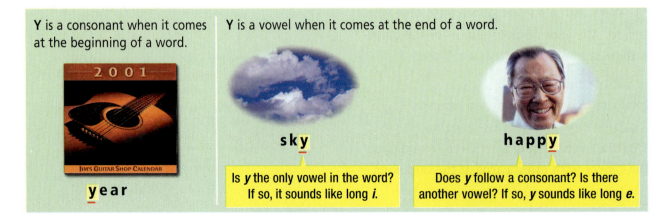

**Y** is a consonant when it comes at the beginning of a word.

2001

JIM'S GUITAR SHOP CALENDAR

**y**ear

**Y** is a vowel when it comes at the end of a word.

sk**y**

Is *y* the only vowel in the word? If so, it sounds like long *i*.

happ**y**

Does *y* follow a consonant? Is there another vowel? If so, *y* sounds like long *e*.

## READING STRATEGY

**Follow these steps to read words that end in *y*.**

**1** Does the word have one vowel or more than one vowel?

tr**y**

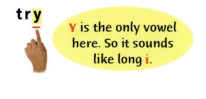

**Y** is the only vowel here. So it sounds like long **i**.

twen**ty**

I see two vowels, **e** and **y**. So the **y** sounds like long **e**.

**2** If there is one vowel, start at the beginning of the word and blend the sounds.

t**r**y      t + r + y = try

If there are two vowels, divide the word into syllables. Blend the syllables. Say the long **e** sound for the **y** at the end.

twenty      **t**wen + ty = twenty

## READING AND SPELLING PRACTICE

**Use what you learned to read the sentences.**

1. In fifty years, people can look back at your life today.
2. Just make a time capsule that tells your story. Try it!
3. Get a box. On top, write "My Year 2002," for example.
4. Put in your school yearbook, along with things from your hobbies or sports.
5. Include funny things, like an old pair of dirty sneakers.
6. Write words that explain what each thing means to you.

<u>7.–11.</u> **Now write the sentences that your teacher reads.**

**Spelling Help**

For words that end in a **consonant + y**, change the **y** to **i** and add **-es** to form the plural.

| | |
|---|---|
| sky | skies |
| penny | pennies |

## WORD WORK

<u>12.</u> **Read these words. Then write each word on a card.**

| | | |
|---|---|---|
| puppy | penny | why |
| sky | candy | funny |
| twenty | by | sticky |
| fly | try | my |

Example: **12.**

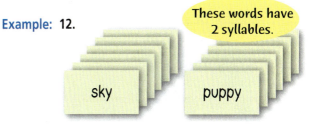

These words have 2 syllables.

sky      puppy

**Put the words with the long *i* sound in one group.**
**Put the words with the long *e* sound in another group.**
**What do you notice?**

# Read on Your Own

KidBrowse: Kidworks for Peace-PeaceChat

Back    Forward    Reload    Home    Search    Print    Stop

Location: http://www.kidworks-for-peace/peace_chat.html

# Kidworks for Peace
### The more we know, the more we understand each other.

HOME | PEACE CHAT | PEACE PROJECTS | PEACE NEWS | PEACE LINKS | COUNTRY INFO

### KIDWORKS for PEACE chat line

### Subject of the Day: Can kids make history?

**Misako Kimura:** Good question! I say YES! In my school, kids are making history. We have a radio show just for kids. We explain news stories in easy words. We try to help kids understand the news. That way more young people will know what's happening in the world.

**Mary Boltman:** Hello, Misako. A kid's radio show is a great example of making history! I have my own Web site. It tells people where to send food for needy children. My Web site makes me happy. I know I'm helping babies get a good start in life.

**Sal Sánchez:** Thank you so much, Mary! I'll pass along your Web address to my buddies. I belong to a lucky group of kids. Each year we work at the State House for two weeks. We study government while we are there. Those weeks fly by! I want to get a job in government someday. Then I can really make history.

**Misako Kimura**
**Japan**

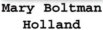

**Mary Boltman**
**Holland**

**Sal Sánchez**
**USA**

## CHECK YOUR UNDERSTANDING

**Answer each question.**

**Example:** **1.** Misako tries to help kids understand the news.

1. Misako, Mary, and Sal all have goals. What are they? Finish these sentences:

    Misako tries to _____.

    Mary wants to help _____.

    Sal wants to get _____.

2. How are their goals alike? How are they different? Finish this sentence:

    Both Misako and _____ want to help _____, but Sal wants to find a _____.

3. Do Misako, Mary, and Sal all like what they do? How do you know?

4. Work with your class to complete this chart.

    Then compare ideas. Which ones do you agree with?

| Can kids make history? | |
|---|---|
| Yes | No |
| My friend Olga sings. She made an album and is famous now. | Kids are too young to make history. |

## EXPAND YOUR VOCABULARY

<u>5.</u>  **Copy this word map. Work with a group to complete it.**

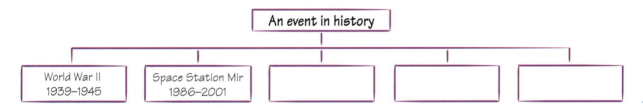

**Choose two events from the map. Tell your group about them.**
**Tell how they are alike or different. Use words from the green box.**

> alike    and    but
> same    both    different

**Example:** World War II was a horrible time when countries fought each other, but countries worked together on Space Station Mir.

## WRITE ABOUT KIDS AND HISTORY

<u>6.</u>  **Pretend you are part of the on-line chat on page 224.**
**Write an e-mail to say what you think: Can kids make history?**

**Example:** **6.** Yes! My class painted a mural at school. It will be there for a long time!

# Learn About the U.S. Government

## THE THREE BRANCHES OF THE U.S. GOVERNMENT

**LEGISLATIVE BRANCH: CONGRESS**
Senate
House of Representatives

**EXECUTIVE BRANCH**
President
Vice President
cabinet members

Franklin D. Roosevelt was President during World War II.

**JUDICIAL BRANCH**
Supreme Court
Chief Justice

KIDWORKS for PEACE created a Web page to explain the kinds of governments in each country. Read their page. Then do the Review.

KidBrowse: Kidworks for Peace-Country Info

Location: http://www.kidworks-for-peace/country-info/usa.html

# Kidworks for Peace
The more we know, the more we understand each other.

HOME | PEACE CHAT | PEACE PROJECTS | PEACE NEWS | PEACE LINKS | COUNTRY INFO

## The United States 🇺🇸

The structure of the U.S. government has not changed very much since it was established in 1789. The U.S. government is a democracy. That means the people choose the leaders. There are three branches in the U.S. government:

| The **Executive Branch** carries out laws. | |
| --- | --- |
| President and Vice President | Cabinet |
| • The President and Vice President are elected by the people. <br> • Term: 4 years | • The President appoints the members of the cabinet. Members include the Secretary of State and the Attorney General. |

| The **Legislative Branch** is the Congress. It makes laws. | |
| --- | --- |
| Senate | House of Representatives |
| • The people of each state elect two Senators. <br> • Term: 6 years | • The number of Representatives from each state depends on its population. <br> • Term: 2 years |

| The **Judicial Branch** listens to legal cases and interprets laws. |
| --- |
| Supreme Court |
| • The nine Justices of the Supreme Court are appointed by the President and approved by the Senate. One is the Chief Justice. <br> • Term: lifetime |

### REVIEW

1. **Check Your Understanding** Name the three branches of the U.S. government. What is the role of each branch?
2. **Vocabulary** Who is elected every 2 years? Every 4 years? Every 6 years?

# Writing Project — COMPARISON POSTER

**How was life different in the past? Compare your own life to life in the 1940s. Then make a poster with the information.**

## COLLECT INFORMATION

What do you know about the 1940s? Get more information from books or an interview. Make a chart to compare life in the 1940s with your life today.

| 1940s | Today |
|---|---|
| People needed special stamps to buy things. | We can just use money. |
| Lots of people had gardens for food. | Some people grow gardens for food. |
| People collected old paper and aluminum. | We recycle paper and aluminum. |
| People ate powdered eggs and potatoes. | We eat some powdered food, but not eggs. |

## MAKE AND SHARE YOUR POSTER

What will you show? Find or draw pictures. Write sentences to explain how life is the same or different. Check and correct your work.

> ✔ **Check Your Work**
>
> Do your sentences make comparisons?
>
> Did you use the correct forms of the past tense?
>
> Did you use the correct pronouns?

Put your pictures on a poster. Copy your sentences below the pictures. Tell the class about your poster.

In some ways, life in the 1940s and life today is the same. In other ways, it is different. In the 1940s, people had to use special stamps to buy things, but today we just use money. In the 1940s, a lot of people had gardens to grow their food. Today most people grow food in a garden just for fun. In the 1940s, people collected old paper and aluminum, and people still do that today.

UNIT
14

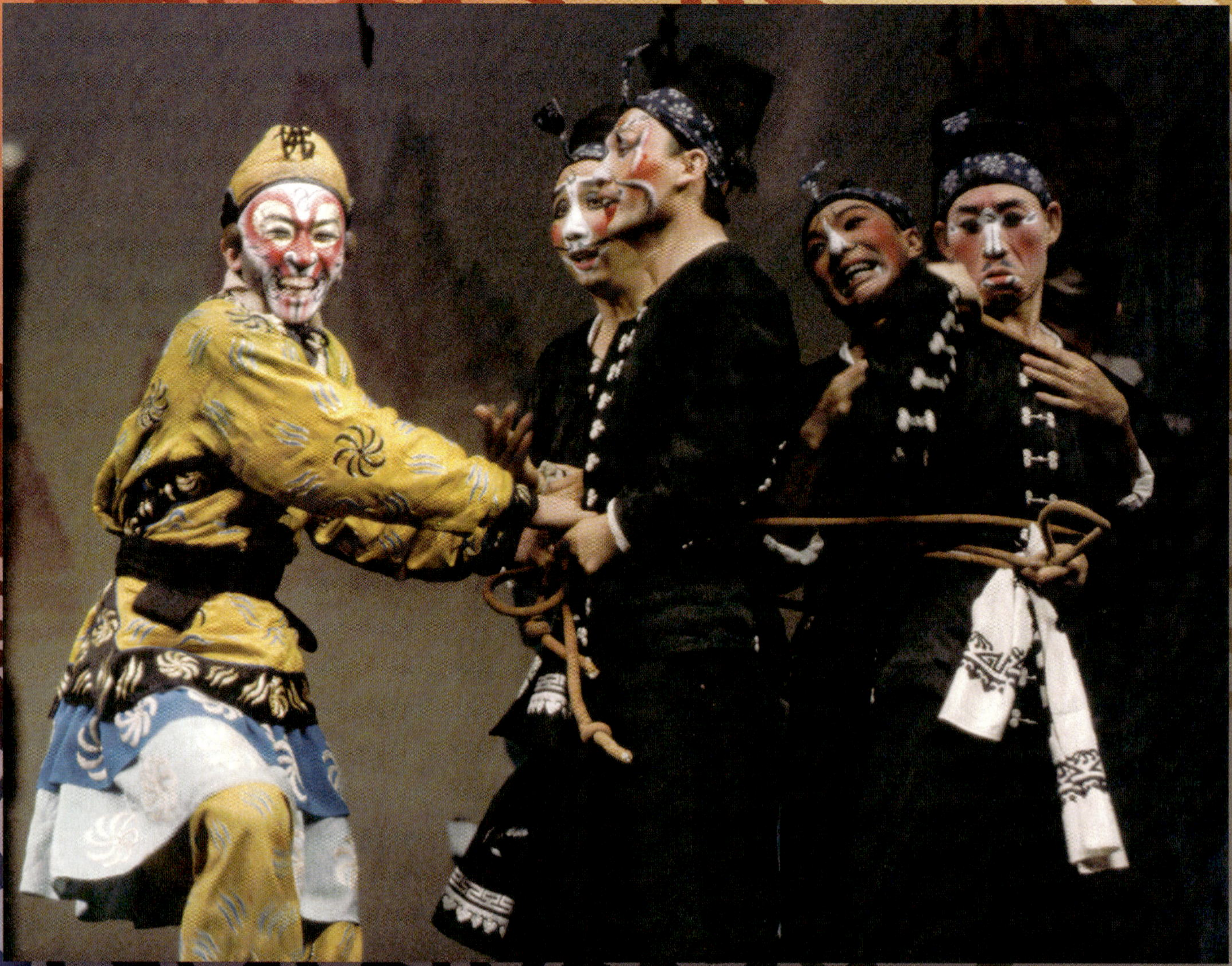

# Tell Me More

What is happening in this play? What are
the people saying? What will happen next?
Discuss your ideas with your classmates.
Then act out the scene together.

## In This Unit

### Vocabulary
- Story Elements
- Opposites
- Phrases for Times and Places

### Language Functions
- Ask for and Give Advice
- Ask for and Accept a Favor
- Describe Actions

### Patterns and Structures
- Prepositions
- Commands

### Reading
- Diphthongs and Variant Vowels
- Comprehension:
  Story Elements—Characters (character map),
  Setting, Plot

### Writing
- Notes
- Commands
- Story Endings

### Content Area Connection
- Language Arts (myths)

# How to Make a Story

Listen and chant.

**RECIPE FOR A STORY**

villain

superhero

monster

**B**egin with characters,
Some evil, some kind.
Put them in settings
That you have designed.

Throw lots of action
Into the mix.
Stir in a problem
That you can fix.

Cook it for hours
And get to the end.
Share your new story
With all of your friends.

**What's in a Story?**
A **character** is a person or animal in a story.

The **setting** is the time and place that the story happens.

The **plot** is what happens in the story from the **beginning** to the **middle** to the **end**.

## EXPRESS YOURSELF ▶ ASK FOR AND GIVE ADVICE

**1.–2.** Imagine that you are the superhero in the picture. Ask a partner:
*What should I do to get away*? **Your partner gives you advice. Then change roles.**

Example:  **1.** What should I do to get away? You should use your rope and climb the mountain.

## WRITE SENTENCES WITH ADVICE

**3.–6.** Talk with a partner. What advice would you give the monster in the picture? Write 4 sentences.

Example:  **3.** You should drive toward the mountain.

# Two Sides of the Story

**MAKE-BELIEVE CHARACTERS**

evil pirate

good fairy

tall giant

strong bear

weak mouse

short elf

young child

brave girl

old woman

frightened dragon

**REAL PERSON**

## WHO'S TALKING? ▶ ASK FOR AND ACCEPT A FAVOR

**1.–4.** Listen.

Which two characters are talking? Point to them.

Act out each scene with a partner. Ask for a favor.

## WRITE A NOTE

**5.** Write a note to one of the characters above.

Ask for a favor. Read your note to the class.

**Example: 5.**

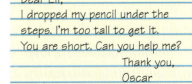

Dear Elf,
I dropped my pencil under the
steps. I'm too tall to get it.
You are short. Can you help me?
        Thank you,
        Oscar

# A Time and a Place for Everything

Read the story. Look for phrases that tell `when` and `where` things happen.

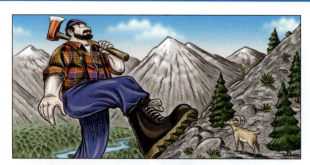

In the morning, Paul went up Eagle Mountain.
After his walk, he went back home.

During breakfast, Paul sat beside the other men.
He ate 275 pancakes.

At 12:00, Paul began to plant trees near his home.
He worked from noon to 3:00 and made the
North Woods!

Before dinner, Paul walked across Minnesota.
He walked until 6:00. His footsteps made
10,000 lakes.

## EXPRESS YOURSELF  ▶ DESCRIBE ACTIONS

1.–4. Make up settings for 4 new stories about Paul Bunyan.
Use words from each column to make a sentence that tells the setting.

| At 7:00 a.m.,<br>During lunch,<br>In the afternoon,<br>Before dinner, | Paul went | around the lake.<br>into the river.<br>up the mountain.<br>through the forest. |
|---|---|---|

Example: 1. At 7:00 a.m., Paul went up
the mountain.

## WRITE A DESCRIPTION 🖊

5. Choose a setting you made above. Draw a picture
to show it. Then describe the action. Tell the class
what happened next.

Example: 5. At 7 a.m., Paul went up the
mountain. He walked up the
mountain with just three steps.

# A Genie at Your Command

**A command tells someone to do something.**

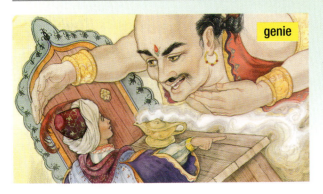

genie

A command can end with a **period** or an **exclamation mark.**

Listen to my wish**.**
Go to the kitchen**.**
Make something for me to eat**!**

## BUILD SENTENCES

Aladdin gave the genie a new command every day. Choose the correct word to complete each command. Then say the command.

1. "_____**(Get/Paint)**_____ some slippers for me."

2. "_____**(Put/Build)**_____ a gold ring on my finger."

3. "_____**(Swim/Bring)**_____ gold and jewels to me."

4. "_____**(Put/Sing)**_____ me a song."

5. "_____**(Build/Put)**_____ a new castle for me."

6. "_____**(Take/Paint)**_____ me to the princess."

**Example:** **1.** Get some slippers for me.

## WRITE COMMANDS ✏️

<u>7.–12.</u> Imagine you have your own genie. Work with a partner to write 6 commands for the genie. Put a period or an exclamation mark at the end of each command.

**Example:** **7.** Do my homework.

# Read and Think Together

Make a character map for the characters in *The Eagle and the Moon Gold*. Follow these steps.

**1** Draw a character map like this.

| Character | What the Character Does | What the Character Is Like |
|---|---|---|
| Yaoh | | |
| the eagle | | |
| Gwa | | |

**2** Read the story again. Think about Yaoh's actions. List them in the second column. What do Yaoh's actions show about his character? Write words to describe Yaoh in the third column.

| Character | What the Character Does | What the Character Is Like |
|---|---|---|
| Yaoh | He chops wood to stay warm. | hard-working |

**3** Now think about the eagle and Gwa. Complete the character map for each character.

**4** Use your finished map to tell a partner about the three characters in the story.

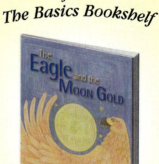

*from*
## The Basics Bookshelf

**THEME BOOK**

This Hmong fable has a lesson about the cost of greed.

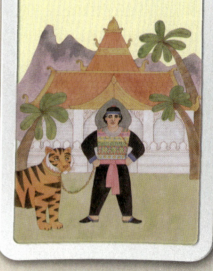

# Words to Know

## REVIEW WORDS YOU KNOW

**Read the words aloud. Which word goes in each sentence?**

| study | story |
|-------|-------|
| our | over |
| before | because |

1. He tells a _____.
2. It was first told by _____ grandfathers.
3. They told the story _____ we were born.

## LEARN TO READ

**Learn new words.**

| as | Listen carefully **as** I tell you a story. |
|----|------|
| sentence | Pay attention to every **sentence** I say. |
| idea | I got the **idea** for this story from my grandfather. |
| plants | A frog lived in the garden among the tall **plants**. |
| into | One day, it jumped and fell **into** a pail of cream. |
| until | The frog swam and swam **until** its legs got tired. |
| but | The frog was tired, **but** it did not stop swimming. |
| seemed | Then the cream **seemed** a little thicker. |
| each | With **each** kick, the cream got thicker and thicker. |
| made | In a few minutes, the frog **made** a pail of butter! |

**How to Learn a New Word**

- Look at the word.
- Listen to the word.
- Listen to the word in a sentence. What does it mean?
- Say the word.
- Spell the word.
- Say the word again.

## WORD WORK

**Write each sentence. Add the missing word.**      **Example: 4.** The children listen as the man tells a story.

4. The children listen __ __ the man tells a story.
5. The first __ __ __ __ __ __ __ __ in the story starts with "A frog lived…".
6. The frog came out of the tall __ __ __ __ __ __ where it lived.
7. The frog fell __ __ __ __ a pail of cream.
8. The frog got tired, __ __ __ it did not stop swimming.
9. __ __ __ __ time it kicked, the frog __ __ __ __ the cream thicker.
10. The frog kicked __ __ __ __ __ the cream turned to butter.
11. The children laughed. They __ __ __ __ __ __ to like the story.

# Reading and Spelling

## Tell Me a Tale

Tell me a tale of a sword and a crown
and a boy who becomes a king.

Tell me a tale of a cat with a ball
and a girl with a magical string.

Tell me a tale of an owl in the night
under a cloud-covered moon.

Tell me a tale of jewels and coins
owned by a band of baboons.

Tell me a tale, an old tale or new.

Tell me a tale, and I'll tell you one, too.

## CONNECT SOUNDS AND LETTERS

**Read the words. How do you spell each vowel sound?**

1. coin    boy

2. cloud    crown

3. laundry    saw

4. salt    ball

5. moon    screw

▶ Transparencies 68–72

## READING STRATEGY

**Follow these steps to read a word.**

**1** Look for pairs of letters that make a vowel sound.

**t o y**

When **o** and **y** are next to each other, they combine to make a new sound, like the **oy** in **boy**.

**m o o n**

When **o** and **o** are next to each other, they combine to make a new sound. Here they sound like long **u**.

**2** Start at the beginning. Blend the sounds in your head. Then say the word.

**t o y**     **t + oy = toy**

**m o o n**     **m + oo + n = moon**

## READING AND SPELLING PRACTICE

**Use what you learned to read the sentences.**

1. My mother is an author. She writes stories for teens.
2. She also draws pictures to go with each story.
3. I enjoy all of Mom's stories. They are very cool.
4. When she needs a new idea for a story, she goes out.
5. Sometimes I join her. We go to the mall or into town.
6. Mom jots down notes as she watches the crowd.

<u>7.–11.</u> **Now write the sentences that your teacher reads.**

## WORD WORK

<u>12.</u> **Write each of these words on a card.**

| coin | now | joy | boil | oil |
| town | toy | moist | count | point |
| out | loud | owl | clown | boy |

**Then say each word. Sort the words by vowel sound. Make 2 groups. What do you notice about each group?**

<u>13.</u> **Now make 4 new groups. Put the words with the same vowel sound *and* spelling together.**

Use **oy** to spell the sound at the end of a word. Use **oi** in the middle.

Example: **13.**

toy    coin

Language and Literacy   **237**

# Read on Your Own

"Welcome to your new home, Paul!" Mr. Brown handed Paul a story on tape and a set of keys to his room.

"Thank you! I love stories on tape," said Paul. "Come in and join me for tea."

"I can't tonight," said Mr. Brown. "I hope you enjoy the tape. It's a great story."

Paul nodded. He knew the author. He liked all of her stories.

Paul waited until 9:00. He made himself a cup of tea and put the tape into his tape deck. The story was about a small boy who lived in a haunted house. Each time the boy saw an owl, someone died.

As Paul listened, something started to pound on the pipes inside his walls. The sound seemed to grow louder and louder as the room grew cooler. Paul was so scared that he called Mr. Brown.

"There is something awful inside the walls!" he cried.

"It's just me," said Mr. Brown. "I was working on the pipes. I had to turn off the heat to fix them. I hope you don't mind."

## CHECK YOUR UNDERSTANDING

**Copy and complete the story map. Tell what happens in the beginning, in the middle, and at the end of the story on page 238.**

**Beginning**

1. Paul moved into his new _____.
2. Mr. Brown gave Paul _____.
3. Paul asked Mr. Brown _____.

**Middle**

4. Paul listened to _____.
5. It was about _____.
6. Each time the boy saw an owl, _____.

**End**

7. Something started to pound on _____.
8. Paul felt _____.
9. The sound was caused by _____.

**Example:**

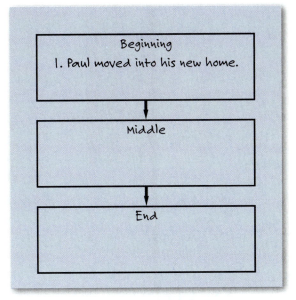

## EXPAND YOUR VOCABULARY

**Read the sentences.**

10. The story was about a <u>small</u> boy.
11. Paul was so <u>scared</u>.
12. "There is something <u>awful</u> inside the walls!" he cried.

**Work with a group to think of other words that mean *small*, *scared*, and *awful*. Make a list. Then say each sentence with a new word.**

## WRITE ABOUT CHARACTERS ✏

<u>13.</u> **Choose a character from a story you know. Write sentences to describe the character.**

**Example:** **13.** Yaoh was a poor boy. He was wise to listen to the eagle. He was content with a few coins.

# Learn About Myths

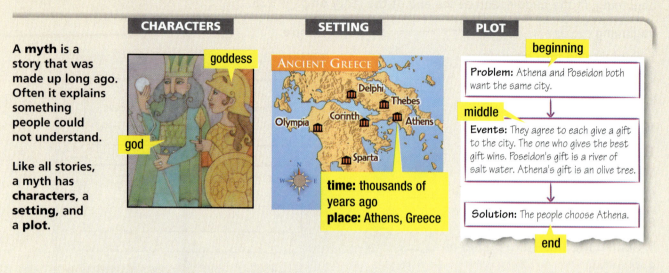

**CHARACTERS**     **SETTING**     **PLOT**

A **myth** is a story that was made up long ago. Often it explains something people could not understand.

goddess

god

Like all stories, a myth has **characters**, a **setting**, and a **plot**.

ANCIENT GREECE

Delphi

Thebes

Corinth

Olympia

Athens

Sparta

**time:** thousands of years ago
**place:** Athens, Greece

beginning

**Problem:** Athena and Poseidon both want the same city.

middle

**Events:** They agree to each give a gift to the city. The one who gives the best gift wins. Poseidon's gift is a river of salt water. Athena's gift is an olive tree.

**Solution:** The people choose Athena.

end

**Listen to the myth. Then answer the questions.**

# THE BEGINNING OF ATHENS

Thousands of years ago, the gods were dividing up the land. Poseidon, the god of the sea, found a city that he liked. He wanted it for his own. Athena, the goddess of wisdom, saw the same city. She wanted it, too.

Poseidon and Athena agreed to a contest. They decided to each give a gift to the city and let the people choose the best gift. The winner could have the city.

Poseidon touched the rocky mountainside. A river gushed out. Athena touched the dark earth. An olive tree sprang up.

The people looked at the gifts. They tasted the water. It was salty, like the sea. It was of no use to them.

Then they studied the tree. They saw that they could eat the fat olives or make oil from them.

Poseidon's gift is a river of salt water.
Athena's gift is an olive tree.

They knew that they could use the tree's wood to build things. They chose Athena.

Athena named the city Athens. The people built a large building to honor her, but they never forgot Poseidon. For many years, a salty pond and an olive tree remained near the building to remind people of the contest.

## CHECK YOUR UNDERSTANDING

1. Who are the two main characters in this myth?
2. What is the setting of this story?
3. Which paragraph tells about the problem in the myth? What happens next? How does the myth end?

# Writing Project  NEW STORY ENDING

Write a different ending for *The Eagle and the Moon Gold*.
Then share it with the class.

## CHOOSE AN IDEA

Think about different endings for
*The Eagle and the Moon Gold*. Choose one.

Gwa gets a ride home from a passing rocket.
✔ Eagle and Yaoh return to save Gwa.
Yaoh goes with the eagle to the stars.

## WRITE THE NEW ENDING

Draw pictures on a storyboard to plan your ending.
Write a sentence under each picture to tell what happens.
Work with a partner to check your work.

Before sunrise, Yaoh rides to the moon.

Gwa and Yaoh ride back to Earth. They get home in the morning.

Gwa gives Yaoh a tiger. He thanks Yaoh for his help.

Gwa changes from an evil man to a good man.

### ✔ Check Your Work

Is your ending different from the one in the book?

Did you describe the characters' actions?

Did you use words that tell the time and place?

## TELL YOUR STORY

Read aloud your new ending. Listen to the endings that your
classmates wrote. Tell which endings you like the most.

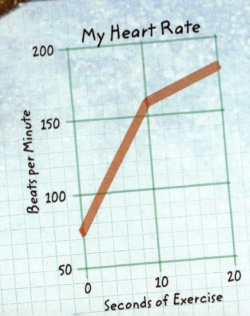

My Heart Rate

Beats per Minute

200

150

100

50

0        10       20

Seconds of Exercise

# Personal Best

Surfers and other athletes work hard.
Their hearts beat fast. How is your heart?
Sit in a chair and take your pulse.
Hop on one foot for 20 seconds.
Then take your pulse again.
What do you notice?

## In This Unit

### Vocabulary
• The Body
• Sports

### Language Functions
• Ask for and Give Information
• Express Thanks

### Patterns and Structures
• Present Tense Verbs
• Pronouns

### Reading
• Phonics: Variant Vowels and Consonants
• Comprehension:
  Relate Main Idea and Details
  (main-idea diagram)

### Writing
• Facts
• Thank-You Speech
• Paragraph for a Healthy-Habits Book

### Content Area Connection
• Language Arts (how to build a paragraph)

# Body Basics

**Listen and chant.**

Busy Body

Your skeleton helps you stand upright.

Your heart pumps blood all day and night.

Your lungs breathe air out and in.

Your muscles let you turn and spin.

Your stomach digests the food you eat.

Your nerves sense feelings down to your feet.

Your brain tells your body how to act.

Your body is busy, and that's a fact!

### The Body

| | |
|---|---|
| skeleton | stomach |
| heart | nerves |
| lungs | brain |
| muscles | |

## EXPRESS YOURSELF ▶ ASK FOR AND GIVE INFORMATION

**Ask a partner a question about each of these parts of the body. Answer your partner's questions in complete sentences.**

1. skeleton
2. heart
3. lungs
4. muscles
5. stomach
6. brain

**Example:** 1. What does the skeleton do?
It supports your body and protects the heart and lungs.

## WRITE FACTS ABOUT THE BODY ✏

**7.–10. Write 4 facts about the body.**    **Example:** 7. Muscles help you move.

# Our Workout Routine

**Use present tense verbs to tell what happens all the time.**

We always **exercise** to stay healthy.

Every morning we **run** two miles.

We **stretch** before every run.

Every day we **make** our bodies strong.

## BUILD SENTENCES

**Say a sentence for each picture below. Choose words from each column.**

| Each Every | day morning afternoon Saturday week month | I the boys the girls the people the athletes they | bike. exercise. play. practice. run. swim. |
|---|---|---|---|

**Example: 1.** Every afternoon the girls practice.

1.

2.

3.

4.

## WRITE SENTENCES ✏️

<u>5.–8.</u> **Tell a partner about some sport or exercise you do all the time. Work together to write 4 sentences about it.**

**Example: 5.** Every day I play basketball.

# Meet the Athletes

She **bowls**.

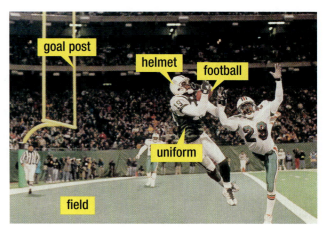

They play **football**.

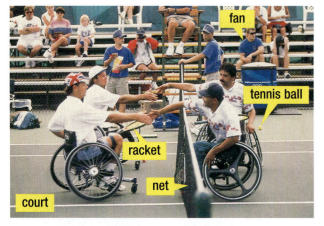

They play **tennis**.

She plays **basketball**.

## WHO'S TALKING? ▶ EXPRESS THANKS

1.–3. Listen.

Who is talking? Point to the correct athlete. Act out the roles you hear on the tape. Thank your teammate, coach, or another player.

## WRITE A THANK-YOU SPEECH

4. You are a champion athlete and just won an award. Write a thank-you speech. Tell who helped you play the sport so well.

Example: 4. Thank you for the basketball trophy. My coach helped me a lot. I also want to thank my teammates. We have the best basketball team in the city!

# Watch Them Play

**Use the correct pronoun when you talk about a person, place, or thing.**

goalie

Use these pronouns to tell who does the action.

| I | you | he | she | it | we | they |

**He** kicked the ball.

Use these pronouns after an action verb or after a word like *to*, *for*, or *with*.

| me | you | him | her | it | us | them |

The goalie missed **it**.
The goalie kicks the ball to **her**.

## BUILD SENTENCES

**Say each sentence. Add the correct pronoun.**

Example: **1.** Our coach talked to us at half time. She gave us a plan.

1. Our coach talked to us at half time. _____(She / Her)_____ gave us a plan.
2. Randy got ready. I passed the ball to _____(he / him)_____.
3. _____(He / Him)_____ missed the ball!
4. The other team got the ball. _____(They / Them)_____ raced away.
5. We chased _____(they / them)_____.
6. Our goalie got the ball. She kicked it to _____(I / me)_____.
7. I saw Farnez. I shouted to _____(she / her)_____.
8. Another player knocked _____(she / her)_____ down!
9. I had no choice. _____(I / me)_____ shot at the goal.
10. We scored! The crowd cheered for _____(we / us)_____.

## WRITE SENTENCES ✏️

<u>11.–15.</u> **Write 5 sentences. Tell about a sport you like to watch.**
**Use at least 3 pronouns.**

Example: **11.** I watch hockey with Hari Amrit.

**12.** She likes the team from San Jose.

# Read and Think Together

**Work in a group. Make diagrams to show the main ideas and details in *Body Works*. Follow these steps.**

**1** Read pages 6–7 of *Body Works*. What is the most important idea in this section? Write it inside a box, like this:

> **Main Idea**
> The skeleton helps your body work.

**2** What details in these pages help to support, or explain, the main idea? Write them in boxes connected to your main-idea box, like this:

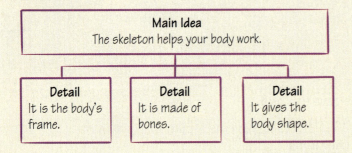

**3** Make diagrams for more sections of *Body Works* to show the main idea and details.

| | |
|---|---|
| The Muscles | pages 8–9 |
| The Blood | pages 12–13 |
| The Lungs | pages 14–15 |

**4** Use your completed diagrams to tell the class what you learned about the body.

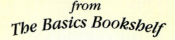

*from*
*The Basics Bookshelf*

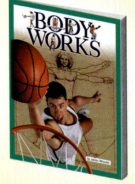

**THEME BOOK** 📼

Learn about parts of the body and how to keep your body in good shape.

# Words to Know

## REVIEW WORDS YOU KNOW

**Read the words aloud. Which word goes in each sentence?**

| | |
|---|---|
| along | also |
| into | again |
| any | very |

1. They walk _____ the trail.

2. It goes _____ the mountains.

3. Their packs are _____ big.

## LEARN TO READ

**Learn new words.**

| | |
|---|---|
| **friends** | My **friends** and I love to hike. |
| **asked** | "Will you help me put on my pack?" **asked** Celia. |
| **walked** | We **walked** to the start of the trail. |
| **trees** | We passed pines, oaks, and other **trees**. |
| **air** | We breathed the crisp mountain **air**. |
| **talked** | We **talked** about the hike. |
| **if** | "**If** you feel tired, stop and rest," I said. |
| **even** | "Drink water **even** if you're not thirsty." |
| **while** | We drank water **while** we walked. |
| **such** | I have **such** a good time when I hike! |

**How to Learn a New Word**

- Look at the word.
- Listen to the word.
- Listen to the word in a sentence. What does it mean?
- Say the word.
- Spell the word.
- Say the word again.

## WORD WORK

<u>4.–13.</u> **Make a map for each new word. Write the word in the center. Complete the other boxes.**

**Example: 4.**

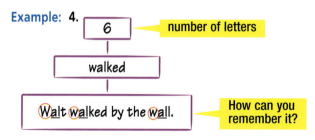

6 ← number of letters

walked

Walt walked by the wall. ← How can you remember it?

# Reading and Spelling

## LISTEN AND LEARN

# Good Advice

If you want to feel great,
Here's my advice:
Eat healthy food
Such as corn, meat, and rice.

With ice cream and cake
Or too many snacks,
You'll be dragging your heels
As you run down the track.

## LOOK FOR LETTER PATTERNS

When **c** comes before **a**, **o**, or **u**,
it makes a hard sound.

**Joe has a new baseball cap.**

When **g** comes before **a**, **o**, or **u**,
it makes a hard sound.

**He got it!**

When **c** comes before **e** or **i**,
it makes a soft sound.

**Look at Dawn's face mask.**

When **g** comes before **e** or **i**,
it usually makes a soft sound.

**Dawn swings the bat
in the batting cage.**

## READING STRATEGY

**Follow these steps to read words with *c* and *g*.**

**1** When you see the consonant *c* or *g* in a word, look at the vowel that comes next. It will tell you how to say the consonant.

r a c e — The *c* is soft. An *e* comes after it.

g a m e — The *g* is hard. An *a* comes after it.

**Reading Help**

Look for these letter patterns in words:

wr  kn  gn
dge  mb

One consonant is silent.

write    write
knife    knife
gnat     gnat
badge    badge
thumb    thumb

**2** Start at the beginning. Blend the sounds in your head. Then say the word.

r a c e    r + a + c + e̶ = race        g a m e    g + a + m + e̶ = game

## READING AND SPELLING PRACTICE

**Use what you learned to read the sentences.**

**1.** Ginny stood in the center of the huge diving board.

**2.** She walked to the edge of the board and bounced twice.

**3.** She took a deep breath. Then she jumped.

**4.** Below her, the water looked like blue glass.

**5.** She cut through the water like a knife!

**6.** Her friends had never seen such a good dive.

**7.–11.** Now write the sentences that your teacher reads.

## WORD WORK

**12.–23.  Copy the chart. Then read the words in this box:**

| catch | page | golf | good | age | gel |
|-------|------|------|------|-----|-----|
| center | place | contest | cup | ice | gate |

| cap | race | game | huge |
|-----|------|------|------|
| 12. | 15. | 18. | 21. |
| 13. | 16. | 19. | 22. |
| 14. | 17. | 20. | 23. |

**Write each word in the chart. Put it under the word that has the same sound for *c* or *g*.**

Example: **12.**

| cap |
|-----|
| 12. catch |

# Read on Your Own

# Summer Games Are a Big Hit

Athletes try for gold at Bridge Park on Saturday.

GARDEN CITY— The Special Olympics State Summer Games were a big hit this weekend at Bridge Park. About 3,000 athletes, coaches, and volunteers came from around the state. Tents were set up in a football field by the park to make an Olympic Village.

The rock band Thumbs Up gave a concert at the edge of the park to open the games. A huge crowd came to see the band. Some lucky fans even got to go on stage and sing with the band.

The next day, athletes competed in different sports. They rode bikes, ran, threw a softball, and raced in wheelchairs. Cindy Collins, a 20-year-old from Garden City, won the wheelchair race.

"My next goal is to win at the World Games," Cindy said. "I'm in training now. I move my wrists to make them strong. I also race around traffic cones. If I knock a cone over, I try again."

"I met so many nice people while I was here," Sam Wong, another winner, said. "We're all good friends now!"

## CHECK YOUR UNDERSTANDING

**Copy the paragraph. Add the missing words or phrases to tell the main idea and important details in the news story.**

**Example: 1.–2.** The article is about the Special Olympics State Summer
Games in Garden City.

The article is about the ___(1)___ ___(2)___ State Summer Games in Garden City. About 3,000 athletes, ___(3)___, and volunteers came for the games. They stayed in tents in the Olympic ___(4)___. On opening day, a band gave a ___(5)___ in the park. The next day, the athletes competed. They rode bikes, ran, threw a softball, and ___(6)___ in wheelchairs. The winner of the wheelchair race was ___(7)___ ___(8)___.

## EXPAND YOUR VOCABULARY

**Read the sentences.**

9. The runners <u>race</u> around the track.
10. Crowds of people watch them and <u>cheer</u>.
11. Everyone has a <u>good</u> time.

**Work with a group to think of other words that mean *race, cheer, and good*. Make a list. Then say each sentence with a new word.**

race
run
move

cheer
clap
yell

good
wonderful
great

## WRITE ABOUT SPORTS

<u>12.</u> **Choose a sport. Give information about it.**

**Example: 12.** You need two teams to play softball.
You use a bat. You use a ball. You use mitts.
One team is at bat.
The other team is in the field.
Players hit the ball and run around the bases.

# Learn About Paragraphs

**PARAGRAPHS**

A **paragraph** is a group of sentences.
All the sentences tell about one main idea.

indent → **A triathlon is a race that includes three different sports.** Athletes start with a swim race. Next they hop onto bicycles for a bike race. The last part of a triathlon is a running race.

The **topic sentence** tells the main idea.

The other sentences give **supporting** details. They tell more about the main idea.

**Study the lesson. Then do the Exercise.**

# Practice Your Paragraphs

## Think and Discuss

Follow these steps to write a paragraph.

**1** Think about your main idea.
What details support it? Make a diagram.

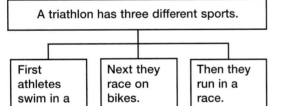

A triathlon has three different sports.

| First athletes swim in a race. | Next they race on bikes. | Then they run in a race. |

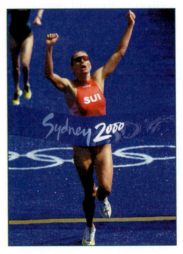

Brigitte McMahon, of Switzerland, races in the women's triathlon in Sydney, Australia.

**2** Write a topic sentence to tell the main idea. Be sure to indent it.

**3** Add the detail sentences.

**4** Read your paragraph. Make sure all the sentences tell about one main idea.

## Exercise

Write a paragraph. Use ideas in this diagram.

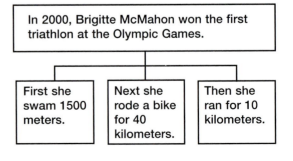

In 2000, Brigitte McMahon won the first triathlon at the Olympic Games.

| First she swam 1500 meters. | Next she rode a bike for 40 kilometers. | Then she ran for 10 kilometers. |

# Writing Project  CLASS BOOK ON HEALTHY HABITS

What are some of your healthy habits? Write a paragraph about something that you do to take care of your body. Draw a picture. Then add your page to a class book.

## CHOOSE A HEALTHY ACTIVITY

List the healthy things you do each day. Choose one to write about.

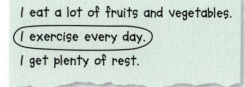

I eat a lot of fruits and vegetables.
I exercise every day.
I get plenty of rest.

## PLAN AND WRITE A PARAGRAPH

Make a diagram to show your main idea and details:

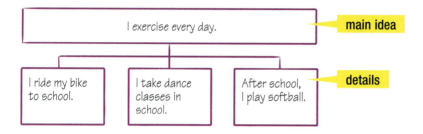

I exercise every day. ◄ **main idea**

| I ride my bike to school. | I take dance classes in school. | After school, I play softball. | ◄ **details** |

Then follow the steps on page 254 to write your paragraph.

Work with a partner to check your paragraph.
Look in *Body Works* if you need to check a word.

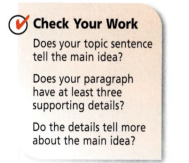

✔ **Check Your Work**

Does your topic sentence tell the main idea?

Does your paragraph have at least three supporting details?

Do the details tell more about the main idea?

## MAKE A CLASS BOOK

Copy your paragraph or type it on a computer. Make a drawing or add a photo. Put your page together with your classmates' pages to make a "Healthy Habits" book.

I exercise every day to keep my body strong and healthy. I ride my bike to school. I take special dance classes in school. After school, I get to play softball with my friends.

# UNIT
## 16

MIDWEST/Wisconsin

MIDWEST/Illinois

NORTHEAST/New York

SOUTHEAST/Kentucky

WEST/California

WEST

MIDWEST

NORTHEAST

SOUTHWEST

SOUTHEAST

SOUTHWEST/Arizona

WEST/Hawaii

SOUTHEAST/Georgia

# This Land Is Our Land

There are many kinds of music played in the United States. Listen to some. Which music do you like the most? On a map, find the place where it is played.

## In This Unit

### Vocabulary
- American History
- Landforms and Bodies of Water
- Geography

### Language Functions
- Ask and Answer Questions
- Give Directions

### Patterns and Structures
- Questions with *How?* and *Why?*
- Capitalization: Proper Nouns (geographical names)

### Reading
- Multisyllabic Words
- Comprehension: Classify (category chart, concept map)

### Writing
- Questions and Answers
- Directions
- Biographical Sketch

### Content Area Connection
- Social Studies (regions of the U.S.)

# Who Built America?

**Listen and chant.**

# The Builders of Our Nation

The Pilgrims sailed across the sea
To practice their religion in Plymouth Colony.

Colonists built new American towns.
They won their liberty from the British crown.

Explorers traveled across the land
So our growing nation could expand.

To reach the Pacific, in long wagon trains,
The pioneers traveled from the golden plains.

Immigrants escaped from hunger and strife
To seek work, education, and a better life.

All of us here in our nation today
Are the many faces of the U.S. of A.

**People in History**

Pilgrims
colonists
explorers
pioneers
immigrants

## EXPRESS YOURSELF ▶ ASK AND ANSWER QUESTIONS

<u>1.–6.</u> **Work with a partner. Ask each other 6 questions about the chant. Then answer your partner's questions.**

**Example:** **1.** Who sailed across the sea? The Pilgrims sailed across the sea.

**Question Words**

who      when
what     where

## WRITE QUESTIONS

<u>7.–12.</u>  **Write the questions you made above.**      **Example:**  **7.** Where did the Pilgrims practice their religion?

# People of America

You can use the word `how` or `why` to ask a question.

**Use *how* to ask about the way people do something.**

> **How** did the pioneers travel?
> They traveled in wagons.

**Use *why* to ask for a reason.**

> **Why** did the pioneers travel west?
> They traveled west **because** they wanted land to farm.

> You can use ***because*** to answer a question with *why*.

## BUILD QUESTIONS

Read each answer. Then ask 2 questions to go with the answer: *How* _____? *Why* _____?

Example: **1.** How do scientists do experiments?
Why do they do experiments carefully?

**1.**

Scientists do experiments carefully because they want to get correct results.

**2.**

Soldiers fight bravely because they want to protect their country.

**3.**

Most cowboys ride horses very well because they spend a lot of time on horseback.

**4.**

Farmers use machines to harvest their crops because machines work quickly.

## WRITE ANSWERS

Work with a partner. Use the chant on page 258 to find the answer to each question below. Write your answer as a complete sentence. Use the word *because*.

Example: **5.** The Pilgrims left home because they wanted to practice their religion.

**5.** Why did the Pilgrims leave home?

**6.** Why did explorers travel across the land?

**7.** Why did immigrants come to the United States?

**8.** Why did pioneers leave the plains?

# Our Natural Treasures

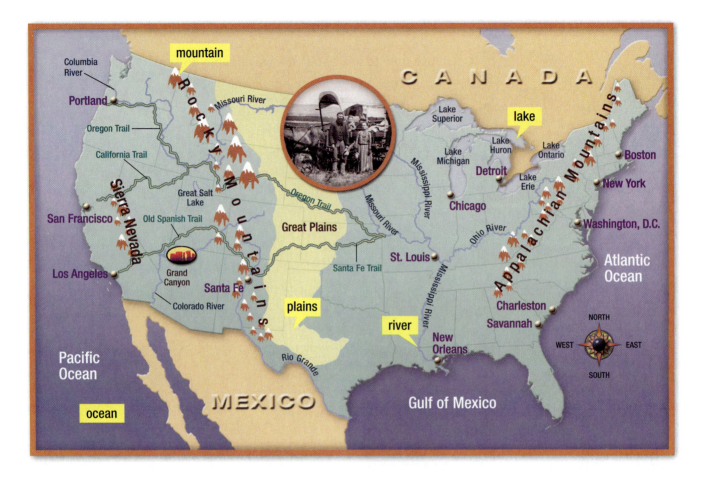

## WHO'S TALKING? ▶ GIVE DIRECTIONS

<u>1.–2.</u> **Listen.** 🎞️

Two students are giving directions to the pioneers.

What route is each student describing? Trace it on the map.

## WRITE DIRECTIONS ✏️

<u>3.</u> **Work with a partner. Draw the outline of the United States. Mark where you are now. Where do you want to go? Label the landforms and cities along the way. Then write directions to get there.**

Example: **3.** How to go to Washington, D.C., in the northeastern part of the country:

- Start in New Orleans. Go north along the Mississippi River.
- Follow the Ohio River east. Keep going east until you get to Washington, D.C.

# Americans from Other Lands

A **proper noun** names a particular person, place, or thing.

| Capitalize the proper names of: | Examples |
|---|---|
| countries, cities, and states | John Muir was born in **Scotland** in 1838. He moved to **Portage, Wisconsin,** when he was 11 years old. |
| bodies of water | Muir walked 1,000 miles to the **Gulf of Mexico.** |
| landforms | Muir studied the plants and animals of the **Yosemite Valley.** |

## STUDY SENTENCES

Say the sentences. Look at the <u>underlined</u> words. Do they need capital letters? If so, tell why.

**Example:** 1. *Guangzhou* needs a capital letter. It is the name of a city.

1. I. M. Pei was born in <u>guangzhou</u>, China.
2. In 1935, he came to <u>massachusetts</u> to study architecture.
3. One of the buildings he designed is at the foot of the <u>rocky mountains</u>.
4. Another is next to <u>boston harbor</u>.
5. He designed other buildings across the <u>country</u>.

6. Alexandra Nechita was born in <u>romania</u>.
7. Now the young artist lives in Los Angeles, California, near the <u>pacific ocean</u>.
8. In 2000, she designed a giant angel sculpture in the <u>city</u>.
9. Her other artwork is in galleries from <u>hawaii</u> to <u>new york</u>.
10. When she was 12 years old, she met the Emperor of <u>japan</u>.

## WRITE SENTENCES ✏

<u>11.–20.</u> Write the sentences above with the correct capitalization.

**Example:** 11. I. M. Pei was born in Guangzhou, China.

# Read and Think Together

Make a category chart about the people in *All Across America*. Follow these steps.

**1** Draw a chart with two columns, like the one below. In column 1, write the categories of people from pages 2–3 of *All Across America*.

| Category | Examples |
|----------|----------|
| explorers | |
| pioneers | |
| cowboys | |
| inventors | |

**2** Read the book again. As you read, put the name of each person you read about in the correct category. (Some people may belong in more than one category.)

| Category | Examples |
|----------|----------|
| explorers | Meriwether Lewis, William Clark, Sacagawea, York, John Wesley Powell, Sally Ride |

**3** Compare your finished category chart with a classmate's chart. Did you list the same people? Talk about the people you included in the chart.

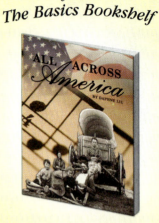

*from*
*The Basics Bookshelf*

**THEME BOOK**

This song about America tells about the many different people who built this nation.

# Words to Know

## REVIEW WORDS YOU KNOW

**Read the words aloud. Which word goes in the sentence?**

| lives | life |
|-------|------|
| my | by |
| no | knows |

1. This girl _____ in Alaska.
2. Her home is _____ a frozen lake.
3. She _____ how to keep warm.

## LEARN TO READ

**Learn new words.**

| state | Alaska is the largest **state** in the United States. |
|-------|-----------------------------------------------------|
| than | It is much bigger **than** Texas. |
| high | Alaska has very **high** mountains. |
| million | It has about 51 **million** acres of parks. |
| form | The Aleutian Islands **form** a long chain of islands. |
| sea | They stretch far out into the **sea**. |
| near | Little Diomede Island in Alaska is **near** Russia. |
| miles | It is only 2.5 **miles** away! |
| explore | To **explore** Juneau, the capital city, go in summer. |
| earth | Alaska is one of the coldest places on **earth**. |

**How to Learn a New Word**

- Look at the word.
- Listen to the word.
- Listen to the word in a sentence. What does it mean?
- Say the word.
- Spell the word.
- Say the word again.

## WORD WORK

**4.–13. Work with a partner. Write each new word on a card. Mix your cards together for the game. Turn them so the words are down. Then:**

- Turn over 2 cards.
- Spell the words. Are they the same?
- If so, use the word in a sentence and keep the cards. If not, turn them over.
- The player with more cards at the end wins.

**Example:**

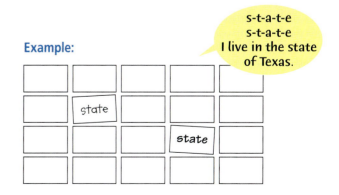

s-t-a-t-e
s-t-a-t-e
I live in the state of Texas.

# Reading and Spelling

## LISTEN AND LEARN

## Town in the Desert

One hundred fifty years ago,
Families lived here.
Children played here.
Covered wagons rolled past the gates
where cactus flowers bloomed.

Now the doors bang in the wind.
No one plays here.
No one lives here.
Dry winds open the broken gates
where cactus flowers bloom.

## STUDY LONG WORDS

How should you divide each word into syllables? Look for the pattern.

1. cactus  2. hundred  3. open gate  4. wagon  5. asleep

## READING STRATEGY

**Follow these steps to read long words.**

**1** Look for the pattern of vowels and consonants in the middle of the word.

**canyon** — There are two consonants between two vowels.

**music** — There is one consonant between two vowels.

**2** Blend the syllables together to read the word.

You can break words like music either way. See which way sounds right

**canyon**
▲

**can** + **yon** = **canyon**

**music** or **music**
▲            ▲

**mu** + **sic** = **music**

This one sounds right. The u is long.

## READING AND SPELLING PRACTICE

**Use what you learned to read the sentences.**

1. About one hundred fifty years ago, California became the thirty-first state.
2. Adults and children traveled over 2,000 miles to build homes there.
3. They built cabins in the high mountains and in the low deserts.
4. They built farms all across the open lands.
5. They built cities near the lakes, the rivers, and along the coast.
6. Today, millions of people enjoy living in this sunny state.

**7.–11.** Now write the sentences that your teacher reads.

## WORD WORK

**12.–20.** Read the newspaper article. Find all the words with two syllables.
Copy the chart. Write each word under the word that has the same pattern.

### Boy Wins Essay Contest

Chen Lu is on his way to Boston! He won first place in an essay contest called "This Land is Our Land." The contest was open to all students in grades 5 through 8. Chen won a medal and a visit to Boston. Chen's essay, "The Broken Wagon," was based on a book he read.

| canyon ▲ | event ▲ | cabin ▲ |
|---|---|---|
| 12. | 15. | 18. |
| 13. | 16. | 19. |
| 14. | 17. | 20. |

**Example: 12.** essay

# Read on Your Own

# DEEP CANYON

The Grand Canyon is located in the northwestern corner of Arizona.

Would you like to go back millions of years in time? A visit to the Grand Canyon will take you there. It took the Colorado River millions of years to cut through the land that is now the Grand Canyon. The river cut so deep into the earth that you can see nine thick layers of rock. These layers sit one on top of the other, like pancakes. The bottom layer is the oldest. At this level, you may see some of the oldest rocks on Earth.

There is a lot to do in the Grand Canyon. Take a boat ride where the Colorado River runs slow. Take a raft across rapids where the river runs fast. Enjoy a picnic near a waterfall. Explore 400 miles of trails. Look for tiny birds. At the end of the day, relax in a cabin or a tent. There is no limit to what you can see and do in the Grand Canyon!

## CHECK YOUR UNDERSTANDING

1. Copy this concept map. Work with a partner to add other details.
Use the finished map to discuss what you learned about the Grand Canyon.

## EXPAND YOUR VOCABULARY

Work with a partner. Read each sentence aloud.
Add different words. Make as many new sentences
as you can.

2. The Grand Canyon _____.
3. The Colorado River _____.
4. There is a lot to do at the Grand Canyon.
   You can _____.
5. It is fun to be outdoors, where you can see _____.

Example: 2. The Grand Canyon is very old.
The Grand Canyon has a river
and waterfalls.

## WRITE ABOUT A VISIT TO THE GRAND CANYON

6. Imagine you are at the Grand Canyon.
Write a postcard to a friend. Tell what you
see and do there.

Example: 6.

Dear Kashmir,

   I am in the Grand
Canyon! The rocks are
beautiful. Yesterday, I hiked
on a trail. I took a lot of
photos. Some day, I want to
take a raft down the river.

       Your friend,
       Alex

Kashmir Komanapali
300 S. Orange Street
Miami, FL 33109

# Learn About Regions of the U.S.

## THE SOUTHWEST

A **region** is a part of a country.

The **geography** of a region includes its physical features, like mountains, rivers, forests, or deserts.

product map

state

ARIZONA

NEW MEXICO

OKLAHOMA

TEXAS

product

🐂 Cattle
🜨 Copper
⚪ Cotton
🔥 Natural Gas
⛽ Oil

The **climate** of a region is what the weather is usually like there. In the Southwest the weather is usually hot and dry in the summer.

**Listen to the article. Then do the Review.**

# The Southwest: A Region of Richness

• What is the southwestern region of the United States like?

The southwestern region of the United States is made up of Arizona, New Mexico, Texas, and Oklahoma. It covers over 572,300 square miles.

Most of the region has a warm and dry climate in the summer. For example, it is about 83°F in Houston, Texas, in July. Only 3.3 inches of rain fall there at that time.

You can see interesting landforms in the region. One of the most famous is the Grand Canyon. Flat-topped hills called *mesas* are in Arizona and New Mexico. Texas has many dry plains.

Mesa

The Southwest produces useful products. There is a lot of oil and natural gas throughout the region. Many people raise cattle, too. Cotton and copper are two other important products from the region.

Oil Well

The Southwest was once part of Mexico. Cities, rivers, and other places still have Spanish names. Mexican celebrations are important in the culture of the region. Many Mexican Americans live in the Southwest.

Midwest    Northeast

West

Southwest    Southeast

Most people who live in the Southwest live near the major cities. For example, more than 1,992,000 people live in the Houston, Texas, area.

The Southwest is a region of richness from its geography to its products.

## REVIEW

1. **Check Your Understanding** What is the Southwest like?
2. **Use Product Maps** What does Arizona produce? What does Texas produce?
3. **Vocabulary** Name the other regions in the United States. In which region do you live?

# Writing Project  BIOGRAPHICAL SKETCH

A biography tells about a person's life. Write a paragraph to give
the biography of a famous American. What makes the person special?

## FIND INFORMATION

**1** Choose a person to study. Look through
*All Across America*, or ask your teacher
or a librarian for help.

> Stephanie Kwolek
> Jonas Salk
> (Dr. Sally Ride)
> Duke Ellington

**2** Brainstorm questions. Put
each question on a card.
Then find the answers.
Ask a teacher, look in
a book, or use the
Internet.

> How has Dr. Ride helped
> the United States?

> Why is Dr. Ride famous?

> Where does Dr. Ride live?

> When was Dr. Sally
> Ride Born?
> She was born on
> May 26, 1951.

## PLAN AND WRITE YOUR PARAGRAPH

Use the information you learned to write your paragraph.
First write a **topic sentence.** Tell the person's name
and what he or she did. Then give the **details**:
- Tell when and where the person lived.
- Tell why the person is famous.
- Tell how the person helped the United States.

> ✔ **Check Your Work**
>
> Does your biography
> give facts about a
> famous American?
>
> Does your paragraph
> follow the plan above?
>
> Did you capitalize the
> names of people and
> places?

### Dr. Sally Ride

Dr. Sally Ride is a scientist and
astronaut. She was born on May 26,
1951, and lives in
California. She
was the first
American woman
in outer space.
She was a mission
specialist in
space. Later she
wrote three
books about space.
Now she is a physics teacher at a
university in San Diego.

## SHARE YOUR BIOGRAPHY

Copy your paragraph or type it on a computer. Add illustrations,
if you like. Read your paragraph to the class. Then display it on
a bulletin board.

UNIT
17

SELL AND BUY

WATER

HARVEST

PLANT

PLOW

TRANSPORT

# HARVEST TIME

Work with a partner.
What is the correct order for the pictures?
Use the pictures to tell how broccoli comes
from the farm to your table.

## In This Unit

### Vocabulary
- Farming
- At the Restaurant
- Plants

### Language Functions
- Buy or Sell an Item
- Give Information
- Order an Item

### Patterns and Structures
- Questions with *How many?*
  and *How much?*
- Sensory Adjectives

### Reading
- Suffixes: *-ly, -y, -less, -ful*
- Prefixes: *un-, re-*
- Comprehension: Make Comparisons
  (comparison chart, concept map)

### Writing
- Questions and Answers
- Descriptions
- Crop Comparison Report

### Content Area Connection
- Science (plants)

# The Market Price

**Listen and sing.**

## At the Farmers' Market

Every day, my customers say,
"How many apples are in a bag?"
Every day my customers say,
"How much does one bag cost?"

"How many? How much?" is all I hear.
I answer a hundred times,
"Three dollars, please, for a bag of twelve.
In bills or quarters or dimes."

Every day my customers say,
"How much does one bag cost?"
I put a tag on every bag,
But the tags keep getting lost!

### Questions

Use *how many* to ask about things you can count.

**How many** apples are in a bag?
**How many** bags can I buy
   for $6.00?

Use *how much* to ask about a price.

**How much** do the apples cost?
**How much** are the apples?

## EXPRESS YOURSELF ▸ BUY OR SELL AN ITEM

**Work with a partner. Act out a scene at a farmers' market.
Buy and sell the food shown below.**

**Example: 1. Buyer:** How much are the apples?
**Seller:** They are $3.00 a bag.

1.
   **apples**
   $3.00 for a bag

2.
   **green peppers**
   3 for $1.00

3.
   **carrots**
   50¢ per pound

4.
   **lettuce**
   $1.00 each

## WRITE QUESTIONS

**5.–8.** Write 4 of the questions you made above on index cards.
Trade cards with a partner. Write answers to your partner's questions.

**Example: 5.** How much are the apples
   They are $3.00 a bag.

# Down on the Farm

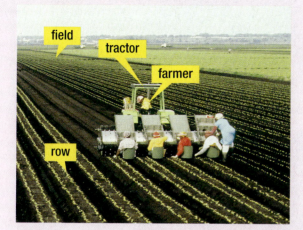

field
tractor
farmer
row

The farmer plows the field and plants the lettuce.

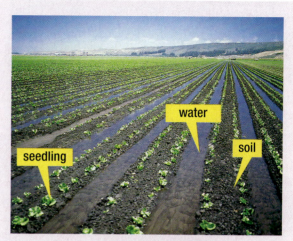

water
soil
seedling

The farmer waters the field.

crop
crate

The farmer gets help to harvest the crop.

## EXPRESS YOURSELF ▶ GIVE INFORMATION

**1.–3.** Work with a partner. Use farming words to tell about each picture.

**Example: 1.** The farmer drives a tractor. The tractor makes rows in the field.

## WRITE QUESTIONS AND ANSWERS ✏

**4.–6.** Write 3 questions about farmers' work. Trade papers with a partner. Write answers to your partner's questions.

**Example: 4.** What does a farmer do first?
        The farmer plows the field.

# Place Your Order

At the Restaurant

server

He takes an order.

check

customer

table for three

place setting

menu

**LAKESIDE CAFE**

# MENU

| Appetizers | | |
| --- | --- | --- |
| • Nachos | | $2.75 |

| Main Courses | | |
| --- | --- | --- |
| • Hamburger | | $4.50 |
| • Chicken Salad | | $4.50 |
| • Individual Pizza | | $5.75 |

| Desserts | | |
| --- | --- | --- |
| • Brownie | | $1.50 |
| • Ice Cream | | $1.75 |

| Beverages | | |
| --- | --- | --- |
| • Juice | | $1.75 |
| • Soda | | $1.50 |
| • Milk | | $1.00 |

## WHO'S TALKING? ▶ ORDER AN ITEM

**1.–3. Listen.**
Who is talking? Point to the correct person.
Then work in a group of four. Act out the scene. One person
is the server. Three people are customers. Order items from the menu.

## WRITE AN ORDER

**4.** Work with a partner. Order some food.
Your partner writes down the order. Then
change roles.

**Example: 4.**

*I want some chicken salad and milk, please.*

| 102 | Guest Check | |
| --- | --- | --- |
| date April 18 | waiter David | |
| 1. 1 chicken salad | | $4.50 |
| 2. 1 milk | | $1.00 |
| 3. | | |
| 4. | | |
| | **TOTAL** | $5.50 |
| | *Thank You!* | $5.50 |

# Describe the Food!

An **adjective** can tell how something looks, feels, smells, sounds, or tastes.

These nachos smell **delicious**. The cheese is **soft** and **warm**. The peppers are **green** and **shiny**. The chips taste **salty**. They sound **loud** and **crunchy**, too!

## BUILD SENTENCES

Look at the pictures below. Study the sensory adjectives on pages 310–311 of your Handbook. Use them to describe these foods.

**Example: 1.** The cinnamon rolls are sticky, sweet, and warm.

1. cinnamon rolls

2. noodles

3. grapefruit

4. chili

5. vegetables

6. banana split

7. hamburger

8. orange juice

9. corn

## WRITE A DESCRIPTION ✏️

<u>10.</u> Write a description of your favorite food. Share the description with a group. Make a chart of all the sensory adjectives your group used.

**Example: 10.** Chili tastes spicy and delicious. It is hot. It smells really good.

# Read and Think Together

**Work with a partner. Make a comparison chart for *Crops*.**
**Follow these steps.**

**1** Set up a chart like the one below.

| Crop | Planting | Harvesting | Products |
|---|---|---|---|
| cranberries | | | |
| wheat | | | |
| cotton | | | |
| potatoes | | | |
| oranges | | | |
| sugar cane | | | |

**2** Read the book again. As you read, fill in the
rest of the chart. Tell how farmers plant and
harvest each crop. Tell what products are
made from the crops.

| Crop | Planting | Harvesting | Products |
|---|---|---|---|
| cranberries | in bogs | by machine | juice, sauce |
| wheat | | | |

**3** Use your completed chart to compare the
crops. Talk to a partner. Discuss how some
of the crops are alike. Discuss how they
are different. Use words like these:

| alike | same | but |
|---|---|---|
| and | both | different |

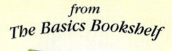

*from*
*The Basics Bookshelf*

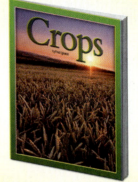

**THEME BOOK**

Learn how six crops
are planted, harvested,
and made into products.

# Words to Know

## REVIEW WORDS YOU KNOW

**Read the words aloud. Which word goes with the sentence?**

| too | good |
|-----|------|
| way | why |
| each | earth |

1. She takes _____ care of the garden.
2. This is the _____ she does it.
3. She gives _____ plant what it needs.

## LEARN TO READ

**Learn new words.**

| weigh | Ana buys tomatoes that **weigh** over 2 pounds. |
|-------|-------------------------------------------------|
| beautiful | The **beautiful** tomatoes are firm and bright red. |
| special | They come from a **special** market across town. |
| own | "I want to grow my **own** tomatoes," Ana thought. |
| any | She did not have **any** seeds, so she bought some. |
| indoors | She planted them **indoors**, by her kitchen window. |
| warm | It was winter, but her kitchen was **warm** and sunny. |
| healthy | Soon, she had strong and **healthy** seedlings. |
| cold | By the end of April, the **cold** weather was over. |
| outdoors | It was time to put her plants **outdoors** in the yard. |

### How to Learn a New Word

- Look at the word.
- Listen to the word.
- Listen to the word in a sentence. What does it mean?
- Say the word.
- Spell the word.
- Say the word again.

## WORD WORK

**Write each sentence. Add the missing word.**     **Example:** **4.** You can grow your own flowers at home.

4. You can grow your _ _ _ flowers at home.
5. Sunflower seeds can be planted _ _ _ _ _ _ _ _ in the garden at the start of spring.
6. Sunflowers are big. The flowers can _ _ _ _ _ more than a pound!
7. Other seeds must be planted inside the house. The pots stay _ _ _ _ _ _ _ for a few weeks.
8. In the summer when it gets _ _ _ _ outside, you can put the young plants in your garden.
9. Plant many colorful flowers. They will make your garden look _ _ _ _ _ _ _ _ _!

<u>10.–13.</u> **Find the 4 words you didn't use.**     **Example:** **10.** It is too cold to grow vegetables in the winter.
**Write sentences with those words.**

# Reading and Spelling

## Young Corn

We replant, and then we wait
for corn to sprout from healthy seeds.
The unseen roots push silently
deep into the earth.

We replant, and then we wait
for corn to grow from healthy seeds.
The graceful plants reach proudly
toward the endless sky.

## STUDY WORD PARTS

You can add a **prefix** to the beginning of a word.

| Prefix | Meaning | Example |
|--------|---------|---------|
| **un-** | not | unseen |
| | the opposite of | unlock |
| **re-** | again | replant |
| | back | repay |

You can add a **suffix** to the end of a word.

| Suffix | Meaning | Example |
|--------|---------|---------|
| **-ly** | in a certain way | proudly |
| **-y** | full of | healthy |
| **-less** | without | endless |
| **-ful** | full of | graceful |

▶ Transparencies 83–87

Follow these steps to read a word with a prefix or suffix.

**1** Look for a prefix or a suffix. Cover it. Then read the root word.

**un**tie          tie

When I cover the prefix **un–**,
I see a word I know: **tie**.

**2** Uncover the prefix or the suffix. Blend the syllables to read the entire word.

**un** + **tie** = **untie**

**Untie** means
"the opposite of tie."

## READING AND SPELLING PRACTICE

**Use what you learned to read the sentences.**

1. Insects are killing the healthy plants in Matt's garden.
2. He will not use insect sprays. They are messy and unsafe.
3. So he buys ladybugs that eat the harmful insects.
4. When he replants each spring, he fills his garden with these wonderful red bugs.
5. In a few months, Matt will proudly show you his garden.
6. It will be full of vegetables and harmless red bugs!

**7.–11. Now write the sentences that your teacher reads.**

## WORD WORK

**12.–16. Read the newspaper article. Find words with the prefix *un-*.**
**Copy the chart. Write each word next to its meaning.**

### The Top Tomato

Tomato lovers from all over the county unpacked crates of big, juicy tomatoes for the Tomato Festival on Sunday.

Fernando Robles, of Oak Park, grew a tomato unlike any other. It weighed 6.4 pounds! Pat Tanaka, also of Oak Park, was unhappy. Her 5.1 pound tomato won second place. Fernando remains unbeaten three years in a row.

"My secret is to find the best tomato on the vine, and then take off the unwanted ones," says Fernando.

| Words with *un-* | Meaning |
|---|---|
| 12. | emptied |
| 13. | not beaten |
| 14. | not wanted |
| 15. | sad |
| 16. | different from |

**Example: 12.** unpacked

# Read on Your Own

# Many Places to Plant a Plant

Farmers plant on a big scale! They fill huge fields with millions of seeds. Plants grow well in these open fields, but not all plants are grown there. Many plants are first grown indoors, in greenhouses and in nurseries. Unlike open fields, these shelters protect plants from too much heat or cold. They also protect young plants from harmful diseases, insects, and weeds.

Greenhouses have glass walls that let the sunshine in. Plants that like heat grow well inside the warm, sunny space. On really cold days, steam pipes heat and reheat the greenhouse to keep the plants healthy. Summer crops, such as peppers and eggplant, can be grown year-round in greenhouses.

A nursery is another place where plants grow in a sheltered place. Some nurseries grow priceless plants and collect their seeds. They sell some of the seeds and use others to grow more plants.

Some nurseries are huge, with a shop that sells plants and gardening tools. After people buy plants from the nursery, they replant them outdoors in gardens at home. Visit a nursery! Get a daisy plant and some roses. Buy a rake. You'll be ready to start a garden of your own.

## CHECK YOUR UNDERSTANDING

<u>1</u>. **Copy the concept map. Work with a partner to add details to it. Use your finished map to compare places to grow plants.**

**Example:** 1. A greenhouse has glass walls, but an open field is unprotected. Both places are often sunny and warm.

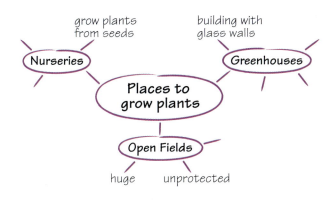

## EXPAND YOUR VOCABULARY

<u>2</u>. **Work with a group to collect words and phrases related to plants. Put the word or phrase and a picture on each card. Put the cards in groups and store them in a file.**

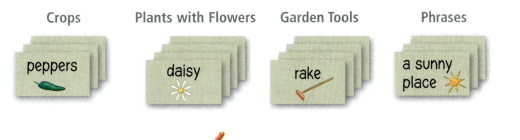

## WRITE MORE COMPARISONS

<u>3.–8.</u> **Choose cards from your word file. Find things to compare. Write 6 comparisons. Use the words in the box to tell how the things are alike or different.**

| both | alike | different |
|------|-------|-----------|
| and | same | but |

**Example:** 3. Peppers and carrots are both vegetable crops. Carrots taste sweet, but peppers are hot and spicy.

# Learn About Plants

## LIFE CYCLE OF A PLANT

The **seed** sprouts. It grows into a **plant**.

The **plant** forms a **bud**.

The **bud** blooms into a **flower**.

The **flower** has the **seeds** that start the cycle over again.

**Listen to the article. Then do the Review.**

# Oranges: From Tree to Market

• How are oranges grown?

Although farmers start some crops with seeds, farmers grow orange crops in a different way. Growers start by planting young **grafted** trees.

A grafted tree is made of two trees. The farmer takes a part of one young tree and attaches it to the roots of another young tree. The trees grow together to make a stronger tree. A grafted tree also produces fruit that is better than the fruit of an ungrafted tree. The grafted trees start producing oranges after about 2 years.

When the oranges are ripe, farmers harvest the fruit. Most farmers pick oranges by hand. Then they take the oranges to a storage area.

Farmers sell almost half of the harvested oranges to people who make orange juice. They also sell oranges to people who make perfumes, oils, jams, and candies. Some oranges go directly to a market where you can buy them.

### Development of an Orange Tree

A grafted tree ready to be planted

A young orange tree

A mature orange tree

## REVIEW

1. **Check Your Understanding** Why do farmers graft orange trees?
2. **Check Your Understanding** What are some of the ways that people use oranges?
3. **Vocabulary** Draw a diagram of a sunflower. Add these labels: *stem*, *leaf*, and *flower*.

# Writing Project  CROP REPORT

**Use a Venn diagram to compare two crops. Then write a report.**

## RESEARCH TWO CROPS

Choose two crops to compare. Use *Crops* or ask a librarian to help you find another book.

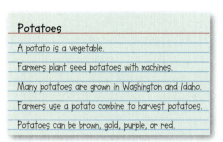

**Potatoes**

A potato is a vegetable.

Farmers plant seed potatoes with machines.

Many potatoes are grown in Washington and Idaho.

Farmers use a potato combine to harvest potatoes.

Potatoes can be brown, gold, purple, or red.

## PLAN YOUR REPORT

Use a Venn diagram to compare the two crops.

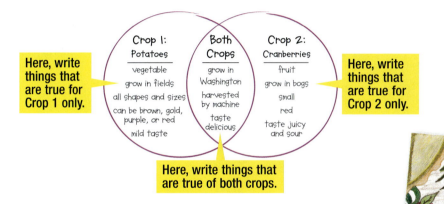

Here, write things that are true for Crop 1 only.

**Crop 1: Potatoes**
vegetable
grow in fields
all shapes and sizes
can be brown, gold, purple, or red
mild taste

**Both Crops**
grow in Washington
harvested by machine
taste delicious

**Crop 2: Cranberries**
fruit
grow in bogs
small
red
taste juicy and sour

Here, write things that are true for Crop 2 only.

Here, write things that are true of both crops.

## WRITE AND SHARE YOUR REPORT

Use your completed Venn diagram to write the report. Tell how the crops are alike. Tell how they are different. Use sensory adjectives to describe how the crops look and taste. See pages 310–311 of your Handbook. Then work with a partner. Check and correct your work.

### ✔ Check Your Work

Did you tell how the crops are alike and different?

Did you use signal words like *both, but,* and *and*?

Did you use sensory adjectives?

**Crop Report: Potatoes and Cranberries**

Potatoes and cranberries are two crops. Potatoes are vegetables that grow in fields. Unlike potatoes, cranberries are fruits that grow in bogs. Cranberries are small and red. They are juicy and taste sour. Potatoes come in different sizes. They can be brown, gold, purple, or red. Both crops grow in Washington. They both are harvested by machine. They both taste delicious!

Copy your report or type it on a computer. Add pictures. Read your report and put your it on a bulletin board.

LIVE in CONCERT!

SHERIFF
8

# Superstars

There are all kinds of stars! Work with a group. Draw a star you like. Describe your star to the class.

## In This Unit

### Vocabulary
- Idioms
- Space

### Language Functions
- Agree and Disagree
- Give Information

### Patterns and Structures
- Future Tense Verbs
- Verb Tense Review (present, past, future)
- Contractions

### Reading
- Multisyllabic Words
- Comprehension: Relate Goal and Outcome (goal-and-outcome map)

### Writing
- Opinions
- Description
- Diamante Poem

### Content Area Connection
- Science (outer space)

# Music Stars

**Listen and chant.**

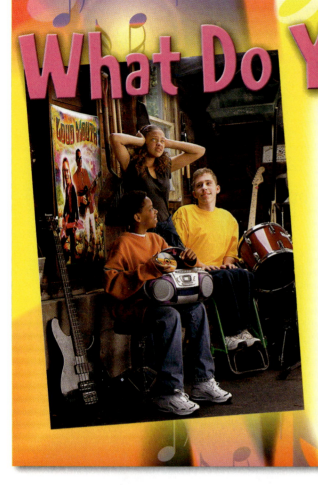

## What Do You Think?

**This band is great! They sound alright!**

Yes, I agree! I think you're right!

*No way, I don't enjoy this band!*

*It's just no good. In fact, it's bad!*

But listen to their great new song!

It is the best!

*You are so wrong!*

**Their music is one of a kind.**

**They leave all other bands behind.**

*I disagree! That isn't true!*

**OK. Let's find something else to do.**

**Idioms**
No way!
no good
one of a kind
leave all other
  bands behind

## EXPRESS YOURSELF ▶ AGREE AND DISAGREE

**Read each opinion. Say if you agree or disagree.**

**Example:** **1.** I agree. Jazz music is great. I disagree. I don't like jazz music.

1. Jazz music is great.
2. CDs are better than tapes.
3. All kids like the same music.
4. Music videos are beautiful.

## WRITE OPINIONS

<u>5.–7.</u> **Work with 2 partners. Each of you writes an opinion about rock stars. Then one partner writes a statement that agrees with your opinion. The other partner writes a statement that disagrees with it.**

**Example:** **5.** Rock stars have a hard life.
I agree because they are never alone.
I disagree. They have a lot of money.

# You Will Be a Star Some Day!

**A verb in the future tense tells what will happen later, or in the future.**

**Here are some ways to show the future tense.**

| | |
|---|---|
| **will** + verb | Our band **will play** at the park next week. |
| **am** **are** + **going to** + verb **is** | I **am going to play** the guitar. You **are going to sing**. The concert **is going to be** great! |
| **we'll** + verb | We will practice tonight. **We'll practice** tonight. The contraction for *we will* is *we'll*. |
| **won't** + verb | We will not stop until we know every song. We **won't stop** until we know every song! The contraction for *will not* is *won't*. |

## BUILD SENTENCES

**Change each sentence to tell about the future. Say each sentence 2 different ways.**

1. We practice at Ana's house.
2. You and Ana learn a new song.
3. It sounds great.
4. Many people hear our music at the park.
5. We become superstars!

**Example: 1.** We will practice at Ana's house.
We are going to practice at Ana's house.

**Use the contraction *won't* to make each sentence negative. Say the new sentence.**

6. I will sing.
7. You will play the guitar.
8. Ana will get worried.
9. We will forget the songs.
10. The audience will want to leave.

**Example: 6.** I won't sing.

## WRITE ABOUT YOUR FUTURE ✏

<u>11.</u> **You, too, can become a superstar! Maybe you'll be a star in music, maybe in math. Write what you will do to become a superstar.**

**Example: 11.** I am going to learn to write computer games.
I'll write every day.
I will make a popular game.

Language Development   **287**

# Stars in the Sky

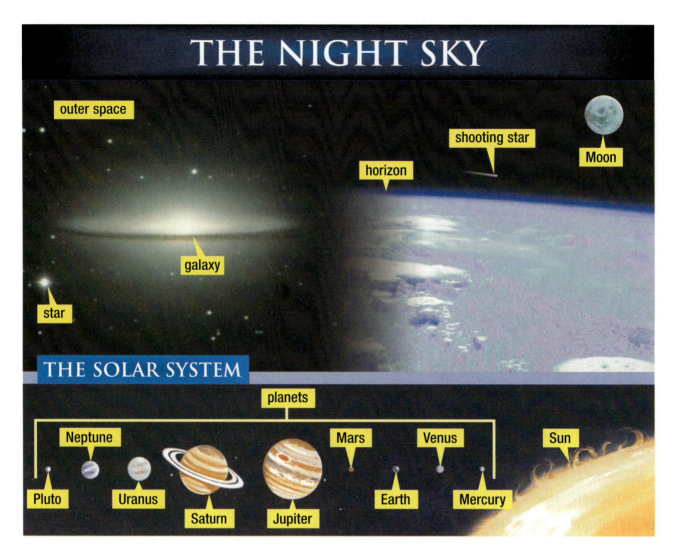

THE NIGHT SKY

outer space

shooting star

Moon

horizon

galaxy

star

THE SOLAR SYSTEM

planets

Neptune

Mars

Venus

Sun

Pluto

Uranus

Earth

Mercury

Saturn

Jupiter

## EXPRESS YOURSELF ▶ GIVE INFORMATION

**1.–6.** Study the pictures. Tell a partner 3 facts about the night sky and 3 facts about the solar system.

Example: **1.** Earth is the third planet from the Sun.

## WRITE ABOUT A TRIP INTO SPACE ✏

**7.** Work with a partner. Write about a trip to outer space. Use future tense. Describe what you will see on your trip.

Example: **7.** I will go to outer space.
I'll see many stars.
I will fly by Venus and Mars.

# Star Power

The tense of a **verb** shows when the action happens.

| Tense | Tells | Example |
|---|---|---|
| Past | what happened earlier | The star Antares **formed** millions of years ago. |
| Present | what is happening now | It now **shines** with a bright orange light. |
| Future | what will happen later | Some day Antares **is going to explode**. It **will turn** into a supernova, or exploding star. |

## BUILD SENTENCES

**1.–9.** Read the words below. Choose words from each column to make a sentence. Use each verb correctly.

| | | | |
|---|---|---|---|
| | traveled<br>revolved<br>moved | | in the past. |
| Mars | travels<br>revolves<br>moves | in outer space<br><br>around the Sun | today. |
| | will travel<br>is going to revolve<br>will move | | in the future. |

Example: **1.** Mars moved around the Sun in the past.

## WRITE A DESCRIPTION ✏️

**10.–15.** Work with a partner. Write 2 sentences to describe the Moon in the picture. Then write 2 sentences to describe the Moon last night. What will the Moon look like tomorrow night? Write 2 more sentences to describe it.

Example: **10.** The Moon is big and bright.

# Read and Think Together

**What does Moonshine want? Make a goal-and-outcome map for *Sunny and Moonshine*. Follow these steps.**

**1** Draw a map like the one below.

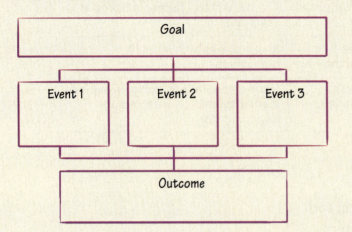

```
                          Goal
        ┌──────────────────┼──────────────────┐
   ┌─────────┐        ┌─────────┐        ┌─────────┐
   │ Event 1 │        │ Event 2 │        │ Event 3 │
   └─────────┘        └─────────┘        └─────────┘
        └──────────────────┼──────────────────┘
                        Outcome
```

**2** Read pages 4–8 of *Sunny and Moonshine* again. Write Moonshine's goal in the top box.

```
                          Goal
             Moonshine wants to meet Sunny.
        ┌──────────────────┼──────────────────┐
```

**3** Read the rest of the book again. What happens when Moonshine tries to reach her goal? Write an event in each of the small boxes. Write what happens at the end of the story in the last box.

**4** Use your completed goal-and-outcome map to retell the story to a partner.

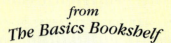

*from*
*The Basics Bookshelf*

**THEME BOOK**

This fantasy tells about a meeting between the Sun and the Moon.

# Words to Know

## REVIEW WORDS YOU KNOW

**Read the words aloud. Which word goes in each sentence?**

| great | large |
|-------|-------|
| Do | Does |
| most | might |

1. I think this band plays _____ music.
2. _____ you like it, too?
3. They _____ play a song for you!

## LEARN TO READ

**Some words have more than one meaning. Read each sentence. Think about the meaning of the word in dark type.**

| | | |
|---|---|---|
| **show** *verb* | Let me **show** you my new guitar. |
| **show** *noun* | I am going to play it in the **show** tonight. |
| **right** *adverb* | I need to practice to play the songs **right**. |
| **right** *adjective* | I strum the strings with my **right** hand. |
| **close** *adverb* | I keep the music book **close** to me while I play. |
| **close** *verb* | **Close** it now and see if I can play the song. |
| **watch** *verb* | Many people will come to **watch** us perform. |
| **watch** *noun* | I have to check my **watch** so I won't be late. |
| **kind** *noun* | I wonder what **kind** of music people will like. |
| **kind** *adjective* | I hope the audience will be **kind** and won't shout "Boo!" |

## WORD WORK

**Write each sentence. Add the missing word.**   **Example: 4.** The show will start at 7:30.

4. The _ _ _ _ will start at 7:30.
5. Come at 7:00 so you can sit _ _ _ _ _ to the stage.
6. My _ _ _ _ _ broke. I don't know what time it is.
7. I can't wait to _ _ _ _ you how well we play.
8. Sometimes I _ _ _ _ _ my eyes while I play.
9. I hope I sing all the _ _ _ _ _ words to the songs.
10. Look for me on the _ _ _ _ _ side of the stage.

# Reading and Spelling

## Starship Earth

Safely,
And silently,
Earth goes around the Sun.
And each time our Earth circles that Sun
Another year is done.

Gracefully,
Silently,
Earth spins while she rings the Sun.
And each time our Earth has completely spun
Another day is done.

## STUDY LONG WORDS

How many syllables are in each word? Look for letter patterns and word parts.

**eagle**          **fifteen**          **telescope**          **hold carefully**

## READING STRATEGIES

**There are several ways to read a long word.**

**1** Look for familiar parts—prefixes, suffixes, or endings like *-ed* or *-ing*. Cover them.

**completely**          **complete**

**2** Figure out how to divide the root word.

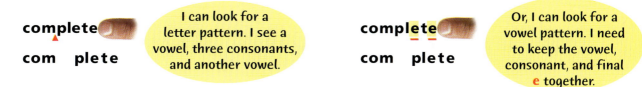

**complete**

**com   plete**

> I can look for a letter pattern. I see a vowel, three consonants, and another vowel.

**complete**

**com   plete**

> Or, I can look for a vowel pattern. I need to keep the vowel, consonant, and final **e** together.

**3** Blend the syllables to say the root word. Then uncover the suffix and read the entire word.

**com + plete**          **com + plete + ly = completely**

## READING AND SPELLING PRACTICE

**Use what you learned to read the sentences.**

1. Chan waited on the rooftop beneath the night sky.
2. He carefully checked his watch. It was close to midnight.
3. The North Star twinkled in the middle of the night sky.
4. Chan was able to see Venus. Then he saw a flash of light!
5. Was it a rocket launch? No! It was just lightning.

**6.–10.** Now write the sentences that your teacher reads.

## WORD WORK

**11.–16. Read the newspaper article. Find the words with 3 syllables. List them. Divide them into syllables.**

**Example: 11.** important   im por tant

### A Star in Space

Here is some news for fans of Kim Mills. The film star will go to Houston to train for an important space flight with NASA. She will hopefully blast off sometime in June.

"I have to prepare for the flight." Ms. Mills said with excitement.

The star plans to act in two different films this fall: *A Terrible Surprise* and a remake of *The Forbidden Planet*.

# Read on Your Own

Many Native American calendars divide the year into thirteen moons.
Each moon has its own story. Read this one about the Fifth Moon.

## Fifth Moon's Story

In the Old Time, Winter stayed on Earth forever. Rain and snow fell on the land. Fields and rivers were covered with snow. The Earth Children asked the kind Sun for help, "Please send Winter away!"

Sun went to Winter's house. Winter sat all alone. He was huddled close to a cold fire. He recognized Sun. "Go away!" Winter shouted.

"No!" Sun exclaimed. "It is you who must go. Leave the Land of the Earth Children, now!"

Winter frowned. He blasted Sun with icy rain, but he was not able to make Sun leave.

Thirteen moons on Turtle's back

Sun just watched and smiled happily. He kept shining and shining. At last, Winter began to melt away. He grew smaller and smaller until he became the size of a snowflake. Sun then called to Owl. Owl flew into the room. Sun said, "Take Winter to the snows in the far north. He will remain there a long time." Owl did as Sun asked.

Suddenly the Land of the Earth Children began to grow warm. Green leaves reappeared on the trees.

The people came together to celebrate. They danced joyfully as gentle Spring came back into their land.

## CHECK YOUR UNDERSTANDING

1. Copy this goal-and-outcome map and complete it. Use the completed map to retell "Fifth Moon's Story" to a partner.

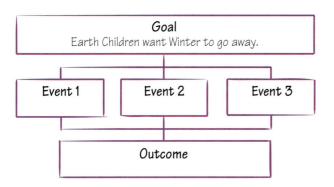

## EXPAND YOUR VOCABULARY

2. Copy the chart. Work with a group to add words. Tell about the weather and what you do in each season.

| Season | Weather | Activities |
|---|---|---|
| winter | cold, snowy, icy | ice skate, eat soup |
| spring | | |
| summer | | |
| fall | | |

## WRITE ABOUT THE SUN

3. Talk with a partner about how the Sun helps people. Can the Sun be bad for people, too? Write sentences to tell about the Sun.

Example: 3. The Sun helps people grow crops.

The Sun is bad for your skin when you stay out too long.

# HIGH POINT
## Handbook

# ▶Handbook Contents

# Strategies for Learning Language

These strategies can help you learn to use and understand the English language.

## 1 Listen actively and try out language.

| WHAT TO DO | EXAMPLES |
|---|---|
| Repeat what you hear. | You hear: *Way to go, Joe! Fantastic catch!* You say: *Way to go, Joe! Fantastic catch!* |
| Recite songs and poems. | My Family Tree<br><br>Two grandmas, one brother,<br>Two grandpas, one mother,<br>One father, and then there's me.<br>Eight of us together<br>Make up my family tree.<br><br>*Two grandmas, one brother,...* |
| Listen to others and use their language. | You hear:<br>"When did you know that something was missing?"<br><br>You say:<br>"I knew that something was missing when I got to class." |

## 2 Ask for help.

| WHAT TO DO | EXAMPLES |
|---|---|
| Ask questions about how to use language. | *Did I say that right?* *Did I use that word in the right way?* *Which is correct, "bringed" or "brought"?* |
| Use your native language or English to make sure that you understand. | You say:<br>"Wait! Could you say that again more slowly, please?"<br><br>Other options:<br>"Does 'violet' mean 'purple'?"<br>"Is 'enormous' another way to say 'big'?" |

### ❸ Use gestures and body language, and watch for them.

| WHAT TO DO | EXAMPLES |
|---|---|
| Use gestures and movements to help others understand your idea. | *I will hold up five fingers to show that I need five more minutes.* |
| Watch people as they speak. The way they look or move can help you understand the meaning of their words. | *Let's give him a hand.*  *Everyone is clapping. "Give him a hand" must mean to clap for him.* |

### ❹ Think about what you are learning.

| WHAT TO DO | EXAMPLES |
|---|---|
| Ask yourself: Are my language skills getting better? How can I improve? | *Was it correct to use "they" when I talked about my grandparents?*  *Did I add 's to show ownership?* |
| Keep notes about what you've learned. Use your notes to practice using English. | **How to Ask Questions** <br> • I can start a question with "who," "what," "where," "when," "how," or "why": <br> What will the weather be like today? <br><br> • I can also start a question with "do" or "does": <br> Do you have my math book? |

# Sentences

A sentence is a group of words that expresses a complete thought.

| TYPES OF SENTENCES | EXAMPLES |
|---|---|
| A **statement** tells something. It ends with a period. | The football game was on Friday. <br> The coach made an important announcement. |
| A **question** asks for information. It ends with a question mark. | What did the coach say? |

### Kinds of Questions

**Questions That Ask for a "Yes" or "No" Answer**    **Answers**

| | |
|---|---|
| **Can** you tell me what he said? | Yes. |
| **Does** everyone know the news? | No. |
| **Is** it about the team? | Yes. |
| **Did** the team win the game? | Yes. |
| **Are** the players sad? | No. |
| **Were** the fans surprised? | Yes. |

**Questions That Ask for Specific Information**

| | |
|---|---|
| **Who** heard the announcement? | The team and the fans heard the announcement. |
| **What** did the coach say? | He said the team will play in a special game. |
| **Where** will the team play this game? | In Hawaii. |
| **When** did the coach find out? | Right before the game. |
| **How** did he feel? | He felt so happy! |
| **Why** was our team chosen? | Our team was chosen because we won a lot of games. |
| **How many** games did the team win this year? | All ten of them. |
| **How much** will the tickets to the game cost? | Fifteen dollars. |

| | |
|---|---|
| An **exclamation** shows surprise or strong feeling. It ends with an exclamation mark. | That's fantastic news! <br> I can't believe it! |

| TYPES OF SENTENCES, continued | EXAMPLES |
|---|---|
| A **command** tells you what to do or what not to do. It usually begins with a verb. It often ends with a period. | Give the team my congratulations. Buy a ticket for me, too. |
| If a command shows strong emotion, it ends with an exclamation mark. | Don't forget! |

| NEGATIVE SENTENCES | EXAMPLES |
|---|---|
| A **negative sentence** uses a <mark>negative word</mark> like *not*. | |
| • Add ***not*** after *am, is, are, was,* or *were*. | The game in Hawaii **was** <mark>not</mark> boring! |
| • Add ***do not, does not,*** or ***did not*** before all other verbs. | The other team **did** <mark>not</mark> **play** well. |
| • Combine the verb and ***not*** to make a **contraction**. | Our team **did<mark>n't</mark> make** any mistakes. |

### Contractions with *not*

To make a **contraction**, take out one or more letters and add an **apostrophe (')**.

| | |
|---|---|
| are + not = aren't | The fans of the other team **aren't** happy. |
| is + not = isn't | Their coach **isn't** happy either. |
| can + not = can't | The other team **can't** believe they lost. |
| was + not = wasn't | The game **wasn't** fun for them. |
| were + not = weren't | The players **weren't** playing their best. |
| do + not = don't | They **don't** want to go to practice on Monday. |
| does + not = doesn't | The quarterback **doesn't** want to hear about his mistakes. |
| did + not = didn't | The other team **didn't** want to lose. |

| CAPITALIZATION IN SENTENCES | EXAMPLES |
|---|---|
| Every sentence begins with a <mark>capital letter.</mark> | **O**ur team was very proud. |
| | **W**hat do you think of all this?  **I**t's a wonderful story! |

# Nouns

A noun names a person, place, or thing.
There are different kinds of nouns.

| COMMON AND PROPER NOUNS | EXAMPLES |
|---|---|
| A **common noun** names any person, place, or thing. | A **teenager** sat by the **ocean** and read a **book**. |
| A **proper noun** names one particular person, place, or thing.<br><br>The important words in a proper noun start with a <u>capital letter</u>. | Daniel sat by the **Atlantic Ocean** and read *Save the Manatee.*<br><br>A manatee |

| SINGULAR AND PLURAL NOUNS | EXAMPLES |
|---|---|

> **A singular noun names one thing.**
> **A plural noun names more than one thing.**

Follow these rules to make a noun plural:

- Add **-s** to most nouns.

| | | | | |
|---|---|---|---|---|
| desk | book | teacher | apple | line |
| desk**s** | book**s** | teacher**s** | apple**s** | line**s** |

- If the noun ends in **x**, **ch**, **sh**, **s**, or **z**, add **-es**.

| | | | | |
|---|---|---|---|---|
| box | lunch | dish | glass | waltz |
| box**es** | lunch**es** | dish**es** | glass**es** | waltz**es** |

- Some nouns change in different ways to show the plural.

| | | | | |
|---|---|---|---|---|
| child | foot | tooth | man | woman |
| **children** | **feet** | **teeth** | **men** | **women** |

| POSSESSIVE NOUNS | EXAMPLES |
|---|---|
| A **possessive noun** shows ownership. It often ends in **'s.** | Daniel**'s** book was very interesting. |

# Nouns that Name People

## Family Words

### Girls/Women

great-grandmother
grandmother
mother
stepmother
sister
stepsister
half-sister
daughter
granddaughter
aunt
cousin
niece

### Boys/Men

great-grandfather
grandfather
father
stepfather
brother
stepbrother
half-brother
son
grandson
uncle
cousin
nephew

My family includes my grandmother, mother, father, sister, cousins, aunts, uncles, and me.

## People at Work

architect

artist
astronaut
athlete
baker
bank teller
barber
bus driver
business person
cab driver
cashier
coach
construction worker

cook
custodian

dancer

dentist
designer
doctor
editor
eye doctor
farmer
firefighter
flight attendant
florist

gardener
guard
historian
lawyer
letter carrier
librarian
mechanic

messenger

model
mover
musician
nurse
office worker

painter
photographer

pilot

plumber
police officer
reporter
sailor
salesperson
scientist
stylist
teacher
veterinarian
writer

# Nouns, continued

## Nouns that Name Places

### At Home

bathroom
bedroom
dining room
garage
garden

kitchen

living room

yard

### In Town

airport
bank
basketball court
beauty shop
bookstore

bus stop

cafe
city hall
clothing store

fire station
flower shop
garage
gas station

hardware store

hospital
intersection
jewelry store
library

mall
market
motel
movie theater
museum
music store
nursing home
office building
park
parking garage
parking lot
pet shop
police station
pool

post office
restaurant

school

shoe store
sports stadium
supermarket
theater
toy store
train station

### On the Earth

beach
canyon
desert
forest
hill
island
lake

mountains

ocean

plains
pond
rain forest
river
sea
seashore
valley
wetland

# Pronouns

**A pronoun takes the place of a noun or refers to a noun.**

| PRONOUN AGREEMENT | EXAMPLES |
|---|---|
| Use the correct **pronoun** for a person or thing. |  |
| • To tell about yourself, use **I**. | |
| • When you speak to another person, use **you**. | |
| • To tell about a boy or man, use **he**. | Scott likes art. **He** wants to be a photographer. |
| • For a girl or woman, use **she**. | Anna likes animals. **She** wants to be a veterinarian. |
| • For a thing, use **it**. | What about music? Is **it** a good career? |
| • For yourself and other people, use **we**. |  |
| • When you speak to more than one other person, use **you**. | 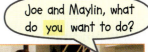 |
| • To tell about other people or things, use **they**. | Joe and Maylin love children. **They** want to be teachers. |

# Pronouns, continued

## SUBJECT PRONOUNS

Some pronouns tell who or what does the action. They are called **subject pronouns.**

### EXAMPLES

Anna likes animals.

**She** works at a pet shop.

Ernesto works there, too.

**He** is in charge of the fish section.

**It** is a big area in the store.

Anna takes care of the birds.

**They** are in cages.

**Subject Pronouns**

| Singular | Plural |
|---|---|
| I | we |
| you | you |
| he, she, it | they |

## OBJECT PRONOUNS

Some pronouns come after an action verb or after a word like *to*, *for*, or *with*. They are called **object pronouns.**

### EXAMPLES

The parrots get hungry at 5 o'clock.

Anna feeds **them** every day.

The parrots are nice to **her.**

One day, Ernesto fed the parrots.

They didn't like **him.**

The parrots took the food and threw **it** on the floor.

Now only Anna can feed **them.**

**Pronouns**

| Subject Pronouns | Object Pronouns |
|---|---|
| I → | me |
| you → | you |
| he → | him |
| she → | her |
| it → | it |
| we → | us |
| you → | you |
| they → | them |

## POSSESSIVE PRONOUNS

A **possessive pronoun** tells who or what owns something.

It is sometimes called a **possessive adjective.**

### EXAMPLES

Anna's favorite parrot is a red-and-blue male.

**His** name is Repeat.

Repeat knows how to say **her** name.

Repeat knows Ernesto's name, too.

The bird says **their** names over and over again.

**Pronouns**

| Subject Pronouns | Possessive Pronouns |
|---|---|
| I → | my |
| you → | your |
| he → | his |
| she → | her |
| it → | its |
| we → | our |
| you → | your |
| they → | their |

# Adjectives

An adjective describes, or tells about, a noun. Many adjectives tell what something is like. An adjective can also tell "how many" or "which one".

| ADJECTIVES | EXAMPLES |
|---|---|
| Usually an **adjective** comes before the **noun** it describes. | You can buy **fresh food** at the market.<br><br>You can buy **colorful** fruit.<br><br>You can buy **delicious** vegetables. |
| An **adjective** can come after the **noun** in sentences with verbs like *is, are, was,* or *were*. | The **bananas** are **yellow**.<br><br>The **tomato** is **round**.<br><br>The **market** was **busy**.<br><br>The **shoppers** were **happy**. |
| Some **adjectives** tell "how many." They always come before the **noun**. | This farmer has **six** kinds of tomatoes.<br><br>My mom wants **three** tomatoes.<br><br>She has **five** dollars. |
| Some **adjectives** tell the order of persons or things in a group. They usually come before the **noun**.<br><br>They can come after the noun in sentences with verbs like *is, are, was,* and *were*. | Mom looks at the tomatoes in the **first** basket.<br><br>Then she looks at the tomatoes in the **second** basket.<br><br>My **mom** is **first** in line to buy them! |
| Never add *-s* or *-es* to an **adjective,** even if the **noun** it describes is plural. | Look at the **green** cucumbers.<br><br>Mom wants **two** cucumbers.<br><br>The **vegetables** tonight will be **delicious**! |

# Adjectives, continued

## Sensory Adjectives

An adjective can tell how something looks, sounds, tastes, feels, or smells.

**How Something Looks**

beautiful

fluffy

colorful
dark

messy
shiny

The red apple is big.

**Colors**

- red
- pink
- purple
- blue
- green
- yellow
- orange
- brown
- tan
- black
- gray
- white

**Sizes**

big
huge
large

little
small
tiny

long

medium
short
tall
thin

**Shapes**

curved
oval
rectangular

round

square

triangular

## How Something Sounds

blaring
crunchy
loud
noisy
quiet
soft
rattling

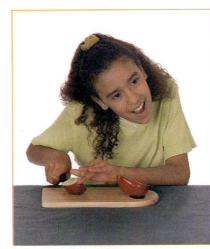

I like crunchy apples.

## How Something Feels

bumpy
dry
hard
hot
rough
sharp
slimy
smooth
soft
sticky
warm

The outside of a pickle feels bumpy.

These cinnamon rolls are very sticky!

## How Something Tastes

bitter
delicious
fresh
juicy
salty
sour
spicy
sweet
tasty

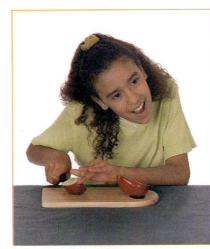

These vegetables will taste fresh.

Chili can be very spicy.

## How Something Smells

fishy
fragrant
fresh
rotten
sweet

It smells very fragrant here!

# Adjectives, continued

## Feelings

An adjective can tell how someone feels.

angry

embarrassed

sad

annoyed

excited

scared

bored

happy

shy

confused

nervous

surprised

curious

proud

worried

# Numbers

Numbers are a special kind of adjective. They can tell how many.
They can also tell the order of things in a sequence.

## Number Words

| | | | |
|---|---|---|---|
| 0 | zero | 30 | thirty |
| 1 | one | 40 | forty |
| 2 | two | 50 | fifty |
| 3 | three | 60 | sixty |
| 4 | four | 70 | seventy |
| 5 | five | 80 | eighty |
| 6 | six | 90 | ninety |
| 7 | seven | 100 | one hundred |
| 8 | eight | 500 | five hundred |
| 9 | nine | 1,000 | one thousand |
| 10 | ten | 5,000 | five thousand |
| 11 | eleven | 10,000 | ten thousand |
| 12 | twelve | 100,000 | one hundred thousand |
| 13 | thirteen | 500,000 | five hundred thousand |
| 14 | fourteen | 1,000,000 | one million |
| 15 | fifteen | | |
| 16 | sixteen | | |
| 17 | seventeen | | |
| 18 | eighteen | | |
| 19 | nineteen | | |
| 20 | twenty | | |

## Order Words

| | |
|---|---|
| 1st | first |
| 2nd | second |
| 3rd | third |
| 4th | fourth |
| 5th | fifth |
| 6th | sixth |
| 7th | seventh |
| 8th | eighth |
| 9th | ninth |
| 10th | tenth |
| 11th | eleventh |
| 12th | twelfth |
| 13th | thirteenth |
| 14th | fourteenth |
| 15th | fifteenth |
| 16th | sixteenth |
| 17th | seventeenth |
| 18th | eighteenth |
| 19th | nineteenth |
| 20th | twentieth |

This woman is the first customer. She buys two heads of broccoli for $1.98.

# Verbs

**Every complete sentence has a verb.**

| THE FORMS OF *BE* | EXAMPLES |
|---|---|
| The words **am, is,** and **are** are **verbs.** They are forms of the verb **be**. They tell about something that is happening now, or in the present. | I **am** in New York with my mom.<br><br>She **is** here for the first time.<br><br>We **are** excited to see the buildings.<br><br>They **are** amazing! |
| The **verbs was** and **were** are also forms of the verb **be**. They tell about something that happened in the past. | I **was** in Central Park yesterday.<br><br>It **was** beautiful.<br><br>We **were** with some friends.<br><br>They **were** very helpful. |

**Forms of the Verb** *be*

| Present | Past |
|---|---|
| I **am** | I **was** |
| you **are** | you **were** |
| he, she, it **is** | he, she, it **was** |
| we **are** | we **were** |
| you **are** | you **were** |
| they **are** | they **were** |

| CONTRACTIONS WITH VERBS | EXAMPLES |
|---|---|
| You can shorten the verbs *am, is,* and *are* to make a **contraction**. | Today **we're** going to Lincoln Center. |

### Contractions with Verbs

To make a **contraction,** take out one or more letters and add an **apostrophe (').**

| | |
|---|---|
| I + am = I'm | **I'm** glad to be in New York. |
| you + are = you're | **You're** going to meet my brother. |
| he + is = he's | **He's** staying with my aunt. |
| she + is = she's | **She's** in a performance at Lincoln Center. |
| it + is = it's | **It's** a ballet. |
| we + are = we're | **We're** going to watch a ballet practice. |
| they + are = they're | **They're** coming to our hotel at 3:00. |

| ACTION VERBS | EXAMPLES |
|---|---|
| Most verbs are **action verbs.** They tell what a person or thing does. | The dancers **hop** and **spin.** |
| When you tell what another person or thing does, use **-s** or **-es** at the end of the **verb**. | The spotlight **shines** on them.<br><br>One dancer **twirls** around and around.<br><br>Then she **stretches** a leg and **leaps** gracefully. |

# Action Verbs

act
add
answer
arrive
ask
bake
bathe
boil
bounce
brush
burn
call

dance

deliver
discuss
drop
dry
enter
erase

carry

change
check
chop
circle
clap

clean

climb
close
comb
cook
copy
count
cross
cry

exercise

fill
finish
fix
fold
hammer
help
introduce
invite
jog
join

jump

kick
laugh

learn
listen
look

mail

mark
mix
mop
move

open

paint
plant
play
point
pour
pull
push
raise
rake
repair
repeat
skate
slice
spell
start
stir
stop
stretch

talk

tie
turn
type
underline
use
vote

walk

wash
watch
water
wipe

work

# Verbs, continued

| THE VERBS *CAN, COULD, MAY, MIGHT* | EXAMPLES |
|---|---|
| You can use the verbs **can, could, may,** or **might** with an **action verb** to express:<br><br>• the ability to do something<br>• a possibility, or the chance that something may happen | A hurricane **can cause** a lot of damage.<br>Several inches of rain **might fall** in just a few minutes.<br>The wind **may blow** at high speeds.<br>It **might knock** over trees.<br>It **could break** windows. |

| PRESENT TENSE VERBS | EXAMPLES |
|---|---|

**The tense of a verb shows when an action happens.**

| | |
|---|---|
| The **present tense** of a verb tells about an action that is happening now, or in the present. | My mom **looks** at her charts.<br>She **checks** her computer screen.<br>She **takes** notes. |
| The **present tense** of a verb can also tell about an action that happens regularly or all the time. | My mom **works** for the local TV station.<br>She **is** a weather forecaster.<br>She **reports** the weather every night at 5 p.m. |
| The **present progressive** form of a verb tells about an action as it is happening.<br><br>It uses **am**, **is**, or **are** and a main verb. The main verb ends in **-ing**. | Right now, she **is getting** ready for the show.<br>"I can't believe it!" she says. "I **am looking** at a terrible storm!"<br>The high winds **are starting** to blow.<br>Trees **are falling** down.<br><br>Wind damage from Hurricane Floyd, 1999 |

| PAST TENSE VERBS | EXAMPLES |
|---|---|
| The **past tense** of a verb tells about an action that happened earlier, or in the past. | Yesterday, my mom **warned** everyone about the hurricane. The storm **moved** over the ocean toward land. We **did** not **know** exactly when it would hit. |
| The past tense form of a **regular verb** ends with **-ed**. | The shop owners in our town **covered** their windows with wood. We **closed** our shutters and **stayed** inside. |
| **Irregular verbs** have special forms to show the past tense. See page 318 for more examples. | The storm **hit** land. The sky **grew** very dark. It **began** to rain. |

**Some Irregular Verbs**

| Present Tense | Past Tense |
|---|---|
| hit | hit |
| grow | grew |
| begin | began |

| FUTURE TENSE VERBS | EXAMPLES |
|---|---|
| The **future tense** of a verb tells about an action that will happen later, or in the future. To show future tense, use one of the following: | |
| • **will** plus another verb | After the storm, people **will come** out of their houses. They **will inspect** the damage. |
| • a **contraction** with **will** plus another verb | **They'll uncover** their windows. **They'll clean** up their yards. Some people **won't have** as much work as other people. |
| • the phrase **am going to, is going to,** or **are going to** plus a verb. | I **am going to take** the tree branches out of my yard. The city **is** not **going to clean** every street. We **are** all **going to help** each other. |

**Contractions with *will***

I + will = I'll
you + will = you'll
he + will = he'll
she + will = she'll
it + will = it'll
we + will = we'll
they + will = they'll
will + not = won't

# Verbs, continued

## Irregular Verbs

These verbs have special forms to show the past tense.

| Present | Past |
|---------|------|
| become | became |
| begin | began |
| bend | bent |
| blow | blew |
| break | broke |
| build | built |

| Present | Past |
|---------|------|
| buy | bought |
| catch | caught |
| come | came |
| cut | cut |
| do | did |
| draw | drew |

| Present | Past |
|---------|------|
| drink | drank |

| Present | Past |
|---------|------|
| eat | ate |
| fall | fell |
| feel | felt |

| Present | Past |
|---------|------|
| find | found |
| fly | flew |
| get | got |

| Present | Past |
|---------|------|
| give | gave |
| grow | grew |
| go | went |
| have | had |
| hear | heard |
| hide | hid |
| hit | hit |

| Present | Past |
|---------|------|
| hold | held |
| keep | kept |
| lead | led |
| leave | left |

| Present | Past |
|---------|------|
| make | made |
| pay | paid |

| Present | Past |
|---------|------|
| put | put |
| read | read |

| Present | Past |
|---------|------|
| run | ran |
| say | said |
| see | saw |
| sing | sang |
| sit | sat |
| speak | spoke |
| stand | stood |
| swim | swam |
| take | took |
| throw | threw |
| wear | wore |

| Present | Past |
|---------|------|
| write | wrote |

# Capital Letters

You can tell that a word is special in some way if it begins with a capital letter.

| TO START A SENTENCE | EXAMPLES |
|---|---|
| Start the first word in a sentence with a **capital letter.** | **O**ur class read four books this month.<br>**W**hat book did you like the most? |

| PROPER NOUNS | EXAMPLES |
|---|---|

> **A common noun names any person, place, or thing.**
> **A proper noun names one particular person, place, or thing.**

All the important words in a **proper noun** start with a capital letter.

| | Common Noun | Proper Noun |
|---|---|---|
| Person | boy | **M**arcos **V**alle |
| Place | city | **M**iami |
| Thing | book | ***B**ody **W**orks* |

**Proper nouns** include:

- names of people

Laura Roberts       Sam Wong

- names of geographic places

**Cities and States**
Dallas, Texas
Miami, Florida

**Countries**
Iran
Ecuador

**Continents**
Asia
South America

**Bodies of Water**
Pacific Ocean
Gulf of Mexico

**Landforms**
Rocky Mountains
Grand Canyon

**Planets**
Earth
Jupiter

- months of the year and days of the week

| | | | | |
|---|---|---|---|---|
| January | May | September | Sunday | Thursday |
| February | June | October | Monday | Friday |
| March | July | November | Tuesday | Saturday |
| April | August | December | Wednesday | |

| PROPER ADJECTIVES | EXAMPLES |
|---|---|
| A **proper adjective** is formed from a **proper noun**. Capitalize proper adjectives. | Miguel is from **Nicaragua**. He is **Nicaraguan.**<br>Miki is from **Japan**. She is **Japanese.** |

# Paragraphs

**A paragraph is a group of sentences that tell about the same idea.**

## PARAGRAPH ORGANIZATION

Most paragraphs begin with a **topic sentence.** It tells the main idea, or what the paragraph is mainly about.

Other sentences give supporting details. They tell more about the main idea.

The first sentence of a paragraph is idented.

## EXAMPLE

indent

topic sentence

There is a lot to do on the pier at our beach.

supporting details

You can watch the surfers in the waves below the pier. You can talk with the people who are fishing from the pier. You can stop in the middle of the pier at the lifeguard station. You can go to a great restaurant at the end of the pier. You can watch the sunset from the restaurant.

## SEQUENCE PARAGRAPHS

A **sequence paragraph** is organized by time.

**Time order words** tell when things happen:

**after**

**finally**

**first**

**next**

**then**

## EXAMPLE

One day I went fishing with my brother. **First** we woke up at 4 a.m. **Next** we rowed our boat to the middle of the lake. **Then** we waited three hours! We **finally** caught one tiny fish. When my brother goes fishing again, I'm staying in bed!

## COMPARISON PARAGRAPHS

A **comparison paragraph** tells how things are alike and different.

Use **comparison words** when you compare things:

- **alike**
- **and**
- **both**
- **but**
- **different**
- **same**
- **unlike**

### EXAMPLE

**Like** human beings, whales are mammals. **Both** give birth to live babies and feed them milk. **Unlike** most mammals, whales can stay underwater for a long time.

## OPINION PARAGRAPHS

An **opinion paragraph** tells your ideas about something.

- Write your opinion in the **topic sentence.**
- Give the reasons for your opinion in the detail sentences.

Here are some words you can use to show your opinion:

- **I think**
- **I believe**
- **We should**
- **We must**

### EXAMPLE

**I think the octopus is a fascinating sea creature.** It can do many unusual things. An octopus can change its color. It shoots an inky cloud when it senses danger. It can fit into small hiding places. Don't you think the octopus is fascinating, too?

# Index of Skills

## Vocabulary

## Language Functions

# Language Patterns and Structures, Mechanics, and Spelling

# Index of Skills, continued

## Learning to Read

**Associate sounds and symbols**
Consonants *See* the Teacher's Edition for Lakeside School.
Short vowels *See also* the Teacher's Edition for Lakeside School.
/a/ *a* 50–51
/e/ *e* 78–79
/i/ *i* 64–65
/o/ *o* 50–51
/u/ *u* 64–65

Short vowel phonograms
*–at, –an, –ad, –ag, –ap* 50–51
*–et, –en, –ed* 78–79
*–ig, –it, –in* 64–65
*–og, –op, –ot* 50–51
*–ug, –up, –ut* 64–65

Double consonants and *ck* 78–79
Blends 92–93
Digraphs
/ch/ *ch, tch* 64–65, 92–93
/ng/ *ng* 92–93
/sh/ *sh* 78–79, 92–93
/th/ *th* 92–93
/TH/ *th* 92–93

Long vowels
/ā/ *a_e* 122–123
*ai, ay* 136–137
/ē/ *ee,* ea 136–137
/ē/ *y* 222–223
/ī/ *i_e* 122–123
*ie, igh* 178–179
/ī/ *y* 222–223
/ō/ *o_e* 122–123
*oa, ow* 136–137
/ū/ *u_e* 122–123
*ui, ue* 178–179
/yo͞o/ *u_e* 122–123
*ue* 178–179

R–controlled vowels
/är/ *ar* 192–193
/ôr/ *or* 192–193
/ûr/ *er, ir, ur* 192–193
/âr/ *air, ear* 192–193
/îr/ *eer, ear* 192–193

Variant vowels and diphthongs
/oi/ *oi, oy* 236–237
/ou/ *ou, ow* 236–237
/ô/ *aw, au* 236–237
/ôl/ *al, all* 236–237
/o͞o/ *oo, ew* 236–237

Variant consonants
Hard and soft *c* 250–251
Hard and soft *g* 250–251
Silent consonants 251

**Decodable text** 51–52, 65–66, 79–80, 93–94, 109–110, 123–124, 137–138, 151–152, 165–167, 179–181, 193–195, 207–209, 223–225, 237–239, 251–253, 265–267, 279–281, 293–295

**Decoding Strategies**
Blending 51, 65, 79, 93, 109, 123, 137, 151, 165, 179, 193, 207, 223, 237, 251, 265, 279, 293 *See also* the Teacher's Edition for Lakeside School.
Divide words into syllables 109, 137, 165, 207, 265, 293
Identify root words and affixes 279, 293
Identify root words and endings 151, 165, 293
Identify syllable types 206–207, 292–293
Sound out words 51, 65, 79, 93, 109, 123, 137, 151, 165, 179, 193, 207, 223, 237, 251, 265, 279, 293
Use letter patterns 93, 137, 193, 223, 237, 251
Use word patterns 108–109, 123, 137

**Divide words into syllables** *See* **Multisyllabic words**.

**High frequency words** 49, 63, 77, 91, 107, 121, 135, 149, 163, 177, 191, 205, 221, 235, 249, 263, 277, 291

**Inflectional endings**
*–ed* 103–104, 144, 150–151, 217, 289, 293
*–ing* 159, 164–165
plurals 125, 223

**Multisyllabic words**
Compound words 137
With inflectional endings 103–104, 125, 144, 150–151, 159, 164–165, 217, 223, 289, 293
With one consonant between two vowels 264–265, 292–293
With two consonants between two vowels 109, 264–265, 292–293
With three consonants between two vowels 264–265, 292–293
With *r*–controlled syllables 206–207
With roots and affixes 278–279, 292–293
With /ə/ *a* in first syllable 264–265

**Phonemic awareness** *See* the Teacher's Edition for pages 50, 64, 78, 92, 108, 122, 136, 150, 164, 178, 192, 206, 222, 236, 250, 264, 278, 292 *See also* the Teacher's Edition pages for the phonics transparencies.

**Phonics** *See* **Associate sounds and symbols** and **Decoding strategies**.

**Plurals** *See* **Inflectional endings**.

**Prefixes** 278–279, 292–293

**Reading and spelling** 50–51, 64–65, 78–79, 92–93, 108–109, 122–123, 136–137, 150–151, 164–165, 178–179, 192–193, 206–207, 222–223, 236–237, 250–251, 264–265, 278–279, 292–293

**Reading fluency** *See* The Teacher's Edition for pages 52, 66, 80, 94, 110, 124, 138, 152, 166–167, 180–181, 194–195, 208–209, 224–225, 238–239, 252–253, 266–267, 280–281, 294–295

**Root words** 150–151, 164–165, 278–279, 292–293

**Sounds for *–ed*** 151

**Suffixes** 278–279, 292–293

**Syllable types**
Open 108–109, 264–265
Closed 108–109, 264–265
Consonant + *le* 292–293
*r*–controlled 206–207
Vowel–silent *e* 292–293
Vowel team 136–137, 292–293

**Word analysis** *See* **Associate sounds and symbols, Inflectional endings, Multisyllabic words,** and **Decoding strategies**.

**Word building** 51, 65, 79

**Word families** 50–51, 78–79, 64–65, *See also* **Decoding strategies,** Use letter and word patterns.

**Word parts** *See* **Prefixes, Suffixes,** and **Root words**.

**Word recognition** *See* **High frequency words**.

**Word sorts** 49, 63, 91, 93, 107, 123, 135, 137, 151, 165, 177, 179, 193, 207, 223, 237, 251, 265

**Word work** 49, 51, 63, 65, 77, 79, 91, 93, 107, 109, 121, 123, 135, 137, 149, 151, 163, 165, 177, 179, 191, 193, 205, 207, 221, 223, 235, 237, 249, 251, 263, 265, 277, 279, 291, 293

# Reading and Learning Strategies, Critical Thinking, and Comprehension

# Writing

# Research Skills